A Crack in the Jar

What Ancient Jewish Documents Tell Us About the New Testament

by *Neil S.*

Paulist Press
New York/Mahwah

Paulist Press gratefully acknowledges the use of one drawing from *Qumran: Cities of the Biblical World* by Philip R. Davies, used by permission of James Clarke and Co Ltd, Cambridge England.

Artist's modified drawing of the plan of the Temple of the Temple Scroll based on the schematic plan presented on page 110 ("The Temple Scroll" by Jacob Milgrom, pp. 105–120) of *Biblical Archeologist,* Vol. 41, number 3, September 1978 is used by permission.

Library of Congress
Catalog Card Number: 85-61752

ISBN: 0-8091-2745-8

Published by Paulist Press
997 Macarthur Boulevard
Mahwah, New Jersey 07430

Printed and bound in the
United States of America

Contents

iii

DEDICATION

to my wife

ACKNOWLEDGEMENT

My deep gratitude is due to the Rev. Lawrence Boadt, C.S.P. for his friendly encouragement and also to my long time friends, the Rev. James Hicks and Dr. T. Muraoka, for their valuable criticism and advice. I am indebted to Mr. George McKee for kindly furnishing the maps and figures.

Abbreviations

Ant.	Jewish Antiquities by Flavius Josephus (Loeb Classical Library)
BA	Biblical Archaeologist
BAR	Biblical Archaeologist Review
BASOR	Bulletin of the American Schools of Oriental Research
CBQ	Catholic Biblical Quarterly
DJD	Discoveries in the Judaean Desert
IDB	Interpreter's Dictionary of the Bible
IEJ	Israel Exploration Journal
JBL	Journal of Biblical Literature
JJS	Journal of Jewish Studies
JQR	Jewish Quarterly Review
JSJ	Journal for the Study of Judaism
JSS	Journal of Semitic Studies
LXX	Septuagint
MT	Masoretic Text
NTS	New Testament Studies
RB	Revue Biblique
RQ	Revue de Qumran
TDNT	Theological Dictionary of the New Testament
TZ	Theologische Zeitschrift
VT	Vetus Testamentum
War	The Jewish War by Flavius Josephus (Loeb Classical Library)
ZAW	Zeitschrift für die Alttestamentliche Wissenschaft
ZNW	Zeitschrift für die Neutestamentliche Wissenschaft

The Hasmoneans
Judas Maccabaeus (B.C. 165–160)
Jonathan (160–143)
Simon (143–134)
John Hyrcanus (134–104)
Aristobulus (104–103)
Alexander Jannaeus (103–76)
Alexandra Salome (75–67)
Hyrcanus II (75–66; 63–40)
Aristobulus II (66–63)
Antigonus (40–37)
Herod the Great (37–4)

*   *   *

Roman Emperors	Procurators
Augustus (31 B.C. – A.D. 14)	Coponius (B.C. 6 – A.D. 9)
	Marcus Ambibulus (9–12)
	Annius Rufus (12–15)
Tiberius (14–37)	Valerius Gratus (15–26)
	Pontius Pilate (26–36)
	Marcellus (36–37)
Gaius Caligula (37–41)	Marullus (37–41)
Claudius (41–54)	Cuspius Fadus (44–46)
	Tiberius Alexander (46–48)
	Ventidius Cumanus (48–52)
	Felix (52–60)
Nero (54–68)	Porcius Festus (60–62)
	Albinus (62–64)
	Gessius Florus (64–66)
Galba (68–69)	*Jewish Provisional Government*
Otho (69)	
Vitellius (69)	
Vespasian (69–79)	
	Fall of Jerusalem (70)
Titus (79–81)	
Domitian (81–96)	
Nerva (96–98)	
Trajan (98–117)	
Hadrian (117–138)	*The Second Jewish Revolt*

Introduction

According to a now well-known story,[1] one day in the early spring of 1947, a Bedouin of the Ta'amire tribe casually threw a stone into a cave near the Dead Sea as he was looking for a stray goat. The stone by chance hit and shattered a jar deep inside the dark hollow—a jar which happened to house scrolls which were two thousand years old! This incident was the beginning of the amazing discovery of the Dead Sea Scrolls. A crack in a jar unexpectedly opened up a vast new treasure of information with regard to the Bible, Jewish political, cultural and religious history around the time of Jesus, and Christian origins.

The discoveries made subsequently in other regions of the Judaean wilderness were certainly inspired by the great impact of the Dead Sea Scrolls. All of these finds have proven to be of enormous significance since they pertain to a vital period in history—the time when rabbinic Judaism was formulated and Christianity was born. Though during this period the Jewish people lost their homeland and saw their temple destroyed, they managed at the same time to canonize the Hebrew scripture and institute the rabbinic system. New tides were developing as well, including the Christian movement and the Gnostic trend in religion.

In what ways, then, would the above-mentioned discoveries contribute to our understanding of critical happenings around the turn of the Christian era? That is the goal of our endeavor in this present book. The scope of our inquiry is set geographically in Judaea, the cradle of Judaism and Christianity. It is aimed toward introducing interested laypersons to a more precise and extensive comprehension of the problems involved.

1

The discussions, therefore, are arranged in five designated chapters. In the first chapter, a general survey is undertaken of the finds in the Judaean wilderness. Chapter Two deals with the historical implications of these finds. The question is raised: In what way would they illuminate conditions of the Jewish people of a few centuries before and after the time of Christ?

The next two chapters consider, by adducing various pertinent examples, how the discovered materials would help us in our biblical studies. Chapter Three concerns Old Testament questions, and Chapter Four deals with New Testament subjects. This investigation is important, because the biblical manuscripts from the Dead Sea caves are the oldest textual evidence in existence. They also attest to the evolvement of Old Testament texts which culminated in the formation of the standard text. The Dead Sea documents show many textual and historical connections to the New Testament as well.

The topic of the final chapter concerns early Gnostic trends. Do the discovered documents provide us with any evidence pertaining to the incipient stage of Gnosticism? If so, in what way? And what of the Jewish mystic tradition? Was the Jewish group that left the Dead Sea Scrolls an early mystic sect? Needless to say, each one of these questions is far from easy to answer. But what we are able to do is to probe into this past world shrouded with mystery, as though attempting to gaze into the darkness by way of the stream of light which enters through a crack in the jar.

Recent archaeological explorations have provided us with a tremendous wealth of information about the biblical land, its history, culture, religions and so forth.[2] And, of course, there will be many more fascinating discoveries to come—including perhaps some more new (old) scrolls from the Dead Sea caves! I recall what an Arab antique dealer who had been involved in the acquisition of the Dead Sea Scrolls since their initial discovery said to me at his shop in Jerusalem right after the Six Day War between Israel and the Arab countries in 1967. With a friendly grin on his face, he assured me that there were still several more scrolls yet to be made known. To prove the point, he produced several recently purchased jars which looked identical to those found in the caves.

In October of that year, the late Y. Yadin, an eminent archaeologist and scholar of the Dead Sea Scrolls, announced the acquisition of a new scroll which he called "the Temple Scroll." Shortly after the announcement, Professor Yadin was generous enough to invite me to his home to discuss the scroll with him, for I was studying the Dead Sea manuscripts for my doctoral dissertation at that time. As he talked to me in his study, he was sitting behind a huge desk on which photographic copies of the scrolls were spread. (How I wanted to have access to copies such as these!) Toward the end of our conversation, he said with a gentle smile, "From ancient jars come many new things." Yes, indeed. Jars are broken and cracks appear; and through them we can learn so many exciting things.

Map of Judaea

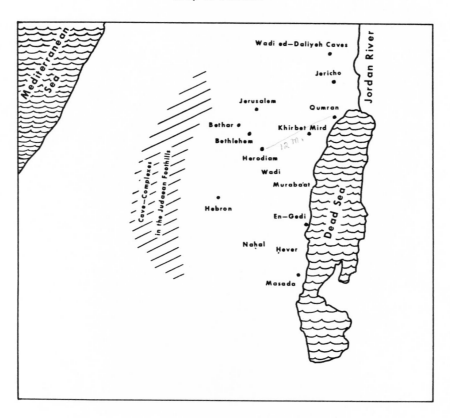

1

Finds in the Judaean Wilderness

1. The Dead Sea Scrolls from Qumran

The Dead Sea Scrolls, comprising several scrolls and hundreds of fragments, were discovered in eleven of the numerous caves honeycombing the cliffs high above the northwestern shore of the Dead Sea. The region, less than ten miles south of Jericho and thirteen miles due east of Jerusalem, is now called "Qumran," taking the Arabic name for a *wadi* (dry river bed) situated there. The rocky wilderness of Judaea, which descends steeply from Jerusalem at 2,400 feet above sea level to the Dead Sea at 1,300 feet below sea level, encompasses the area. Since minimal rainfall keeps the land extremely barren, it is not at all desirable agriculturally but is easily defended. Understandably, therefore, the Jewish sect which left these scrolls had sought ascetic seclusion in that region, and Jewish refugees often found hiding places here and there in the wilderness as well, as they fled foreign conquerors like the Romans.

(1) Cave I

Except for the many fragments from Cave IV which are mostly biblical and are not yet available to the public, the collected documents from these caves have been scrutinized and published by scholars from several countries.[1] Cave I, where the original discovery was made, has proved to be a most fascinating literary treasury. It has yielded seven scrolls of great importance, including a complete book of Isaiah (abbreviated as lQIs³), an incomplete Isaiah manuscript (lQIsᵇ), and a commentary on Habakkuk (lQpHab). (These three documents will be discussed later in Chapter Three.) As far as biblical manuscripts

5

are concerned, fragments of Genesis, Exodus, Leviticus, Deuteronomy, Judges, Samuel, Ezekiel, Daniel, and Psalms were also
acquired from this cave.

Genesis Apocryphon

Also from Cave I came a scroll which is usually called the
Genesis Apocryphon (lQapGen). In the first column of this
badly damaged scroll, Lamech seems to narrate the birth of his
son Noah, a baby so marvelous that (in the second column) he
suspects that his wife has had intercourse with an angel. (This
story coincides with the description of the child in I Enoch
106:2–3: "His body was white as snow. . . . And as for his eyes,
when he opened them the whole house glowed like the sun. . . .
And when he arose from the hands of the midwife, he opened
his mouth and spoke to the Lord with righteousness."[2]) Despite
his wife's denial, Lamech consults his father, Methuselah, who
goes to Enoch, his father, in paradise to learn the truth. The rest
of the story is unfortunately unknown, since columns three
through eighteen have been preserved only in a very fragmentary state. But these portions undoubtedly continue to relate various episodes of Noah's life and then turn to a discussion of
Abraham.

In the better preserved column nineteen, we read Abraham's narration concerning his wife in Hebron, his journey to
Egypt, and his dream of losing his wife Sarah. Column twenty
describes Sarah's beauty, for which she was abducted by the
Pharaoh. The column then tells how the intense prayer of the
distressed husband moved God to send plagues upon Egypt.
Finally the column concludes with the return of the wife and the
couple's departure from Egypt.

Column twenty-one opens with a reference to Bethel, where
Abraham worships God, who promises him that he will grant
him the land encompassing the entire Near East. The patriarch
then decides to travel over the land and he finally settles in
Hebron. Five foreign kings thereupon wage war, involving Lot.
Abraham successfully wreaks vengeance upon them. The story
mentions the blessing of Abraham by Melchizedek, the priest-
king of Salem, here following closely Genesis 14. The column
closes with God's promise of an heir for Abraham.

The whole story resembles pseudepigraphical writings such as Jubilees and I Enoch chapter 106 (most likely written in the second century B.C.) which involve a similar reworking of the Genesis narratives. (The sectarians were quite familiar with the writings which we now call the pseudepigrapha including Jubilees, the Testaments of the Twelve Patriarchs, I Enoch, and many other books. Numerous fragments of these writings, as well as those of hitherto unknown pseudepigraphical literature, were found in the majority of these eleven caves.) Some scholars prefer to call the Genesis Apocryphon a targum (a paraphrastic Aramaic translation of the Hebrew Bible) as it concentrates on the chapters in the Old Testament.[3] Others seek to classify the work as a midrash (rabbinic commentary on the Hebrew scripture).[4] In fact, the Targum of Job (from Cave XI) and Leviticus (from Cave IV), though in a fragmentary state, have been found. But J. A. Fitzmyer, who published an excellent commentary on the Genesis Apocryphon, stresses its independent character—a "free reworking of the Genesis stories, a retelling of the tales of the patriarchs (Lamech, Noah, Abraham, etc.), while displaying traits of targumic and midrashic composition."[5]

The script of this scroll indicates that it was copied during the first half of the first century B.C. Its original composition can most likely be dated to either the early first or second century B.C.

Community Rules

In addition to these writings which directly deal with the Old Testament books, a significant scroll concerning the rules of the sectarian community came from Cave I as well. It comprises three independent collections of regulations: the first and largest one has usually been named "the Manual of Discipline" (1QS, S being the initial of the Hebrew word *serek*, "rule"[6]), which prescribes the sectarian beliefs and life. It ordains the rules for the initiation of new members to the covenant of the community; these new members are required to follow strictly the sect's laws by leaving the outside world which is condemned as being totally defiled and dominated by evil spirits. Their life, instead, is to consist of the sharing of meals and the study of scripture; members are to live under a rigid penal system aimed against sectarian offenses. The community is governed by the legislative and judicial assembly consisting of three priests and twelve lay members who observe the law perfectly. The Manual also teaches the solar calendar as a regulating indicator of the created world, according to which feasts and festivals are to be celebrated.

The second *serek* (rule book), "the Rule of the Congregation" (lQSa), has been preserved only in a fragmentary condition. It concerns an idealized future Israel (the sect) with heavy eschatological overtones—expressly more eschatological in nature than the Manual of Discipline—especially with regard to (1) how members are to be instructed in the Law, (2) the hierarchical organization, and (3) the eschatological banquet led by the messiahs of Aaron and Israel.

The third *serek,* "the Rule of Benediction" (lQSb), survived only in part and that which did was in some thirty-two fragments. It contains blessings for the sectarians, the Zadokite priests, and the prince of the congregation (the messiah of Israel).

When were these manuscripts written? On the basis of paleographical evidence, scholars judge that they were copied sometime during 100–75 B.C.[7] But the date of the original composition remains a matter of scholarly speculation. J. Murphy-O'Connor, for example, has suggested an evolutionary process of formation, comparable to the development of the rabbinic literature—a process ranging from even before the birth of the sect to the final redaction by scribes of the now well-established sect.[8] His approach seems relevant especially as it is correlated with the archaeological evidence regarding the history of the community center of the sect at Qumran (which will be discussed later). The composition most likely dates to the second half of the second century B.C.

War Scroll

Cave I also yielded a unique scroll which describes an eschatological war, the so-called "War Scroll" (lQM, M being the initial of Hebrew *milhaman,* "war"). The sectarians believed that there would be a pre-ordained battle between the powers of good (sons of light) and evil (sons of darkness) at the conclusion of history. The first column of this manuscript, which is made up of a total nineteen columns, opens with the naming of these two forces in conflict and ends with the final victory of the sons of light. After this initial column, there is a long series of regulations concerning the rituals of war, the use of various military equipment, the alignment of the troops and cavalries, and other topics (cols. 2–9). This section is followed by admonitions and prayers offered by the high priest. Column fifteen and the following contain a series of regulations which somewhat parallel the previous prescriptions.

This duplication has prompted many modern scholars to assume this writing to be a composite work. P. Davies, for example, postulates the existence of two major documents preserved in cols. 2–9 and 15–19.[9] The former deals with an eschatological war stemming from the traditions of the Maccabean war, while the latter represents "the end-product of a long history of development from an original Maccabean war-rule."[10] Cols. 10–12 originated from a collection of hymns and prayers of the Maccabean time. These three documents were gradually combined into a single literary entity.

Many other recent researchers also believe that the War Scroll derives from several independent traditions of the Maccabean war.[11] The battle of this scroll is definitely a final war. Y. Yadin, a former army general as well as the author of a superb commentary on this scroll, contends that the military regulations mentioned in the document are based on historical practice during the Roman period.[12] The literature, nonetheless, is not a military manual, but in essence a religious contemplation of the struggle of righteous forces against evil and their final victory. It is reasonable, consequently, to assume that our scroll is a "Qumranized version of the War Scroll" of the Maccabean era.[13] When the older version was "Qumranized," it obtained a decidedly sectarian and eschatological overtone.

Hymn Scroll

A scroll of hymns in the form of a couple of bundles was also discovered in Cave I. They had survived in a very poor condition; many portions were lost, and there were numerous darkened parts and lacunae. Though the second bundle was found in some seventy fragments, modern technological efforts have resulted in the recovery of thirty-two individual psalms. The paleography of the manuscripts indicates that it was copied sometime during the middle of the first century A.D., but the date of original composition is unknown.

The poems of this scroll customarily open with either the sentence "I thank you, O Lord" or "Blessed be you, O Lord." They then continue to describe the poet's distress, a cry for help, and divine deliverance; they are, consequently, songs of thanksgiving and praise of God. The scroll is hence called by modern scholars *Hodayot* ("thanksgiving" in Hebrew) and abbreviated as 1QH.

Another interesting feature is that in every hymn the personal pronoun "I" occurs, indicating either the author or the collective community. Who then is the author? Scholars have often identified the writer with the leader of the sect who is called "the Teacher of Righteousness" in other Dead Sea Scrolls (the Habakkuk Commentary, the Damascus Document, etc.). (We will discuss this figure in the next chapter). It does say, for example, in col. 7, lines 20–21: "And you have made me a father to sons of mercy[14] and a foster father to men of wonder." "Sons of mercy" and "men of wonder" appear to refer to the members of the sect. As we gather from other scrolls, the "Teacher" (perhaps an important priest) condemned the political and religious establishment in the Jerusalem of his time, set up his own group in the wilderness of Judaea, and was persecuted by his foes; the Hymn Scroll probably stemmed from his personal anguish.

This identity of authorship is, however, uncertain. There is no unequivocal indication in support of this theory in the scroll itself. An alternative view is possible—more than one author may have been involved. The Hymns, in fact, contain a variety of feelings and ideas, as well as literary types. The question of authorship awaits further study.[15]

Another area of scholarly debate concerns the poetic style of this scroll. Like other writings from the Dead Sea caves, this literature extensively uses words, concepts, and literary images of the Old Testament, especially from the Psalms and prophetical writings. T. H. Gaster even describes it as "a mosaic of biblical quotations."[16] Such a heavy reliance on scripture occurred because the sectarians devoted themselves to its study, and they believed that the biblical words would be fulfilled by their hand. (This question will be dealt with in Chapter Three.)

As for its poetic style, the scroll does not follow closely the tradition of Hebrew poetry. As characteristically present in the Old Testament poems, parallelism between two or three lines in a stanza can be noticed in the Hymns, but it is not rigidly adhered to. The metrical system of biblical poetry is not observed either. C. F. Kraft terms it "metrical chaos,"[17] while H. Ringgren prefers to define the style as "rhythmic prose."[18] We should note, however, that it is a poetic form developed from its biblical ancestor, and consequently it should stand in its own right.[19] It is significant that our scroll contains Hebrew poetry which was composed around the time of Jesus. Some of the New Testament poems (such as the three psalms in Luke's infancy narratives: the Magnificat in 1:46–55; the Benedictus in 1:67–79; the Nunc Dimitis in 2:29–32) might be based on Jewish poetic sources similar to the Hymn Scroll, although no evidence exists to substantiate any Semitic originals.[20]

The fact that many fragments of the Hymn Scroll were discovered in Cave IV indicates that this poetic literature was valued highly by the members of the sect. In G. Vermes' opinion, it was "recited by the guardian and the new members of the community during the Feast of the Renewal of the Covenant on the Feast of Weeks,"[21] while H. Bardtke assumes that its use was for catechism.[22] Its exact purpose is beyond our determination, but apparently it was not just a private book but cherished literature of the sectarian community.

(2) Minor Caves

Compared to Cave I which yielded these major scrolls, Caves II–III and V–X were found to be not as rich an ancient literary deposit. They are, therefore, often called "minor caves." What was discovered in these caves was a number of fragments of Old Testament texts, sectarian commentaries, pseudepigraphical works, and sectarian liturgical and juridical literature.

Copper Scroll

In Cave III, however, there was a very different kind of find—a scroll made of individual sheets of copper riveted

together. Hence it is usually called the "Copper Scroll." This
scroll is quite unique not only because of the metal material used
but also because of its content in a writing punched out with a
narrow stylus. Surprisingly, what is inscribed turns out to be a
list of treasures of enormous value, including gold, silver, aro-
matics, manuscripts, and other items. They are said to have
been hidden in various places in the areas of the Dead Sea, Jericho, and Jerusalem.

Was this an authentic record? If so, who was the owner of
the treasure? Why and when were the items concealed in the various locations? Some scholars took the record literally and even
embarked upon a treasure hunt, which proved to be utterly
abortive. J. Allegro, a participant in this venture, suggests that
the treasures belonged to the Jerusalem temple and were hidden
by the fanatic nationalists called Zealots shortly before the
Roman conquest of Jerusalem in A.D. 70. The scroll was left by
them in a cave near the sectarians' community center at Qumran, which they occupied until the arrival of the Roman troops.[23]
This theory, however, is totally speculative; there is nothing to
substantiate it.

E.-M. Laperrousaz conjectures that the scroll originated
with Bar-Kokhba's group of Jewish fighters who opposed Rome
in A.D. 132–135.[24] But again there is no evidence; and, in fact,
it is highly doubtful that this group possessed such extraordinary
financial resources.

Is this strange document then just a fairy tale? Many scholars seem to think so; they ascribe it to "popular imagination,"
pointing out its "folkloristic character."[25] Fantasizing such a
treasure, however, not to mention actually possessing such a stu-
pendous fortune of gold and silver, is simply incompatible with
the rigid asceticism of the sectarians. In fact, the amount of the
hoard listed on the scroll seems to be too prodigious even for the
temple treasury.

As Allegro, Laperrousaz and many others feel, the Copper
Scroll seems to have had no connection with the Dead Sea sect.
The script and grammatical features of the scroll are definitely
inferior to those of the rest of the Dead Sea Scrolls. Allegro, a
British scholar, compares some corrupted linguistic forms of
this writing to London Cockney.[26] Its language is the same type

of Hebrew as the one used in the Mishnah (a collection of rabbinic laws codified during the second and third centuries A.D.), whereas the other manuscripts from the Dead Sea caves were written in late biblical Hebrew. (The language of the scrolls will be discussed in Chapter Three.) The very existence of this scroll at Qumran remains an enigma.

(3) Cave IV

Along with Cave I, Cave IV must be cited as a great literary repository. It has yielded tens of thousands of fragments and more than five hundred manuscripts, though many of them have not yet been published. The Cave IV materials available to the public include: (1) biblical fragments of Exodus, Leviticus, Deuteronomy, I Samuel, Isaiah, Jeremiah, Psalms, and Ecclesiastes, and targumic fragments of Job and Leviticus; (2) apocryphal fragments of I Enoch, Jubilees, the Testament of Levi, the Prayer of Nabonidus, the Daniel pseudepigraphon, and Tobit; (3) fragments of sectarian commentaries on Isaiah, Hosea, Micah (?), Nahum, Zechariah, and Psalms; (4) fragments of other sectarian writings such as messianic and eschatological ref-

Qumran Cave IV

erences, astrological documents, sectarian ordinances, as well as some others.

Furthermore, several fragments of the so-called Damascus Document (sometimes referred to as the Zadokite Document) were discovered in Caves IV and VI. This literature has proved to be an important source, supplying us with valuable information concerning the Dead Sea sect.

Damascus Document

Toward the very end of the last century, Solomon Schechter, a great rabbinic scholar, acquired about 100,000 pages of the documents which had been stored in the genizah of an old Karaite synagogue in old Cairo (the Karaites were a medieval Jewish sect).[27] A genizah provided storage for old unusable or disapproved literature, usually attached to a synagogue. Among those numerous manuscripts, Schechter found and later published two medieval (tenth–twelfth century) copies of literature which concerned the ancient sect.[28] They are large incomplete pieces, one of them comprising sixteen pages and the other only two pages.

The document narrates first, drawing from the Old Testament, the historical background of the rise of the sect in the midst of various apostasies of Israel (i.e., in the age of divine wrath). Those who adhered to the Law were able to enter a new covenant with God in the land of Damascus. They were at this stage still in the middle of strife with the powers of Satan (Belial). The covenant community consisted of the sons of Zadok, the Levites, and lay members, and it was led by the "Teacher," who was called the "Interpreter of the Law" as well. The document also presents a series of legal instructions and warnings against wicked outsiders and traitors. As a whole, the context is not coherent, evidence that the extant text is highly composite.

Because of the important references to "Damascus," this writing is usually called the "Damascus Document" (CD). When archaeologists explored the cave nearest to the ruin which was identified as the sect's community center (later named Cave IV), they found fragments of the same document among hundreds of others.[29] Because of this discovery, as well as that of the tenet, laws, and idioms which undeniably parallel those of the Dead Sea Scrolls, scholarly consensus has concluded that this Cairo genizah document represents a medieval copy of a writing which originally belonged to an ancient sect that settled near the Dead Sea or at least a sister group of the same sect.[30]

If the sect of the Damascus Document is to be squarely identified with that of Qumran, then the "Damascus" of this document would be a symbolic name for Qumran.[31] Most scholars, in fact, seem to share this understanding. Some of them, however, favor the view that "Damascus" indeed indicates the well-known city of that name in Syria, where the sect perhaps had a sister group.[32] A third alternative view has also been proposed by others: "Damascus" may symbolically refer to Babylon.[33] (As this view is related to the origin of the sect, it will be discussed in Chapter Two.)

Some differences, in fact, can be noted between the Damascus Document and the major writings from the Qumran caves, including the Manual of Discipline, the Habakkuk Commentary, and others. First, the latter concern themselves strictly with one particular community at Qumran, whereas the former appears to envisage two groups of the sect: one at Qumran and the other whose members are spread throughout various places (called "camps") in the land. Second, the community council at Qumran consists of three priests and twelve laymen (lQS 8:1f.), while at "Damascus" there are four priests and six laymen (CD 10:4ff.). Third, the laws of the Damascus Document, in contrast to the Qumran ordinances, include regulations regarding private property. The exact determination of the relationship of this writing with the remainder of the Qumran literature still lies beyond our reach.

Another difficult question concerns the date of composition. The oldest fragmentary copy of this literature was found in Cave IV, and is dated from paleographical evidence to the first half of the first century B.C. In Cross' estimation, the original work was written during "the late second century B.C., or better, perhaps the early first century B.C."[34]

Cave XI

Several manuscripts of great significance came to light from Cave XI. First, there are biblical manuscripts. Besides some fragments of Leviticus (llQLev) and a seemingly complete scroll of Ezekiel (llQEz) that has been so ossified that little of it is legible, there are a couple of manuscripts of the Psalms (llQPs[a] and llQPs[b]) and a fragment (llQPs[c]). These present intriguing textual evidence. Another document of striking interest is a Targum of Job (llQtgJob), an example of Targum found in Palestine.

The second category of llQ documents is that of the apocryphal writings, including some non-canonical Psalms (llQPsAp) and fragments of Jubilees (llQJub). In the third category of sectarian texts, there are the midrashic text dealing with messianic Melchizedek (llQMelch) and the Temple Scroll. Since the last of them is both unique and the largest known scroll from Qumran, it is proper to accord a brief description here. (The other texts will be also dealt with later.)

The Temple Scroll

During the Arab-Israeli war in 1967, Y. Yadin acquired the hitherto longest (more than twenty-eight feet long and containing sixty-six columns) scroll, which he edited and published in 1977.[35] The general contents of the scroll include the instructions for construction of the temple and its appurtenance (cols. 3–11), the ordinances concerning offerings and sacrifices (cols. 11–30), a description of the temple courts, gates, vessels, and other items (cols. 30–46), the purity laws of the temple, animals, cities, idolatry, priests, Levites, and other subjects (cols. 46–56, 60), the laws of the king (cols. 56–59). and various laws largely based on Deuteronomy (cols. 60–66). Because of the scroll's emphasis on the temple, Yadin named it the "Temple Scroll" (llQTemple).

Curiously, some of these regulations of the scroll find no parallel in either the biblical or rabbinic legislation. For example, the temple is to be surrounded by three concentric square, rather than the standard rectangular, courtyards. The innermost courtyard enshrining the altar and the sanctuary is to be limited to priests wearing their vestments (35:5–9). The middle court is to be accessible only to Israelite men over twenty years old (39:7–10), and the outer court to be available to Israelite men,

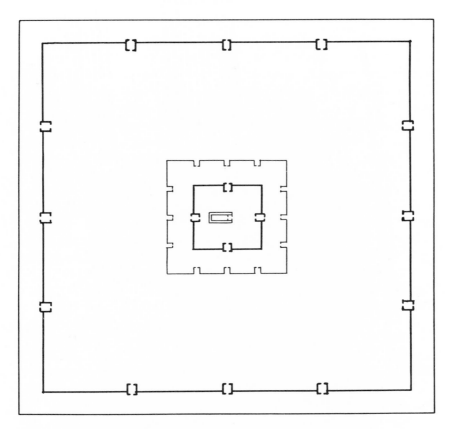

The Temple of the Temple Scroll

women, and children in a state of cleanliness (40:5–6). Also in the scroll new cultic festivals of the New Wine (cols. 19–21) and the New Oil (cols. 21–23) are ordained.

This scroll has another distinctive characteristic, i.e., the text is comprised of what is given as the direct words of God. In other words, it resembles a Torah, a series of laws revealed by God. Here is a new Torah in addition to the biblical one!

Not only because of the above-mentioned peculiarities but also because the calendar of the scroll seems to be the same solar one as that which the sectarians adopted, Yadin and others strongly contend that the scroll has a Qumran provenance.[36]

Who but those in the Qumran community could possibly
espouse distinctive heterodoxies! The discovery of small fragments of this literature also attests to the fact that it was cherished by the people at Qumran.[37] On paleographical evidence,
Yadin assigns the date of the scroll to the Herodian period and
the date of the fragments to the middle Hasmonean time.

To a scholar like B. Z. Wacholder, this scroll represents definitely the "sectarian Torah."[38] He identifies it with the enigmatic "sealed scroll of the Law" hidden since the time of Joshua,
mentioned in the Damascus Document 5:5. That is to say, the
Teacher of Righteousness (Moses redivivus!) opened (but, in
reality, wrote) this secret law book of antiquity, which is superior even to the biblical Torah. The temple of this scroll, consequently, is meant to be final and eternal. (Yadin thinks it is
ideal and real.) According to Wacholder, it was written at the
end of the third century B.C., the era in which he seeks to locate
the origin of the Teacher's sect. (This question will be discussed
in the next chapter.)

Wacholder's theory, though well investigated, does not go
unchallenged. For instance, his identification of the scroll with
the sealed law of the Damascus Document 5:5 does not seem to
be well established. Also, if this scroll was as vitally important
to the sect as he avers it was, why is it not cited more often and
more explicitly in the other Qumran writings?

In L. H. Schiffman's opinion, the scroll did not originate in
Qumran. He points out that the scroll's specifications of the temple and its sacrificial cult were not actualized in the sect's every-
day life and that the document itself does not teach that the ordinances should be practiced outside the temple through the
observance of ritual purity. Furthermore, there is no detectable
polemical intention. Schiffman consequently states that the
author "does not write like a sectarian," but "like a member of
the priestly circles which transmitted and studied the cultic writings of the Pentateuch." The origin and purpose of this literature
remain "an enigma we cannot solve."[39]

Paucity of evidence prevents us from determining the
Qumran provenance of the scroll. Perhaps it was not authored,
but instead inherited by the sect.[40] Wacholder's pre-Maccabean
date of the original composition of this literature may be accurate. It was presumably produced by a priestly group which

influenced (if not directly fostered, as Wacholder suggests) the Qumran sect. The existence of the Temple Scroll is not accidental (unlike the Copper Scroll); the sectarians were willing to accept and preserve in their midst this heterodox "Torah." This very fact may well indicate their polemical intention with regard to their opponents in Jerusalem, even though no explicit antagonism is exhibited in the document itself.

There are many unanswered questions concerning this scroll. It is indeed one of the most controversial documents from Qumran.

2. Finds in Wadi Muraba'at

The continuous treasure-hunt craze of the Bedouins led to the discovery of manuscripts in four caves in the sheer cliffs of the gorge in the desolate mountains of Wadi Muraba'at, about twelve miles southwest of Qumran. These caves were examined by Fr. R. de Vaux and G. L. Harding in 1952, and the reports of the excavation and the texts of the uncovered documents were published in the second volume of *Discoveries in the Judaean Desert* (1961).[41]

These caves yielded traces of human occupation from the Chalcolithic period (the fourth millennium), the Middle Bronze Age (2000–1600 B.C.), the Iron Age (eighth-seventh centuries B.C.), the Roman period (especially the second century A.D.), and the Medieval Age. In two of these caves, important discoveries were made. First of all, there was a palimpsest[42] fragment (Mur 17) from the eighth to seventh centuries B.C., which is the earliest extant Hebrew papyrus we possess. Unfortunately, the text is no longer legible.

Even more exciting materials were discovered which belong to the period of the Second Jewish Revolt. During this time (A.D. 132–135), a desperate struggle against the Romans was led by the man usually known by the name Bar-Kokhba. In fact, some of the man's letters addressed to his subordinates were found. Evidently, these caves were used as a hiding place by these Jewish rebels of that tragic war. A number of other texts include legal documents such as commercial transactions, divorce letters, and marriage contracts, which help in our understanding of the social and economic conditions of that time. These texts were written in Hebrew, Aramaic, Greek, and Latin. (We shall discuss the Second Jewish Revolt in the next chapter.)

Some Hebrew biblical fragments also came from these caves. Of great importance is a portion of a scroll of the Minor Prophets which includes a text from the middle of Joel to the beginning of Zechariah. The manuscript, having been copied apparently in the early second century A.D., presents an identical textual tradition to that of the Masoretic text. This discovery provides us with a significant piece of evidence for ascertaining a crucial stage in the evolution of the Old Testament text. (This question will be dealt with in the third chapter.)

3. Finds at Khirbet Mird

Another of the Bedouins' notable discoveries in the Judaean wilderness was made at Khirbet Mird, some nine miles southeast of Jerusalem. R. de Laughe excavated the site in 1953.[43] It was originally a Hasmonean fortress (called Hyrcanion), which was later reconstructed by King Herod. In A.D. 492, this old, largely ruined, fortress was transformed into the Christian monastery of Kastellion. It was used sporadically down to the third decade of this century.

Greek, Christian Aramaic, and Arabic documents from the sixth to ninth centuries A.D. were found in an underground chamber.[44] These documents included, among others, some fragments of Wisdom, Mark, John, and Acts (copied sometime during the fifth to eighth centuries A.D.). The Christian Aramaic fragments prove to be the earliest literary evidence of this language, which was in daily use by the monks there in the early medieval age.

4. Finds in the Region Between En-Gedi and Masada

Inspired by the tremendous discovery in the Qumran region, in the early 1960's a group of Israeli archaeologists (Y. Aharoni, N. Avigad, Y. Aviram, P. Bar-Adon, and Y. Yadin) undertook a thorough investigation of the caves and ancient sites in the Judaean wilderness between En-Gedi and Masada, where the terrain encompasses many deep, dry ravines (*Naḥal* in Hebrew and *Wadi* in Arabic).[45] The precipitous cliffs of these gorges are dotted with numerous caves, varying in size and shape, yielding traces of the chalcolithic age and also of the period of the Second Jewish Revolt.

As examples of the chalcolithic finds, the excavators discovered in the "Cave of Treasure" in the Naḥal Mishmar, various kinds of objects, including axes, chisels, hammers, mace-heads, hollow stands decorated with knobs, baskets, pots, an ivory box, and many other items. The exact reason why the people of that age chose such an inaccessible locale is still undetermined.

Vestiges of the Second Jewish Revolt against the Romans were found extensively in this area. Like the caves at Wadi Muraba'at, many of the caves of this whole region were used as bases and hideouts by the rebelling Jews, as evidenced by the finds of various kinds of daily utensils, food remains, pieces of fabric, baskets, sandals, lamps, knives, arrowheads, and other objects. The presence of numerous human skeletons, such as those found in the "Cave of Horror" in Naḥal Ḥever,[46] cast a lurid light on the fact that this area also became the final resting place of these seditionaries as the result of Roman search-and-destroy missions.

The multitudinous fragments of documents written in Hebrew, Aramaic, Nabatean, and Greek are also of special value; they, too, were left by the Jewish rebels and refugees. These manuscripts generally consist of biblical and legal materials as well as personal letters. The biblical fragments contain passages from Genesis, Numbers, Jonah, Micah, Nahum, Habakkuk, Zephaniah, and the Psalms. These biblical texts, like those from Muraba'at, exhibit clearly their affinity to the Masoretic text.

The legal materials include deeds, record of law suits concerning matters of property, and other documents, which often concur with Mishnaic legal provisions, and in other cases supply fresh information about the Jewish legal and socio-economic practices of those days.[47] The archives of Babata from the "Cave of Letters" represent an intriguing example of this sort of material. They consist of thirty-five documents from A.D. 93–132, written in Nabatean, Aramaic, and Greek. Babata, a widow of two husbands, kept carefully her marriage contract and other legal documents, including deeds of inheritance and of her son's guardianship. Facing the disastrous end of Bar-Kokhba's war with the Romans, she apparently fled to the cave with other refugees. They met a tragic death there, leaving the documents behind.[48]

Of great interest are the fifteen letters of Bar-Kokhba, which, though written by his scribes, find the leader himself issuing orders to his men, men who called one another "brother." Yadin, excavator of the "Cave of Letters," concluded that these letters were written in the last stage of the war.[49]

5. Finds from the Wadi ed-Daliyeh Caves

New papyrus documents, which came to light in 1962, had been discovered by Bedouin tribesmen in the rugged territory of Wadi ed-Daliyeh, eight to nine miles north of old Jericho. The ravine through which the winter rain flows ultimately into the River Jordan, presents a sheer drop of a hundred feet or more. Along the cliffs on its north side, nature has created numerous caves.

Paul Lapp explored two caves in that region in 1963 and 1964, and identified various deposits from the Middle Bronze Age I (22–21 centuries B.C.), the fourth century B.C., and the period of the Second Jewish Revolt.[50]

The materials from the fourth century B.C. were, above all, astonishing; they included vast quantities of pottery, pieces of fabric, jewelry, remains of food, and close to two hundred skeletons, both male and female, young and old. Moreover, of great significance is the large number of papyri which has proved to be the earliest extensive group of papyri ever found in Palestine.[51]

All of these documents are legal or administrative in content (such as records concerning slaves, sales, real estate transactions, divorce documents and so on), and they originated in Samaria. Some of them contain the names of the city officials (e.g., Sanballat) and are completed with seven seals. Written in the Aramaic cursive (except for two governor's bullae written in

Wadi ed-Daliyeh Caves

Paleo-Hebrew), the earliest dated one is from 375 B.C. and the latest from 335 B.C. According to F. M. Cross who scrutinized them, the documents were left in the cave by refugees who fled from Samaria during its destruction by the troops of Alexander the Great in 331 B.C.[52] Numerous coins found in these caves also bear out this date.

Lapp concurred with the historical reconstruction of Cross and suggested that the numerous skeletons in the cave were due to the refugees' death as a result of suffocation from a huge fire set by the Macedonian soldiers.[53] As the frequent occurrence of Yahwistic names like Yehonur, Nehemiah, and others in the documents demonstrates (with a few exceptions containing names of foreign deities such as the Edomite Qos, the Moabite Kemosh, the Canaanite Baal, and the Babylonian Nabu), most of these victims were worshipers of Yahweh. The existence of governmental documents, fine jewelry, seal rings, and legal material pertinent to slaves indicates the presence of people of means.

As will be discussed in the ensuing chapters, the significance of the discovery at the Wadi ed-Daliyeh caves is enormous; it sheds light on the Samaritan history of the fourth century B.C. and its socio-cultural institutions, the traditions of certain biblical texts (especially the Samaritan Pentateuch), and Hebrew-Aramaic paleographical development.

6. Finds at Masada

The prodigious mesa soaring majestically over the Dead Sea, about ten miles south of En-Gedi, is Masada, the hellenized term for the Hebrew *metsuda* (stronghold). It is appropriately named, as it is well known as the last fortress of the Jewish revolt against Romans in A.D. 66–74. After the initial survey in 1953 and 1955–1956,[54] Y. Yadin conducted a large-scale excavation as well as a partial reconstruction of the site during the years 1963 through 1965.[55] The resulting finds pertained to the Herodian period (37–4 B.C.), the revolt, and the Byzantine era (fifth–sixth centuries A.D.).

King Herod had most of the structures built, including a few palaces, Roman baths, an administrative building, living quarters, and storage and other facilities. The palace, located in the northern cliff, was built on three terraces, representing Herod's personal luxury villa. Some of the palace rooms were decorated with multicolored mosaics and frescoes. A building which was used presumably as a synagogue was also found.[56] If it was indeed a synagogue, as the excavator Yadin claims, it represents one of the oldest remains of a synagogue. (Another one built by Herod has been unearthed at the winter palace in Herodion, east of Bethlehem.[57] Incidentally, the Jerusalem Talmud, Megillah 301 states that there were 480 synagogues in Jerusalem, and the Babylonian Talmud, Ketubot 105a refers to 394 at the time of the destruction of the temple in A.D. 70. In 1913, a limestone block was discovered in the Ophel section of Jerusalem. It has an inscription that names the builder of a synagogue there in the first century A.D.[58])

Several cisterns were hewn in the rock on the slope as well as on the summit to collect and store rain water; they had a total water-retaining capacity of more than 1,400,000 cubic feet. Finally, casemate walls were constructed guarding the edge of the entire summit.

During the Revolt, the Jewish rebels altered the Herodian structures to fit their defensive needs. They strengthened the casemate walls and adapted the administrative and living rooms. As Yadin surmises, the western palace was used for their administrative functions. Hundreds of burned arrows and coins were discovered in the ashes of the tragic ruins. These coins bore the inscription: "For the freedom of Zion."

The remains of domestic utensils, fabric, baskets, and other daily used items were found in the spaces in the casemate walls. Even some of their foodstuffs such as dates, walnuts, salts, grain, and pomegranates were found on the lower terrace. Evidently, the freedom fighters were living in these places. (They burned most of their food supply just before they died.) About twenty-five skeletons of males, females, and children found in a cave near the top of the southern cliff tell us of the grisly catastrophe. They seem to have been thrown there by the Roman soldiers. Other bodies must have been cleared by them, too. (There were almost one thousand Jews in all at Masada.) A Roman garrison was stationed there for some time after the conquest.

The literary deposits at Masada include fragments from Genesis, Leviticus, the Psalms (running from chs. 81 to 85, and 150), Ezekiel, and fragments of the lost original Hebrew text of Ecclesiasticus (hitherto preserved only in translations).[59] Another particularly significant find is a portion of the sectarian literature, "the Songs of Sabbath Sacrifices," identical to the text discovered at Qumran Cave IV.[60] This may well indicate that some of the people at Qumran sought refuge at Masada. In addition to these biblical and other literary deposits, the reuse of the Herodian synagogue (altered somewhat) and the ritual bath *(mikve)* evince the deeply religious nature of the defenders.

During the fifth and sixth centuries A.D., Christian monks built a church there, reusing some of the old structures. Except for this interlude, Masada has been deserted since the Roman conquest.

7. Finds at the Judaean Foothills

In addition to the evidence of Jewish uprising against the Romans that we have observed thus far, other traces of Jewish rebels and refugees have been located in the Judaean foothills. More than one hundred and fifty complexes of caves at seventy sites can be found in the region between the coastal plain in the west and the slopes of the Hebron mountains in the east, and between Naḥal Ayalon in the north and Naḥal Shikma in the south. A team coordinated by the Israeli Department of Antiquities and Museums has been investigating this area since 1978.[61]

Most of these underground complexes were hewn in the chalk rock, comprising chambers (some smaller for family use and others a little larger for communal use), storages, water reservoirs, and other areas. They were connected by passageways which were often low and narrow for crawling from room to room. These facilities were carefully devised so that they could be sealed from the inside. There were also concealed tunnels and cavities. Such a structural feature, as well as small openings, are indicative of the purpose of all the subterranean complexes— defense; they were created as places for refuge and hiding.

The discovered shards of pottery and jars as well as coins suggest that these installations were mostly made and used during the First Jewish Revolt and continued in use until the time of the Second Revolt. A few of them, however, date to the third and second centuries B.C. These were apparently designed mainly for economic and religious functions, with large openings and corridors with no blocking devices, camouflage, or secret hideaways.

According to investigators, the complexes of the time of the Revolts were evidently planned under strategic guidance for the preparation of the entire area for a military uprising. They were equipped to sustain fighters and refugees over a period of weeks or even months.[62] The exploration thus confirms that the entire area of the Judaean foothills was under the control of Bar-Kokhba at the time of the Second Revolt.

2

Judaean Finds and Ancient Jewish History

The task of this chapter is to examine the historical implication of the Judaean finds surveyed in the previous chapter. The materials are thus chronologically arranged into the following three periods: (1) the finds in Wadi ed-Daliyeh (the fourth century B.C.), (2) the finds at Qumran (the second century B.C. to the first century A.D.), (3) the finds at Masada and the Judaean caves (the First Jewish Revolt—the first century A.D., and the Second Revolt—the second century A.D.).

1. The Finds in Wadi ed-Daliyeh and the Samaritans

Samaritans

In 2 Kings 17:29, "Samaritans" refers to the inhabitants of Samaria, the capital city of the Northern Kingdom of Israel during the period of the divided monarchy. It was destroyed by the Assyrians in 722 B.C., but revived as a center of Hellenistic civilization under Greek rule after the conquest by Alexander the Great in 332 B.C. The so-called Samaritans, however, have been connected primarily not with Samaria but with Shechem, an ancient sanctuary, located several miles south of Samaria and near Mount Gerizim.

Even now a small number of Samaritans who claim to be the remnant of the Northern Kingdom of Israel still live in that region of the modern state of Israel, and there are also tiny groups near Tel Aviv. They possess as their scripture an ancient recension of the Pentateuch, the so-called Samaritan Pentateuch. As this recension presents significant textual variation from the rabbinic Bible, so do Samaritan religious tenets and practices differ somewhat from traditional Judaism.

Samaritans were at odds with the Jews in ancient times. The traditional Jewish view was that the Samaritans derived from a gross syncretism, a result of the Assyrian conquest and the subsequent intermarriage with foreign peoples (2 Kings 17:24–41). Consequently, as typically evinced in Ezra and Nehemiah, they were not treated as full-fledged members of Israel. The Samaritan tradition, conversely, insisted that the people were of pure heritage, and not a schismatic branch of Judaism. The Samaritans appealed to the ancient authenticity of the sanctuary on Mount Gerizim on the basis of the Mosaic law, accusing Judaism of being the descendant of Eli's heresy. According to the Samaritan claim, Eli, a priest during the period of Judges (the eleventh century B.C.), withdrew from the legitimate sanctuary to create a rival cult at Shilo, which was succeeded later by the temple in Jerusalem. In New Testament times, the enmity between these two communities was such that the writer of the Fourth Gospel bluntly put it: "Jews have no dealing with Samaritans" (4:9). (Such a feeling does not exist between the contemporary Samaritans and the Israeli government today.)

Samaritan Origins

What was the origin of the Samaritan sect? Does the discovery at Wadi ed-Daliyeh help in our understanding of the sect's history? Ancient sources in regard to this question are extremely scarce and ambiguous, which hampers modern scholarly attempts to reconstruct the past. Some scholars such as M. Gaster[1] and J. MacDonald[2] maintain that Samaritanism was an independent branch of a "common matrix"[3] shared with Judaism. Many others, however, do not concur with this view, though they acknowledge the possible vestige of the old northern Israelite tradition in Samaritanism. They are of the opinion, on the basis of the information found in Ezra and Nehemiah, that the emergence of Samaritanism took place in the Persian period, when the returned Jews refused the Samaritan offer of help in the reconstruction of the Jerusalem temple (Ezra 4:1–5). Animosity between the Jews and the Samaritans persisted through the conflict between Nehemiah and Sanballat and his allies, Tobiah and Geshem (Nehemiah 2:10, 19; 4:1–6:19; 13:29).[4]

This biblical information, however, is opaque and theologically motivated. The Chronicler who wrote the books of Ezra and Nehemiah as well as 1 and 2 Chronicles depicted the returned Jewish community in a highly messianic and idealized way; it was described as the true Israel.[5] The narrative provided by Josephus (a Jewish historian of the first century A.D.) is also historically uncertain and biased about the construction of the Samaritan temple as a rival of the one in Jerusalem (the event which must have been vital to the origin of Samaritanism).[6] He stated that Sanballat built the temple, with permission from Alexander the Great, and placed as its priest his son-in-law, Manasseh, who was once a priest at the Jerusalem temple (*Ant.* 11:321–324). If this Sanballat was Sanballat the enemy of Nehemiah, Samaritanism emerged in the fifth century B.C. If not, either Josephus erroneously connected Sanballat with the temple or there was more than one Sanballat.

Drawing support from the papyri from Wadi ed-Daliyeh, F. M. Cross has proposed a solution to this bewildering question.[7] According to him, there were three Sanballats: (I) Sanballat, a contemporary of Nehemiah, who was also referred to as the governor of Samaria and the father of Dalaiah and Shelemiah mentioned in a papyrus found in Elephantine, Egypt; (II) the Sanballat mentioned in the papyri from Wadi ed-Daliyeh, the grandson of Sanballat I; (III) Sanballat, the grandson of Sanballat II, the son of Hananiah. Sanballat III must have been the governor during the time of Darius III—the last king of Persia (338–331 B.C.)—and also the builder of the Samaritan temple in Josephus' story. (Josephus mistakenly identified the biblical Sanballat with Sanballat III, though he was right on the latter's role.) So, the Sanballat family line goes: Sanballat I—Dalaiah—Sanballat II—Yeshua(?) and his brother Hananiah—Sanballat III.

It follows then that the date of the construction of the Samaritan temple is to be placed in the very early Greek period. This is supported by the archaeological excavation at Shechem led by G. E. Wright from 1956 onward.[8] It furthermore finds confirmation from ancient literary sources. Quintus Curtius, a

We should, however, note, on the one hand, that the information supplied by Philo, Josephus, Pliny, and Dio lacks precision and accuracy, and, on the other hand, that the Damascus Document we possess did not really come from Qumran, as we have mentioned earlier. All in all, the Essene identity of the Qumran sect is most likely. A great majority of modern scholars hold it to be the case, though some elect to be a bit more cautious by calling the sect "Essene-like."[27] Unless proved clearly otherwise, it seems acceptable for us to regard it as an Essene sect (but not as the only Essene group, since sister groups were apparently in existence in other places as well).

A small number of scholars, though, have advanced views still different from the majority opinion which accepts the Essene identity of the sect. The renowned Oxford scholars G. R. Driver and C. Roth have contended that the Qumran sect must have been the Zealots, a group of militant nationalists who were active during A.D. 66–70 in fighting against the Romans.[28] This theory, however, meets with serious difficulties. As we will discuss in the next section, the Jewish struggle with the Romans in those days presented a situation of enormous complexity, and the "Zealots" is an inaccurate umbrella term for several different factions of rebels. Josephus, our main literary source, tenders biased information because of his personal enmity toward them.

The most serious problem of this theory is that the archaeological data from the community center and the caves at Qumran indicate the existence of the sect already in the second century B.C., and the center was destroyed by the Romans in A.D. 68. Seemingly some of the members thereafter fled to Masada because some fragments of a sectarian writing now called the "Songs of the Sabbath Sacrifices" were found at this fortress occupied by a rebel party, the Sicarii (not Zealots).[29] But this does not necessarily mean that the Qumran sect as a whole was a fanatic group as were the Sicarii.[30] Incidentally, the script of this particular document is strikingly similar to that of a fragmentary manuscript of Daniel from Cave I (lQDan[a]).[31] This fact indicates that all of the Qumran scrolls had been written at least prior to the fall of Masada in A.D. 74, since lQDan[a] apparently presents the latest of all the Qumran documents.

Another theory which was once vigorously advocated concerns a Jewish sect called Karaits.[32] This group, originating in the beginning of the eighth century A.D., constituted an anti-traditionalist movement which denied the Talmudic-rabbinic tradition (e.g., rejected the oral laws) and acknowledged the scripture as the sole and direct source of religious law. They claimed their origin from the high priest Zadok and also embraced fervent messianism.

This theory, like the Zealot theory, ignores the available archaeological evidence. The Qumran community could not have existed in medieval times. The script of the scrolls demonstrates its antiquity as well. Moreover, the Karaits were known for their denial of any belief in angels and spirits, whereas this belief was an integral part of the doctrine at Qumran. It is presumable rather that the Qumran-Essene Judaism influenced the medieval Karaits, as they have betrayed intriguing similarities. An interesting fact in this connection is that the manuscripts of the Damascus Document were found in a Karaits' synagogue in old Cairo (as we have noted before).

Lastly, we may add a distinct but long-discarded view which regards the Qumran sect as a Jewish-Christian group (like the Ebionites).[33] Though some interesting connections can be seen between the sect and the early Christian movement (as we will discuss in Chapter Four), the Qumran sectarians were unmistakably Jewish. This Jewish-Christian view also ignores the archaeological and paleographical evidence.

From the foregoing discussion, the Essene identity of the sect of the scrolls should be considered as the most reasonable. As well, we have noted that archaeological data constitute a crucial factor in our understanding of the history and nature of this sect. Let us then proceed in our discussion to the subject of the historical and archaeological investigation of Qumran and the sect.

(3) The Qumran Community Center

Recognizing the great significance of the discovered scrolls and fragments from the caves, archaeologists undertook an exploration of a ruin on the plateau between the cliffs of the caves and the Dead Sea shore. During the period of 1953 to

Qumran Community Center (31 B.C.)

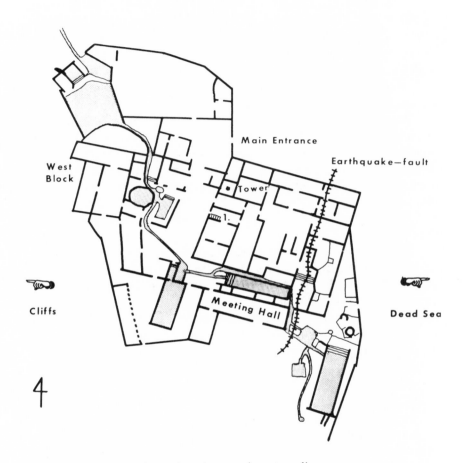

West
Block

Main Entrance

Earthquake—fault

Tower

1.

Cliffs

Meeting Hall

Dead Sea

4

1. Stairs leading to the scriptorium on the upper floor

1956, Fr. R. de Vaux and his team excavated the building site itself and established the fact that it was the place used communally by the people who deposited their scrolls in these caves.[34] Identical types of pottery and coins from the same period, though circumstantial in essence, provided enough evidence to determine that conclusion. The jugs, bowls, lamps, and other kinds of pottery were unearthed in the community building and also in some thirty caves, which is indicative of the fact that the former served as the place for communal activities, while the latter were used as dwelling places. A few other caves appear to have been utilized for storage. The members presumably also lived in tents near the community center but not in the center itself, for there is no trace of the existence of sleeping quarters there.

According to Fr. de Vaux, there were five phases of occupation at the community center. The first phase constituted the Israelite period. He found the evidence of a rather simple rectangular building with a cistern, which he dated to the eighth and seventh centuries B.C. This site is identified with "the city of salt" (mentioned in Joshua 15:62), where the king of Judah, Uzziah (781–740 B.C.), built a settlement.[35] It was subsequently destroyed and abandoned until about the middle of the second century B.C. when it was resettled. And with that, the second phase began.

Those resettlers were the Essene sectarians. The rebuilding of the site seemingly commenced during Simon Maccabaeus' reign (142–134 B.C.). From then until the conquest by the Roman troops in A.D. 68, the sectarians occupied Qumran. De Vaux discerns three different periods (Ia, Ib, and II) during that stretch of time. Period Ia marks the establishment of the sectarian settlement, which appears to have been rather small in size and relatively short in duration. Their building was modest, but three cisterns were created (one of the ancient ones was included in this total of three).

It was during Period Ib, beginning sometime in the reign of John Hyrcanus (134–104 B.C.), that extensive construction was undertaken. An influx of newcomers must have prompted this considerable expansion; the community thrived and reached its climax. The building compound included a watchtower, an assembly hall (for communal meals and the study of scripture), a pantry, a kitchen, workshops, and storage rooms. The scriptorium was apparently located on an upper floor which collapsed. Pieces of a crumbled table were found scattered on the ground, and a couple of ink bottles were also discovered with dried ink in them. The scrolls from the caves must have been written in that room. An impressive installation was the water system—a well-built complex of conduits which channeled rain water into seven large cisterns. The water was of great importance not only because of the dry climate in the region but also because it was used for daily bathing.

Period Ib ended with an earthquake and fire (the traces of which are visible). Josephus reports that there was an earthquake in the seventh year of Herod the Great (31 B.C.). That was most likely the incident which caused the inhabitants to leave the site. (The cause of the fire is undetermined—caused perhaps by the earthquake or a military action.[36]) The place was apparently left abandoned during the major part of Herod's reign (37–4 B.C.). The reason for this long vacancy eludes us.

Most likely at the turn of the Christian era, nonetheless, the community was restored back to its former scale and function, inaugurating Period II. The building and facilities were repaired and strengthened. Catastrophe visited the sectarians when the Roman troops assaulted in A.D. 68. Roman arrowheads and ruins resulting from an intense fire provide us with graphic evidence of the calamity.

Period III comprised the time of the Roman military presence (A.D. 68–87); the soldiers constructed an outpost there by reusing the burned material. After the departure of the Roman troops, the site was occupied very briefly by Jewish rebels during the disastrous uprising led by Bar-Kokhba (A.D. 132–135). It was left deserted from that period until modern times, concealing ancient secrets under the rubble.

(4) Origin and Fate of the Sect

What motivated this group of Jews to settle in Qumran in the second century B.C.? Cryptic references found in the scrolls seem to suggest that there were three major figures who played key roles in the genesis of the sect: the Teacher of Righteousness (or the Righteous Teacher), the Wicked Priest, and the Man of Lies. None of them is identified by name in the Qumran documents. The Teacher was apparently an important Zadokite priest originally at the Jerusalem temple, who was persecuted by his powerful opponent, the Wicked Priest. The person called in the scrolls "the Man of Lies" seemingly acted as a traitor; he was once an ally of the Teacher and subsequently betrayed him. But who were they? And what happened?

Most modern scholars set the scenario in the tumultuous situation in Jerusalem in the middle of the second century B.C. As we read in 1 Maccabees, it was in the time after the defeat of the Maccabean war which had been led by Judas Maccabaeus against the Greeks. Judas' brother Jonathan managed to reclaim the political leadership in Jerusalem by exploiting the turmoil among the international powers including the Greeks and Romans. He eventually became the high priest in 152 B.C.—the highest office which commanded both political and religious rule over the Jews, who had no real political independence under Greek domination. Thus the dynasty of the Hasmonean family was established. Jonathan, however, was killed by Trypho, a Greek marshal, who felt that the Jewish high priest had grown too powerful. The high priesthood was then passed to Jonathan's brother Simon, who stayed in the office from 143 to 134 B.C.

Babylonian Origin?

Now, how do these three figures fit into our historical drama? J. Murphy-O'Connor has proposed a view that traces the provenance of the sect to Mesopotamia; that is to say, it was one of the last groups of Jews who returned from Babylonia, the land of exile.[37] He seeks textual support in the Damascus Document. In 2:18–3:12, the author of the Document relates a summary of the history of ancient Israel, which ends with a reference to the Babylonian exile. The passage goes on to state: "But with those who adhered to the commandments of God, who were left over of them, God established His covenant with Israel by revealing to them the mysteries in which all Israel had gone astray . . ." (3:12–14). In this paragraph, the faithful "Israel" seemingly refers to the Essenes, while the renegade "all Israel" points to the remainder of the Jews. So then, Murphy-O'Connor concludes, the Essene origin should be found in the land of exile. Perhaps inspired by the Maccabean nationalistic fervor, the Essenes (though not all of them, cf. CD 19:33f.) returned to Jerusalem, where, however, they, representing the ultra-conservative branch of Babylonian Jewry,[38] experienced a deep disappointment with the Hellenized society they found, as well as with religious trends which were unacceptable to them.

The Teacher of Righteousness was, according to Murphy-O'Connor, "almost certainly the senior member of the Zadokite family from which high priests were traditionally drawn."[39] Despite his claim of legitimacy, he was ousted when the non-Zadokite Jonathan was placed in office by the Greeks in 152 B.C. With bitter discontent and anger, he fled for his life to the Essenes, and this caused a schism within the sect. Of the two resulting groups, one was led by the Teacher and the other by the "Man of Lies." The Teacher withdrew to Qumran with a small band of his followers to establish a community there.

The Babylonian origin of the Essene sect is indeed a possibility,[40] but this conjecture is not supported by conclusive evidence. Many scholars, consequently, still favor the commonly held view that the Essenes as well as the Pharisees stemmed from a group of pious fighters during the Maccabean uprising. These fighters were called the Hasidim ("pious ones"). In other words, these scholars still affirm that the Essene sect was born in Palestine.

The Wicked Priest

Although disagreeing with others regarding the provenance of the Essene sect, Murphy-O'Connor joins the majority opinion in identifying the Wicked Priest as Jonathan, who usurped the high priest's office by deposing the Teacher.[41] The high priest immediately previous to this incident was Alcimus. Since he was not a Zadokite priest and died in 159 B.C., he could not have been the Teacher. According to Josephus, "the city continued for seven years without a high priest" (*Ant* 20:237). But 1 Maccabees 10:38 refers to a high priest, though not named, at that time. Someone would have officiated at the feasts at the temple at any rate. Who was that person? He must have been the senior member of the Zadokite family—none other than the Teacher. But when the Greeks, with political intention, ignored the Jewish law by appointing Jonathan to the office, the Teacher was ousted.

F. M. Cross and others, however, identify the Wicked Priest with Simon, Jonathan's brother and successor.[42] Based on 1 Maccabees chapter 14, which praises Simon as a great leader of the Jews, Cross points out that Simon was chosen by the Jews while Jonathan had been appointed by the Greeks. Cross also notes that Simon's (and his descendants') authority as high priest was declared so superior and perpetual that all his orders were to be obeyed and no one was to be allowed to convene an assembly without his permission. "Thus in the early years of Simon, the high priesthood was irrevocably transferred from the Zadokites to the Hasmoneans."[43] This situation, according to Cross, occasioned the establishment of the Qumran sect and its persecution at Simon's hand in Jerusalem.

Lack of evidence prevents us from determining which brother should be identified as this accused figure. In the Habakkuk Commentary 8:9, he is said to have been "called by the name of truth (i.e., of good reputation) when he first arose." This reference seems to be applicable to either of the brothers. Jonathan was a war hero, and Simon was accepted by the Jews as a good administrator (1 Maccabees 14).

The Commentary condemns him by saying that "when he ruled over Israel, however, his heart became proud and he forsook God and betrayed the precepts for the sake of wealth. He robbed and gathered the riches of the men of violence who rebelled against God, and he took the wealth of peoples, accumulating sinful iniquity upon himself. And he practiced the ways of abominations in every unclean defilement" (8:9–13). This censure is not specific enough to identify precisely the censured one. A man of authority such as the high priest could have easily abused his power.

According to 9:9–12, his final fate was such that "God gave him into the hand of his enemies to bring him low with a mortal blow in bitterness of soul . . ." (10–11). Again this information can be related to either Jonathan or Simon, since both of them were killed. What complicates the question still further lies in 9:2 which says that the Wicked Priest died from "evil diseases and vengeful acts on his body of flesh." Neither of these Hasmonean brothers died as a result of sickness. To solve this dilemma, scholars often interpret "diseases" symbolically to mean a dreadful death (which both brothers met).[44]

In addition to these paragraphs, some other passages also from the Habakkuk Commentary have been cited to identify the Wicked Priest (e.g., passages dealing with his "drunkenness" in

11:12–17,[45] and with his death "in the midst of many peoples" in 10:3–5).[46] But none of these portions provides any persuasive indication as to the historical identity of the Wicked Priest. Regardless of the choice between Jonathan or Simon, what many modern scholars consider most crucial is concerned with the illegitimacy of the Wicked Priest as a high priest; that is what caused the sect to complain vehemently to the Jerusalem establishment and to withdraw to Qumran. In other words, the "Wicked Priest" actually meant the "illegitimate priest" as against the Teacher of Righteousness, i.e., the legitimate priest. The rituals officiated by illegitimate priests were, the sectarians insisted, not only invalid but also terrible profanations of the temple.

Conflict between the Sect and the Wicked Priest

The issue of non-Zadokite illegitimacy for high priestly office appears to have been one of the most crucial problems about the Teacher and his followers. Curiously, however, as W. H. Brownlee, a Qumran specialist since the time of the scroll's first discovery, points out,[47] this issue does not seem to be underscored in the scrolls as a vital point of the sectarian contention against the Wicked Priest. In its stead, the censure of him mentions his arrogance and violence, his abuse of power, his greedy accumulation of wealth, his drunkenness, and his persecution of the Teacher. Because of these offenses, the Habakkuk commentator returns the verdict that the Wicked Priest had gone astray from God and his Law and would certainly provoke severe divine punishment.

Another significant conflict between the Teacher and the Wicked Priest apparently lay in a calendarial difference: the former's solar calendar (364 days a year) versus the latter's lunar calendar (354 days).[48] The calendar was a rule expressive of divine creation and the preservation of the whole universe. As such, it offered a normative rhythm for people's daily life, including their religious feasts and festivals. It was, therefore, of vital significance; it was not to be altered or modified arbitrarily. The Teacher and his followers argued that the dates on which the festival days were arranged for the practice at the Jerusalem temple were "those in which all Israel was in error" (CD 3:14).

God, however, revealed to the sect "the mysteries in which all Israel had gone astray. The sabbaths of His holiness and the festivals of His glory, the testimonies of his righteousness, the ways of his truth—these are the desires of His will which man should do and live by" (CD 3:14–16).

With such grave differences, it must have been simply impossible for the Teacher and his opponent to have coexisted in the same temple city. The bitter controversies must have resulted in the sect's withdrawal to the wilderness near the Dead Sea. But the wrath of the Jerusalem authorities apparently persisted. The Qumran commentator on Habakkuk wrote that the Wicked Priest pursued the Teacher to "the house of his exile (i.e., Qumran) to devour him with the wrath of his anger. And at the time appointed for the rest, on the Day of Atonement, he appeared before them to confuse them, and to cause them to stumble on the Day of Fasting, the Sabbath of their rest" (lQpHab 11:4–8). This passage seems to indicate the Wicked Priest's attempt to physically terminate the sectarian observance of the festivals according to a calendar different from his "official" one.[49] (He could travel from Jerusalem to Qumran because it was not the high holy day according to his calendar.)

The calendarial difference is indicative of a disagreement of legal interpretation and application. A serious conflict regarding the legal tradition *(halakha)* between the Qumran sect and the Jerusalem religious establishment must also have been a major cause for the sectarian withdrawal to Qumran.[50]

At the International Congress on Biblical Archaeology (the seventieth anniversary of the Israel Exploration Society) held in April of 1984 in Jerusalem, the existence of a letter by the founder and leader of the Qumran sect (the Teacher of Righteousness) was reported.[51] According to the reporter and custodian of this document, J. Strugnell, it was most likely written in approximately 150 B.C. and has survived in six separate copies, though unfortunately in a fragmentary state. The letter, because of its special importance, was copied many times. The names of the addressee as well as the addressor are both missing in the extant texts. But the context of the letter indicates that it was sent to a politically important person (the high priest in Jerusalem, in Strugnell's opinion). It contains about twenty laws, about which the author (the Teacher) differed from the addressee; an uncompromisingly strict position was advanced by the sectarian leader. This letter undoubtedly attests to the fact that the conflict in halakha constituted a significant reason for the departure of the sect.

From the foregoing observation, it seems to be reasonable to say that one single issue was certainly not the reason for the establishment of the Qumran sect. Modern scholars have perhaps overemphasized the question concerning the legitimacy of the high priesthood, and thus are compelled to focus almost exclusively on either Jonathan or Simon. To determine the identity of the wicked Priest is obviously a linchpin of our investigation. Scholars' attempts to pin down the exact historical identity of this figure have not been conclusive. The references to him in the scrolls are highly cryptic and elusive. It is erroneous to interpret the passages with a predetermined identity.

Wicked Priests

Then we come to the question: Was the Wicked Priest really a single individual called by this name? Or did the name imply several persons—influential priests (high priests) at the Jerusalem temple? In recent articles, A. S. van der Woude[52] and W. H. Brownlee[53] contend that we should assume the existence of more than one "Wicked Priest." The former suggests that there are six men who are called by that name in the text of the Habakkuk Commentary. The first reference pertains to Judas Maccabaeus (165–160 B.C.) in 8:8–13. He was the first military leader of the Maccabean revolt and was initially successful against the Greeks. Then, however, he lost his Hasidic allies when they accepted Greek offers to concede to the Jewish people religious (but not political) freedom. The passage criticizes the Wicked Priest who fell into personal greediness despite initial favor. It thus seems to be applicable to Judas. Although he was not a high priest, he was from a priestly family and perhaps could command supreme authority comparable to a high priest.

The next reference to the Wicked Priest (8:16–9:2) may concern Alcimus, who was the high priest (161–159 B.C.) though not a Zadokite. It tells how he was chastised by "judgment of wickedness and of evil diseases" because of his rebelliousness. Alcimus is said to have suffered from a fatal stroke. The third reference (9:8–12) describes the Wicked Priest's receiving a divine scourge, being delivered into his enemy's hand because of the wrong done to the Teacher and his followers. As we have already mentioned, Jonathan was executed by his enemy, and he fits the description well.

Fourth, Simon may be the referred person in 9:16ff. The text has been badly damaged, but we read words speaking of the Wicked Priest's building activity. Simon, according to 1 Maccabees, engaged in constructing fortresses, monuments, and city walls. The Habakkuk Commentary 11:2–8 contains the next mention of the Wicked Priest. We read here of his persecution of the Teacher "at his place of exile" (i.e., Qumran) on the Day of Atonement. Van der Woude considers John Hyrcanus (134–104 B.C.), son of Simon, to be the persecutor, for the Qumran archaeological Period I falls in his reign.[54]

In 11:8–11, we have the author's criticism of the Wicked Priest's habitual drunkenness. The high priest who would fit this description is Alexander Jannaeus (103–76 B.C.), the son of John Hyrcanus, who, according to Josephus (*Ant* 13:398), "fell ill from heavy drinking." Three years after that he died. As Van der Woude points out, the use of the imperfect tense in the Hebrew text suggests that his death had not yet happened when it was written. This is in consonance with the imperfect tense used in reference to his punishment at the hand of God in 12:2–6: "God *will* sentence to complete destruction. . . ." If so, the Habakkuk Commentary was written between 79 and 76 B.C., because Alexander Jannaeus died in 76 B.C.

When understood in this way, our Commentary contains critical comments on a series of serious conflicts between the sect and the Hasmonean rulers. (Among the Hasmonean high priests, only Aristobulus I, 104–103 B.C., the oldest son of John Hyrcanus, does not appear. It is perhaps because he was in office only one year.) This particular view seems reasonable. "The Wicked Priest" most likely refers to several individuals of the high office in Jerusalem, even though the ambiguity of the various passages in question inevitably leaves uncertainty in identifying these people.

The Fate of the Sect

Despite persecutions, the sect not only survived but thrived. As mentioned earlier, the Qumran archaeological Period Ib marks a considerable expansion of the settlement, which indicates an influx of new members. They could have been converts from the Pharisaic party, because bitter animosity developed between the Pharisees and the Hasmonean rulers from the last years of John Hyrcanus and continued on to the time of his successor Alexander Jannaeus.[55]

As we have mentioned before, this prosperous state was, however, suddenly terminated by an earthquake in 31 B.C. The community, though restored sometime around the turn of the Christian era, met with final destruction with the Roman conquest in A.D. 68. What happened to the sectarians who survived it? There is no explicit evidence to clarify the question. Some apparently fled to Masada where they perished (we will refer to this event later), while others perhaps were dispersed to even further places of which we have no knowledge. Did they join rabbinic Judaism or remain as a small, separate group? Were the Karaits a medieval revival of the Essenes? These are possibilities but the answer eludes us now. Did some members convert to Christianity? Perhaps yes. This question and many other aspects of possible connection between the Qumran sect and New Testament Christians will be dealt with in Chapter Four.

At any rate, our knowledge concerning Jewish history between the second century B.C. and the first century A.D. has been enriched by the Qumran documents. Hitherto little-known fringe groups like the Essenes have come to light. The discovery of the scrolls, without a doubt, constituted an epoch-making event. It has spurred enormous interest on the part of contemporary students, among both scholars and lay persons, in events in those particular days of antiquity and in rugged, dry lands like the wilderness of Judaea. This same enthusiasm also predisposed archaeologists and local Bedouins (the latter were perhaps more motivated by money) to discoveries of other documents from the wilderness. These finds and their historical implications are the subject of the following sections.

3. The Judaean Finds and the First Jewish Revolt

After the destruction of the country by the Babylonians in the sixth century B.C., the Jews were forced to live under a series of heavy foreign yokes: the successive rules of the Babylonians, the Persians, the Greeks, and the Romans. Occasionally, a violent rebellion would erupt—the Maccabean Revolt against the Greeks in the second century B.C., the First Jewish Revolt against the Romans during the latter half of the first century A.D., and the Second Revolt in the early part of the second century A.D. The freedom the Jews anxiously longed for, however, did not come; they instead experienced the excruciating agony of struggle and defeat.

(1) Josephus, the Main Literary Source

In this section, we deal with the First Jewish Revolt. In what way would archaeological finds in Judaea help us in our understanding of this traumatic page of Jewish history? Until the excavations of the Judaean caves and Masada, historical sources came solely from the Jewish historian Flavius Josephus (A.D. 38-c. 100).

According to his own account, Josephus was born of an aristocratic priestly family in Jerusalem. He received excellent education and training in Judaism, and then joined the Pharisees. Such a personal background seems to have led him to embrace a moderate political view, as against the militants of his day such as the Sicarii and the Zealots. When the First Revolt broke out, he was reluctantly drawn into the war to become a commander in Galilee. Upon surrendering to Vespasian, the Roman general, his life was spared by virtue of his prediction that Vespasian would soon be emperor, which indeed became a reality in A.D. 69. Now a supporter of the Roman side, he unsuccessfully attempted to mediate between the Romans and the rebels besieged in Jerusalem. Following the fall of the city, he resided in Rome as a Roman citizen to devote his time to writing *the History of the Jewish War, the Antiquities of the Jews,* his auto-

Jerusalem at the Time of Herod the Great

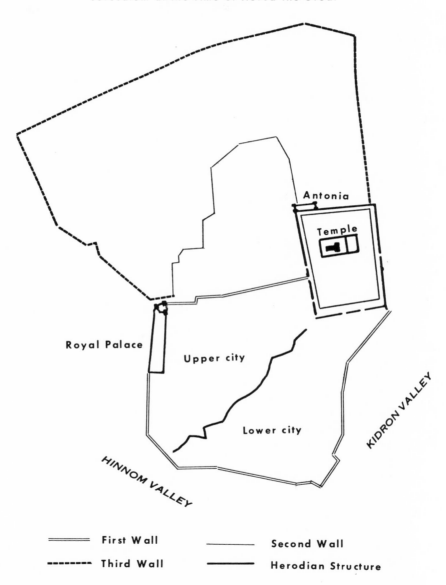

═══════	First Wall	
--------	Third Wall	
────────	Second Wall	
━━━━━━━━	Herodian Structure	

Antonia

Temple

Royal Palace

Upper city

Lower city

KIDRON VALLEY

HINNOM VALLEY

biographical story entitled *Life,* and *Against Apion,* an essay
defending Judaism against Hellenism.

Though undoubtedly these works by Josephus still remain
as the only literary sources of that period of Jewish history, they
contain numerous instances of biased views and unreliable
information. Josephus definitely intended to present in a favor-
able light his own life, his nation, and its heritage to his Roman
readers; he, therefore, did not hesitate to alter or modify historical facts and to make exaggerations. The blame for the war, consequently, he ascribed to militants (whom he called "bandits")
and not to civilized, peace-loving moderates like himself.

Such a self-portrait of Josephus is bound to cause controversy. Was he simply a shameless traitor or a true peace-making
intellect caught in the bloody turmoil? Was he for or against the
war? Scholars' assessment of Josephus varies greatly. For example, S. Freyne, who recently published an excellent study about
the Galilee of those days, insists that Josephus actively pursued
the war, though how much he was driven with militant zeal is
unclear.[56] On the other hand, S. Zeitlin, a noted Jewish scholar,
proposes just the opposite view. He flatly states: "Josephus was
always against the war with Rome,"[57] and contrary to his wish,
"his army became a Frankenstein to him."[58] The majority opinion seems to regard him as representative of the moderate group
which attempted, though it failed, to somehow contain the revolutionary fire. He was indeed the "unfortunate Jew" (Yadin).

The controversial ambiguity pertains not only to Josephus'
personal views and conduct but also to the whole situation of
that period. It was truly a reality of enormous complexity—utter
chaos. Consequently, an historical reconstruction is far from facile. How much of Josephus' information is reliable? Needless to
say, his account of the fight in Galilee and Jerusalem must have
been based on his own experiences. But he did not participate
in the battle at other places in Palestine; he probably never visited Masada, for instance. (He, however, mentioned in *War*
7:404 that two women who survived told the Roman soldiers
what had happened at the Masada summit.)

The accuracy of Josephus' story can be tested by archaeological data. He is often wrong,[58] but in some cases, he is on the
mark. For example, he correctly states that Masada's walls are

seven stadia, i.e., about 1300 meters long, and describes rather accurately the northern palace (*War* 7:286). The perimeter of Jerusalem's wall is said to be thirty-three stadia (6138 m.), which is close to a modern archaeologist's estimate (5550 m.).[60]

What then was his source? He apparently used what he calls "commentaries of the Emperor Vespasian" (*Life* 342) to relate the military drama of the First Revolt. M. Broshi and others think that they were actually field reports of Roman military commanders which were available to Josephus during his literary pursuit in Rome.[61] Consulting Josephus' accounts as well as archaeological data, let us discuss the causes of the First Revolt.

(2) Causes of the First Revolt

The Socio-Economic Factor

There seems to have been no direct and clear-cut cause for the Jews to have waged a massive revolt against the Romans. A number of negative factors accumulated and drifted into a large-scale war. First of all, there were the social and economic factors. The Jewish populace was generally suffering from heavy taxes from both the Roman and Jewish authorities. The procurator Albinus (A.D. 62–64), in fact, even increased the Roman taxes (*War* 2:273). Needless to say, the poor had to bear the greatest burden. Particularly when famine hit the land in A.D. 48 (cf. *Ant.* 15:299–316; Acts 11:28), many of them, having been unable to pay the tribute, were forced either to go into slavery or to take up banditry as a livelihood. The brigandage, in fact, became quite widespread in those days. Josephus declares: "The whole of Judaea was infested with the bands of brigands" (*Ant.* 20:124).

In contrast to the penury of the lower class, the upper class exploited the situation by collecting taxes and by ingratiating themselves with the Roman officials. Josephus mentions, for example, incidents at the time of Albinus: (a) turmoil existed which he calls "class warfare" (*War* 20:179) when the high priests even took advantage of the lower priestly orders (*Ant.* 20:206f.); (b) more turbulence occurred because of the lay aristocracy (Costobar and Saul) who were "plundering the property of those weaker than themsleves" (*War* 20:214).

The brigandage seems to have been a desperate alternative on the part of the poor under such drastic circumstances. As many modern scholars point out, a close link apparently existed between banditry and the peasant revolt.[62] Before and throughout the war, there lay an unbridgeable schism replete with profound resentment and distrust between the aristocracy and the poor. In fact, Simon ben Gioras, one of the leaders of the rebels, not only maltreated the wealthy people of Judaea and ransacked their houses (*War* 2:652), but also burned the public archives in Jerusalem to destroy the moneylenders' bonds (*War* 2:427). Josephus also reports that Simon proclaimed liberty for the slaves (*War* 4:508). These activities of Simon illustrate dramatically the social and economic causes of the Revolt. The war was supported by the general populace from the beginning; it was not a well-organized military venture by one unified group.

Roman Cruelty

The second factor for the Jewish sedition is found with the Romans, that is, the Roman officials' incompetence and cruelty in handling a series of critical events. For example, as Josephus complains in his report (*War* 2:292), when the disturbances occurred in Caesarea between the Jews and the Greeks, Gessius Florus (A.D. 64–66), the last Roman procurator of Judaea, first did nothing to solve the problem, but then later unduly punished only the Jews. He furthermore appropriated money from the temple treasury (*War* 2:293), had his troops sack the city (2:305), and executed innocent inhabitants, including women and children (2:306–308). These occurrences, needless to say, infuriated the Jews; Florus, as Josephus says, "fanned the flame of war" (2:293).

The Religious Factor

The third and last factor of the Revolt was religious in nature. This was first and perhaps most eloquently demonstrated by a revolutionary hero by the name of Judas, who came from the city of Gamala in Gaulanitis (a province east of the Sea of Galilee). In A.D. 6 when the first Roman procurator, Coponius (A.D. 6–9), and the legate of Syria, Quirinius, took a census of the Jews and their properties (*Ant.* 18:2; Lk 2:2), Judas, together with Saddak the Pharisee, refused to subject themselves to the Roman order. Judas claimed that "the assessment carried with it a status amounting to downright slavery, and he appealed to the nation to make a bid for independence" (*Ant.* 18:4). To the Jews, assessment was tantamount to ownership.[63] Judas and his followers insisted that God alone was their leader and master.

Josephus counts this religio-political movement as the last of the four Jewish "philosophies" of his time, listing it with the other three "schools": the Sadducees, the Pharisees, and the Essenes (*Ant.* 18:9, 23). Josephus, however, never mentions the name of this "fourth philosophy" (Judas is called "a sophist who founded a sect of his own" in *War* 2:118), nor does he follow up on its fate in his narratives. A laconic reference in Acts 5:37 informs us that Judas "perished" and the others were "scattered."

It is even uncertain as to what extent Judas' insurrection gained support from his compatriots. His family, however, seems to have played an important role in the course of the Jewish revolt against Rome. Judas himself might have been the same Judas who was the son of the brigand chief Ezekias during Herod's time.[64] The father and son both carried out the fight of resistance in Galilee (*Ant.* 18:271–272). The descendants of Judas of Gauranitis (Josephus calls him "Judas the Galilean") were also fighters. His sons, James and Simon, were crucified under the procurator Tiberias Alexander (A.D. 46–48) (*Ant.* 20:102). Another son, Menahem, was a rebel leader battling with the moderates in Jerusalem only to be killed in A.D. 66 (*War* 2:433). His grandson Eleazar became the Sicarii commander at Masada and committed suicide with the others (*War* 7:253).

This family history suggests an ideological tradition of resistance continuously flowing in the pedigree.[65] Though paucity of evidence hampers decisive historical reconstruction, the Jewish revolt was apparently motivated by such a religious ideology from the outset. Their loyalty to God as the only lord and their devotion to the Law were incompatible with pagan rule. Some scholars hold the view that such a belief perhaps led the freedom fighters of Masada to commit mass suicide to avoid being captured alive to be sold as slaves.[66] The teaching of "no lord but

God" resonates in Eleazar's suicide speech (*War* 7:323, though
written by Josephus) and also in the message of the Sicarii at
Alexandria, Egypt, after the war (7:410–419).

It is beyond reasonable doubt that religious factors were res-
olutely at work among not only the moderates but also such militants as the Sicarii. But this did not result in a united front
against the Romans; the reverse was the case. The Jews were
hopelessly fragmented, one group sanguinarily feuding against
another. Who were these groups? And what happened to them?
These are the questions which will be dealt with in the next
section.

(3) The Course of the Revolt

The years preceding the First Jewish Revolt (A.D. 66–73)
marked a steady deterioration of the conditions among the Jews.
Agrippa II (A.D. 28–c. 100), the Jewish ruler appointed by high-
ranking priests and wealthy landowners, was anxious to avoid
any military confrontation with the Romans while worrying
about the war-minded factions. They seemingly constituted a
moderate group, though they were not well organized.

As for the militants, scholars have often assumed the existence of a single monolithic party called the Zealots. A classical
example of this view was presented by E. Schürer, who published a monumental work on Jewish history during the time of
Jesus.[67] He equated the militant opponents of the Romans singularly with the Zealots founded by Judas the Galilean in A.D.
6. This party also encompassed various smaller, notably fanati-
cal, factions—one of which was the Sicarii. The selfsame understanding has been held by more recent authorities such as Y.
Yadin, who excavated the last stronghold of the rebels at
Masada.[68]

The Sicarii

Josephus, however, did not use these two designations of
the groups interchangeably. As for the name Sicarii, Josephus
wrote: "They employed daggers, in size resembling the scimitars
of the Persians, but curved and more like the weapons called by
the Romans *sicae,* from which these brigands took their name
because they slew so many in this way" (*Ant.* 20:186). This ref-

erence appears to be accurate. According to M. Hengel, the word *cica* (curved dagger) was actually an often-used curse against foes during Roman civil war. The Romans applied the term to the Jewish rebels, and it subsequently became the name of a group of Jewish militants.[69]

The provenance of the Sicarii party is uncertain, but, as we have noted previously, Josephus apparently indicated a connection between the earlier revolutionary Judas the Galilean with the Sicarii (though it is tenuous to assume that he founded the military organization). The Sicarii as a group appears to have arisen during the reign of Anotius Felix, the procurator of Judaea (A.D. 52–60). Josephus stated that "a new species of banditti was springing up in Jerusalem, the so-called Sicarii, who committed murders in broad daylight in the heart of the city" (*War* 2:254). This party continued to be very active—"devastating," according to Josephus (*Ant.* 20:185f.)—in Judaea at the time of Porcius Festus, the successor of Felix (A.D. 60–62). (Incidentally, this Festus was, according to Acts 25, the procurator who sent St. Paul to Rome under custody.) The defenders of Masada were clearly identified by Josephus as the Sicarii (*War* 4:400; 7:253). And that was the final phase of the Sicarii activity as well as of the Revolt itself.

Battles in Jerusalem

By the summer of A.D. 66, the insurgents headed by the temple captain Eleazar were gaining power against the moderates of the high priest Ananias and other aristocrats. The former finally took control of the temple area and the Lower City, while the latter held the Upper City with the help of Agrippa. A fierce battle ensued. The sacrifices offered twice daily on behalf of the Roman emperor were suspended, which meant an open rebellion against Rome. When the Sicarii joined Eleazar's force, the moderates lost ground; the residences of Agrippa and Ananias were burned and the archives destroyed.

The turmoil worsened when Menahem, son of Judas the Galilean, and his followers arrived at Jerusalem with the weapons they took from Herod's armory at Masada. After killing Ananias, the high priest, Menahem himself assumed rule, only to be executed by Eleazar's men. At this juncture, Eleazar, the grandson of Judas, who apparently had supported Menahem, fled to Masada with his partisans.

Eleazar's force also annihilated the Roman guards stationed in Jerusalem. Realizing the crisis, Cestius Gallus, the Roman governor of Syria, marched to Jerusalem after subduing Galilee and the coastal region. A ferocious battle drove the defenders almost to the brink of utter subjugation, but the Roman commander "suddenly recalled his troops, renounced his hopes, without having suffered any reverse, and, contrary to all calculation, retired from the city" (*War* 2:540). This totally unexpected retreat turned the tide of the war; the Romans accepted a miserable defeat. Coins were minted to demonstrate Jerusalem's new-found independence; many of them bore inscriptions such as "Jerusalem is holy," "The freedom of Zion," and "For the redemption of Zion." The discovered coins range from the first year (A.D. 66) to the fifth year (A.D. 70).[70]

Needless to say, this turn of events, on the one hand, stirred up the morale of the insurgents, but, on the other hand, it served as a prelude for the inevitable and massive reprisal from Rome. Josephus described it as follows: "After this catastrophe of Cestius, many distinguished Jews abandoned the city as swimmers desert a sinking ship" (*War* 2:556). Christians were seemingly also among the refugees at that time; according to Eusebius (c. 260-c. 340), the church historian and the bishop of Caesaria, they migrated to Pella in Transjordan *(Ecclesiastical History 3, 5, 3).*

After the victory over Cestius, the Jews established the council and appointed Ananus as high priest, but Eleazar retained supreme authority. Anticipating the imminent Roman onslaught, the rebels fortified the strategic towns of various regions of Palestine. The Roman troops finally arrived under the command of Vespasian and his son Titus. Even the desperate fighting of the Jews could not stop the well-trained and well-equiped Roman force; the towns fell one by one beginning in Galilee, then in Samaria, in the coastal area, and finally in Judaea—Jerusalem was left as the decisive target.

Jerusalem was in utter chaos; numerous refugees as well as the original towns people were segmented, ferociously feuding one against another. Over against the anti-war groups which included the pro-Roman and the moderates, there were several pro-war factions such as the Sicarii and the Zealots.

The Zealots

Josephus' information about the Zealots is ambiguous and thus controversial. M. Hengel detects the earliest reference by Josephus to them in *War* 2:444, which refers to "zealots" who were following Menahem. Upon the leader's death, Hengel further surmises, this party split into two: the Zealots and the Sicarii.[71] M. Smith (who represents perhaps the most severe critic of this German authority) opposes this view, regarding the "zealots" not as a party but simply as "fanatics."[72] As he rightly points out, Josephus clearly states three times that the Sicarii chronologically came first (*War* 7:254, 262, 324). Consequently, Smith concludes that the Zealots became "an organized and important group only late in the revolt" (i.e., mid-winter of A.D. 67–68).[73] Josephus indeed began mentioning the Zealots as a party seemingly around that point of time (see *War* 4:161ff.); they were said to have followed Eleazar, son of Simon (*War* 2:565; 5:5).[74]

Being a moderate, Josephus accused the Zealots vigorously: "For so (Zealots) these miscreants called themselves, as though they were zealous in the cause of virtue and not for vice in its basest and most extravagant form" (*War* 4:161). He then narrates with profound praise and sympathy the counter-measures taken by high priest Ananus and his followers against the Zealots. They, however, with the help of the Idumaeans, defeated Ananus' forces and killed him.

At this juncture, there were three competing factional leaders in Jerusalem: Eleazar son of Simon, John of Gischala (a rival of Josephus in Galilee, who fled from there to Jerusalem), and Simon son of Giora (a late-comer to Jerusalem supported by the Idumaeans)—these two Simons were not related. The Zealot party split into two factions: one supporting Eleazar and the other siding with John. A fierce struggle for hegemony over the entire city continued among those three rivals (which became two as John subjugated Eleazar's group), but they held one thing in common—the desire to eliminate those who spoke for peace (*War* 5:30).

Meanwhile Vespasian was proclaimed emperor in A.D. 69, and his son Titus took over the command of the Roman assault on Jerusalem. A cruel, indeed hellish, battle ensued through the following year; casualties were extremely high on both sides. The Jews died not only from the fighting itself but also from starvation—to the extent that even cannibalism took place (Josephus recorded in *War* 4:205–208 an incident where a mother actually ate her own child).

Catastrophe in Jerusalem

In September of the year A.D. 70, Jerusalem fell to the Romans. Intending to defend his friend and benefactor Titus but writing contrary to historical facts,[75] Josephus in his *War* 6:241 (cf. 6:254ff.) underscored Titus' attempt to save the temple from destruction by blaming soldiers who he said were driven mad and threw torches into the building. Thus ended the magnificient temple of which the Talmudic sages declared later: "He who has not seen Herod's temple has never seen a stately structure in his life" (Baba Bathra 4:5).

Modern excavations at the Southern Wall near the Western Wall (the Wailing Wall) have unearthed in abundance pilasters and their capitals, stone sundials, and other architectural materials. The archaeological finds eloquently demonstrate the lost glory of the city as well as the devastation wrought by the Roman conquest.[76] A vivid illustration of this dreadful tragedy is a burned house which was uncovered by a recent excavation in the Jewish quarter of modern Jerusalem. The house was destroyed by the conflagration at the moment of the Roman invasion. Inside the house, the skeletal remains of the right arm of a woman was found resting on the wall of the kitchen; she was apparently victimized by the intense flame.[77] Josephus' description indicates that the destruction was so thorough that no visitor could have believed that it had been inhabited (*War* 7:3).

The rebel leaders Simon and John were captured; the former was later executed and the latter sentenced to life imprisonment. Archaeological traces of the Roman triumph are found in a section of a broken column unearthed in the south of the Southern Wall with the inscription of the names of Vespasian and Titus.[78] Other evidence is displayed graphically in the Arch of Titus at the Roman Forum (erected in A.D. 81) where a sculptured panel demonstrates the emperor's triumphal procession carrying booty, including the candelabrum (menorah), the trumpets and the altar of Shew-bread taken from the temple.[79]

The Jewish dream of restoring the Holy City, nonetheless, persisted. Though in a muted voice, this dream speaks itself in the inscription carved on a huge stone in the Western Wall by the Jews in fourth century A.D. when the emperor Julian decided to resettle the Jews in the then Christian city of Jerusalem.[80] It is a quotation from Isaiah 66:14; "You shall see, and your heart rejoice; your bone shall flourish like the grass."

Fall of Masada

What happened to the Sicarii who fled to Masada? As we have mentioned earlier, Eleazar ben Jair, the grandson of Judas the Galilean, dissented from the rebel forces in Jerusalem and entrenched himself and his partisans in Masada. By virtue of natural advantage and a remote location, it was indeed a formidable stronghold. Thus in A.D. 74 when the Roman troops led by Flavius Silva arrived at the region, they found themselves in a position which necessitated preparations for a long siege. First, a wall was built encircling the entire mesa to prevent the defenders from escaping, and then a huge ramp was constructed on the western slope for the purpose of an assault. (Its length is about 215 yards, almost leading to the summit.) All this as well as traces of the Roman camp is clearly visible even today.

Finally a strong battering ram was brought up to the top of the ramp. The defense wall could not withstand the violent ramming, but the defenders managed to devise a second wall behind the breached area of the outer wall by using soil and beams to cushion the pounding. The desperate defense mechanism collapsed when the attackers set fire to the wooden support. And that brought an end to this Jewish fortress; the defenders took their own lives.

This crucial happening narrated by Josephus is corroborated by archaeological evidence. Josephus' report, however, has been found inaccurate on some other accounts.[81] For example,

Masada

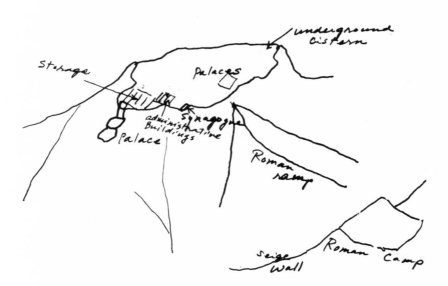

he mentioned only one palace which was destroyed by fire, but there were actually two, and all the public buildings were set ablaze. Our historian also reported that "they quickly piled together all the stores and set them on fire" (7:394), but Yadin's exploration uncovered various items in many different places.

In addition to these discrepancies between Josephus' narratives and the available archaeological data, the skeletons found in the cave as well as the traces of numerous separate fires have led some scholars to doubt his description of the united action taken by the defenders during the final hours. A few even suspect that the Sicarii fighters at Masada were, in fact, massacred by the Romans instead of committing mass suicide.[82] But why did Josephus have to fabricate the story in the face of the experience of thousands of Roman soldiers who actually participated in the conquest? After all, he had related Roman brutality in the war in many places in his book.

Josephus, in spite of his disdain of the Sicarii as "bandits," praised their suicide as an act of bravery. He stated, for example, that the Roman soldiers "admired the nobility of their resolve and the contempt of death displayed by so many in carrying it, unwaveringly, into execution" (*War* 7:406). Such a romantic narrative has induced later Jewish nationalistic fervor, and Yadin's expedition visibly fomented it in modern times. It is well illustrated by the following sentence written by Yadin: "Masada represents for all of us in Israel and for many elsewhere, archaeologists and laymen, a symbol of courage, a monument to our great national figures, heroes who chose death over a life of physical and moral serfdom."[83] It also gave rise to the idea of the so-called "Masada complex" of the Israelis today.[84]

This is quite understandable in view of the long history of the Jewish plight, especially following the Nazi holocaust. However, R. Alter has rightly pointed out, "Jewish tradition, at any rate, has always seen Yavneh and not Masada as the great symbol of national survival against terrible odds—of regeneration."[85] Rabbi Yohanan ben Zakkai chose to survive, instead of dying in Jerusalem under the Roman siege in A.D. 70, in order to perpetuate the Jewish spiritual tradition by founding a rabbinic school in the town of Jamnia. He indeed opted for a life of spirituality rather than an heroic death.[86] Thus the Jewish heritage survived, but, unfortunately, so did their suffering. This leads us to our next subject, the Second Jewish Revolt against Rome.

4. The Judaean Finds and the Second Revolt

Despite the tragic defeat of the First Revolt, the Jewish quest for freedom was never relinquished. Around the turn of the year from A.D. 115 to 116, for example, there was a formidable Jewish rebellion in various places such as Cyrene and Egypt. And then the second and the final desperate struggle with Rome broke out in A.D. 132. The Second Revolt, led by a man usually called Bar-Kokhba against the Emperor Hadrian and his troops, was equal to the First in intensity and in its tragic end as well.

Literary sources attesting to the event are extremely meager—unlike the First Revolt provided by Josephus. The Roman administrator and historian Dio Cassius (A.D. c. 150–235) and the church historian and Bishop of Caesaria Eusebius (c. 260–c. 340) referred to it briefly, though their writings do not totally agree with each other. Other scattered references (e.g., Epiphanius, rabbinic literature, etc.) are considered basically inaccurate by modern scholars.[87] Recent archaeological discoveries from the Judaean caves, Muraba'at, and the underground complexes in the Judaean foothills, consequently, have contributed greatly to our knowledge concerning this calamitous drama.

(1) Causes for the Revolt

What triggered the revolt? What are the immediate as well as general causes for the revolt? It is not easy to answer the question, because ancient sources fail to supply us with a clear-cut picture, and modern scholarly assessment therefore varies. But the following two reasons of which ancient writers make mention seem to contain a good amount of historical accuracy. First, Dio states that Hadrian built a Roman town upon the ruin of Jerusalem and called it Aelia Capitolina. Hadrian then erected a temple of Jupiter on the site of (or in place of) the Jewish temple. Such an overt attempt to paganize the Jewish holy city was so

A silver coin minted in Jerusalem in the second year of the First Revolt. The inscription on the reverse side: "Jerusalem the Holy."

A bronze coin struck in Rome in A.D. 71 to commemorate the Roman victory. The bust of Vespasian, and on the reverse side a victorious Roman soldier and a mourning Jewish woman with the inscription: "Judaea caputa."

A silver coin struck during the Second Revolt showing the Jerusalem Temple with the inscription: "Jerusalem."

intolerable to the Jews that they waged another war against the Romans (*Roman History* 69, 12).

According to Eusebius, however, the Roman construction in Jerusalem was carried out soon after the Second Revolt was quelled (*Ecclesiastical History* 4, 6, 4). While modern scholars like S. Applebaum side with Dio in rejecting totally Eusebius' information,[88] E. M. Smallwood reconciles the two by assuming that Dio records the inception of the plan and Eusebius its fulfillment.[89] A numismatist, Y. Meshorer, reports the discovery of a bronze coin of Aelia Capitolia struck no later than A.D. 130.[90] This evidence, therefore, proves that the Roman colony was already founded in Jerusalem before the war.[91]

The second possible cause for the revolt concerns a prohibition of circumcision. The emperor Domitian (81–96) earlier forbade castration, a decree which was enforced throughout his successor Nerva's time (96–98). Hadrian expanded the law to include circumcision. The fourth century collection of imperial biographies, known as the *Historia Augusta* (wrongly attributed to Aelius Spartianus), cites this imperial order as precipitating the rebellion (*Hadr.* 14, 2). The date of this ban is unknown, which leads Smallwood to suspect that it was a Roman punishment and not a reason for the war.[92] But that possibility is unlikely, and rabbinic references also seem to indicate the Roman suppression of the rite before the uprising.[93]

In addition to these two possible reasons for the revolt, the overall Hellenizing policy of Hadrian constituted a general and indirect cause. The emperor was deeply attached to Hellenistic culture and was eager to demonstrate Roman splendor to the world. Applebaum even believes that "the decision to put an end to Judaism for good and all" was his "major policy decision" at a later stage of his reign.[94]

(2) Bar-Kokhba and His Followers

The name of the leader of the sedition is called *Bar-Chochebas* mainly in ancient Christian sources (Eusebius, Jerome, Justin Martyr, etc.), and *Ben* or *Bar Koziba* often in rabbinic literature. The former must be a nickname, meaning "the son of the star," deriving from a word play on his real name. In fact, according to the Jerusalem Talmud Ta'anit 4, 68d, the foremost rabbi of that time, Akiba, who supported the revolt, reckoned the man (called *Bar Koziva* here) as "the king messiah," citing the oracle of Balaam, "A star *(kokab)* shall come from Jacob" (Num 24:17).[95] This passage is interpreted messianically also in the Septuagint, the Targums, the Qumran documents (CD 7:18f.; 1QM 11:5–7; 4QTest 12–13), the Testament of Levi 8:3; and the Testament of Judah 24:1.[96] This messianic nickname was known among Christians as well (see Eusebius, *Eccl. His.* 4, 6, 2).

The above-quoted Talmudic paragraph also refers to Rabbi Yohanan ben Torta, who retorted Akiba's claim, associating the rebel leader's name not with *kokab* (star) but *kozeb* (liar). Though the historical accuracy of the dispute between these rabbis has not been fully ascertained, the story suggests the controversial character of Bar-Kokhba's attempt at revolution.[97] These rabbis' names, incidentally, never occur in Bar-Kokhba's documents and letters. There is no way to verify personal contact between Akiba and Bar-Kokhba. What then was his real name? The question has been satisfactorily answered by the recent archaeological discoveries from the Judaean wilderness.

The documents from Muraba'at and the caves at Naḥal Ḥever tell us that his real name was Simon (or Simeon) bar (or ben) Kosiba(h), i.e., Simon the son of Kosiba.[98] While some rabbinic references to him suggest kosibah as a locale (the place of his origin), in these Judaean sources it appears to indicate his father's name. Again, despite the rabbinic "koziba," the name should be Kosiba(h). Finally, the name "Shim'on (simon)" is visible on the coins struck by the fighters during the revolt.[99]

Religious Nature of the Revolt

Even with Akiba's messianic endorsement, Bar-Kosiba's name does not appear with title of messiah or king on these coins nor in the Judaean documents. He is called instead "prince *(nasi)* of Israel" in those archaeological finds. (See Documents B, C, D, E, F, G, I, J, in Milik's *DJD* II, pp. 124ff.; Documents 42, 44, 45 in Yadin, *IEJ* 12 (1962) pp.249ff.; for coins, see Meshorer, *Jewish Coins,* nos. 169–170A, 172A, 193.) This name, of course, signifies that he is the supreme leader of the revolt. In the biblical prophet Ezekiel's vision of eschatological restoration, Davidic *nasi* plays the role of a messianic ruler (34:24; 37:25; 44:3). We may recall at this juncture that the symbol of a star is struck on many coins of Bar-Kokhba during the second year of the revolt. The grape cluster is also used on the coins from all three years. These signs, albeit not conclusive evidence, have messianic association.[100] It seems to be safe, therefore, to conclude that his mission was messianic. Its sole aim was the liberation of Jerusalem and Israel. His followers indeed acknowledged him as the liberator.

The liberation war bore not only political but also heavily religious purport as such a messianic overtone of the movement indicates. The war's religious character was eloquently attested to on the coins of Bar-Kosiba; some distinctive symbols struck on them include the Jerusalem temple with the ark, musical instruments (e.g., lyres, harps, trumpets, etc.) used in the temple, the sacred vessels such as amphrac and jugs, and so on. The slogan of the revolt inscribed on the coins minted in the third year of the war explicitly declared; "For the freedom of Jerusalem." (The inscription from the previous two years read: "For redemption/freedom of Israel.") This sounds as though they did indeed succeed in taking hold of the capital city.

Another notable inscription is "Eleazar the priest" on some coins from the first year. The identity of this person eludes us—Eleazar of Modi'in or Eleazar ben Azariah, both of whom were noted rabbis—but he, at any rate, appears to have been an eminent priestly leader in support of the political leader Bar-Kosiba. Incidentally, such a dual leadership corresponds interestingly to the Qumran sectarians' notion of two messiahs, priestly and kingly (see lQS 9:10–11; lQSa 2:11ff.).

All these bits of evidence unmistakably indicate the religious nature of the uprising. Meshorer states that "the main aspiration of the freedom fighters was the reinstitution of the temple service and the restoration of the capital of the land of Israel after it had lain desolate for sixty-two years."[101]

The Followers of Bar-Kosiba

Who were the followers of Bar-Kosiba? We have already mentioned Akiba's support, although no evidence is available as to his activities during the sedition besides his endorsement of Bar-Kosiba. The rabbi's heroic death has been also well-known. But as Applebaum contends,[102] the backbone of the dissident movement derived from the rural population, among whom fervent loyalty to the ancestral heritage was kept alive. Some of these men were organized in brotherhoods as they were called "brothers" in several letters written in Greek.[103] This designation of a group had not been found previously, but such a common bond reminds us of the tightly knit community at Qumran. The Bar-Kosiba's brotherhood certainly was bound together in strong solidarity, sharing the same religious belief and zeal for its military venture. A rabbinic legend relates that men were initiated into the group by having one of their fingers cut off!

There seem to have been, however, somewhat heterogeneous groups as well. In a Greek letter addressed to Yohanan ben Be'ayan and Masabala, the sender, seemingly a non-Jew (whose name is not well preserved: "So . . .ios"), referred to "the camp of the Jews" and stated: "The letter is written in Greek as we have no one who knows Hebrew (or Aramaic)."[104] Dio Cassius also wrote: "Many outside nations, too, were joining them (the Jews) through eagerness for gain" (*Rom. Hist.* 69, 13). The people of the Second Revolt were not a clear-cut monolithic entity. Nonetheless, the personal authority of Bar-Kosiba was apparently uncontested.

The letters of Bar-Kosiba, in fact, demonstrate his tough leadership; many of them were written in an abrupt and stern style. For example, his letter to the two men mentioned above (who were stationed at the rebel base in En-Gedi) harshly reprimands them: "And if you do not do accordingly, you shall be punished severely."[105] Such parlance as this betrays his forceful nature, though his desperate situation perhaps precipitated it (it was written toward the end of the war). Nevertheless, a document from Muraba'at shows his fair-minded control over his men as he scolded his deputy for mistreating the people from Galil. His soldiers were called "brothers." He was also a very devout Jew, as his documents bear witness. In the midst of tumult, for instance, he paid attention to the palm branches and fruits for use in the Feast of Tabernacles.

(3) The Course of the Revolt

The Revolt broke out in the spring of A.D. 132. Not only Dio and Eusebius point to this date, but a document from Muraba'at (Mur 24), which consists of title-deeds written by a deputy of Bar-Kosiba most likely in early February in the second year of the Revolt, provides us with valuable evidence thereof.[106] The first series of Bar-Kosiba's coins with the inscription: "Year One of the Redemption of Israel" was minted most likely in A.D. 132. The date of his documents also begins with the same year. Likewise, the series of both coins and documents ends in 135. (The coins of the first two years are clearly dated, and the undated coins must have been struck in the third year.) Yet, isolated battles seemingly continued on until early 136 in the area of the Judaean caves. The entire length of the Revolt, therefore, lasted three and a half or even close to four years. The rabbinic literature (*Seder 'Olam Rabba* 30) also mentions the three and a half year duration.

Battlefields

The preparation for the uprising before 132 must have been rather extensive.[107] The installation of the underground complexes in the Judaean foothills illustrates the desperate efforts on the part of the Jewish fighters. This confirms Dio's statement:

> To be sure, they (the Jews) did not try engagements with the Romans in the open field, but they occupied the advantageous positions in the country and strengthened them with mines and walls, in order that they might have places of refuge whenever they should be hard pressed, and might meet together unobserved underground, and they pierced these subterranean passages from above at intervals to let in air and light (*Rom. Hist.* 69, 12).

As for the Roman military presence, there were two legions in Judaea by that year; Tineius Rufus was the consular of the territory (appointed in 127). According to recent scholarly opinion, this deployment of troops was necessitated by the widespread uprising of Diaspora Jews during 115–116.[108]

The area of the fight was confined within the territory of Judaea.[109] As the above-mentioned underground complexes evince, the entire Judaean foothills were under the control of Bar-Kosiba. The locales referred to in the Bar-Kosiba documents include 'Ir Naḥash, Rimmon, ha-Luḥit, En-Gedi, Maṣad Ḥasidim (Qumran), Herodium, Tekoa, Qiryat 'Aravaya, Kefer ha-Barukh, Bet Mashikho, Tel Arazin, and some other places. All of them were located in that region, except for ha-Luḥit, which was on the east side of the Dead Sea. Among them, En-Gedi and Herodium, in particular, constituted two of the important rebel bases; the former, an oasis located on the Dead Sea, served as a vital supply port for them, and the latter where King Herod had previously built a citadel, which is still visible, was a (if not the) headquarters of Bar-Kosiba.

Several more significant places should be remembered: Bethlehem, Hebron, Bethar, Wadi ed-Daliyeh, and Jerusalem. The strategically located fortress of Bethar (southwest of Jerusalem) became the very last one to fall into Roman hands as we know from Eusebius (*Eccl. Hist.* 4, 3). Refugees managed to find their way to the caves in Wadi ed-Daliyeh and also to the caves in the cliffs near the Dead Sea, where they were mercilessly attacked and perished.

As for Jerusalem, as already pointed out, the recapture of the holy city was the main goal of the Revolt. The question, however, is whether or not they indeed succeeded in this goal. And if they did, how long did they hold onto the city? Unfortunately, neither reliable literary sources of antiquity nor archaeological evidence is available to verify the facts conclusively. Muraba'at document 25 mentions "the year three of the liberation of Jerusalem," and some of the undated coins attributed to the third year of the Revolt (A.D. 134–135) have the inscription: "For the Freedom of Jerusalem." But it is not certain whether these literary deposits really refer to the actual regaining of the city or represent simply the aspiration for that grand goal.[110] It is, in fact, quite puzzling that only a couple of coins of Bar-Kosiba have been found in Jerusalem itself.[111] Some modern scholars consequently doubt the Jewish reoccupation of the city.

However, as Smallwood points out, some ancient authors such as Appian (a historian from the second century A.D.), and

Justin Martyr (c. 100–c. 165), and Jerome (c. 347–c. 420) did make mention of Hadrian's destruction of Jerusalem.[112] These references seem to suggest the rebels' presence in the city. It is now beyond our reach to reconstruct exactly the Jewish military activities in that region.[113]

The Battles

Soon after its outbreak, the Revolt developed into a large-scale war because "at first the Romans took no account of them (the rebels)" as Dio says in his *Roman History* (69, 13). Realizing the seriousness of the situation, Hadrian sent "his best generals" (Dio); above all, Julius Severus was dispatched perhaps in 134 all the way from Britain. Altogether twelve legions, some in their entirety while others partially, were involved in the operation.

The battles were fierce and cruel. But the arrival of Severus apparently marked the outset of the decisive victory of the Romans. Dio reports:

> Fifty of their most important outposts and nine hundred and eighty-five of their most famous villages were razed to the ground. Five hundred and eighty thousand men were slain in the various raids and battles, and the number of those that perished by famine, disease and fire was past finding out. Thus nearly the whole of Judaea was desolate. . . .

The Roman search-and-destroy mission continued into the Judaean caves, where refugees were hunted down one by one. Many of them also died from thirst and starvation. The gory sight of forty skeletons in the Cave of Horrors ruefully illustrates the fate of some of the victims. They include not only adult males but women and children as well. The excavator of the cave, Y. Aharoni, observes: "The graves in the Cave of Horror show that the siege was of considerably long duration and that the occupants did not surrender even when death had begun to take its toll of them." At last, however, "the besieged occupants therefore evidently decided to make a great bonfire in the center of the cave and destroy all of their belongings—apart from the great scroll of the Twelve Minor Prophets which, together perhaps with some important documents, was buried between the rocks of the end chamber."[114] This fire was so intense that a glass bowl was found warped. Thus ended the desperate Jewish struggle with mighty Rome.

As devastating as the struggle was to the Jews, it was also a costly victory to the Romans. Dio wrote: "Many Romans, moreover, perished in this war. Therefore Hadrian, in writing to the senate, did not employ the opening phrase commonly affected by the emperors, 'If you and your children are in health, it is well; I and the legions are in health'" (*Rom. Hist.* 69, 14).

The people of Israel were subjected to a series of catastrophes by foreign aggressors: the Assyrian conquest of the northern country Israel in the eighth century B.C., the Babylonian exile in the sixth century B.C., the Maccabean Revolt against the Greeks in the second century B.C., and the First and the Second Revolts against the Romans in the first and second centuries A.D. Their tragic history unfortunately continued even thereafter. But they have survived throughout the centuries until today. By contrast, where have all those ancient conquerors gone? What happened to the power and glory of which they so arrogantly boasted? They have long been buried in the documents of antiquity and in the ground. Modern archaeological research has revealed various pieces of valuable evidence to reconstruct these pages of past history. It helps in unfolding not only the ever-repeated human drama of pain and futility but the tenacious human struggle for hope as well.

3

The Significance of the Judaean Finds for Old Testament Studies

1. The Evolution of the Hebrew Biblical Text

The Hebrew text of the Old Testament traditionally has been the Masoretic text. During the ninth or tenth century A.D., it was finalized in its present form by rabbinic scholars called Masoretes (*masora,* meaning "tradition").[1] Recently, however, a number of texts of the Old Testament have been found among the caves of Qumran and other Judaean sites. Amazingly, these biblical manuscripts pre-date in antiquity the Masoretic text by nearly a millennium, and they encompass all of the Old Testament books with the exception of Esther. These manuscripts were copied between the third century B.C. and the second century A.D.

Prior to their discoveries, in fact, no ancient pre-Masoretic texts were available (except for a small fragment usually called "the Nash papyrus" from the second or first century B.C.).[2] The Judaean documents, therefore, shed enormous light on the whole problem of the evolution and history of transmission of the Hebrew scripture. How then did the Hebrew text evolve? And in what way do the new finds contribute to modern scholarly investigation in this regard?

Original Biblical Texts

Was there one archetypal biblical text, from which all manuscripts derived? Or, conversely, were there variegated streams of textual traditions which eventually flowed into one authoritative version? P. A. de Lagarde is representative of those who hold the former view—the archetype (Ur-text) theory, i.e., that the presence of the pristine text evolved no earlier than the first century A.D.[3] True, all the biblical fragments from Muraba'at, Naḥal Ḥever, and Masada exhibit the official rabbinic tradition. The evidence from Qumran, however, demonstrates clearly a diversity in textual type which antedates the official text *(textus receptus)*.

The latter position is advanced vigorously by P. Kahle, who asserts the existence of the "vulgar texts" of various kinds prior to the standard Masoretic text.[4] The Hebrew manuscripts from Cairo Geniza, which he published, prompt him to insist that the textual tradition was more variable than de Lagarde theorizes. The Qumran witness, in fact, proves it. The Geniza evidence, however, is much too late (the ninth-tenth centuries A.D.) to adduce in favor of his theory. Also, rabbinic scribal activity was operative in a period earlier than he postulates.

Local Text Theory

Is there then any alternative to these two rival theories? What are more recent scholarly opinions? Drawing upon the variety in the types of biblical texts in the Judaean manuscripts, F. M. Cross puts forward the "local text" theory.[5] According to his analysis, the documents corroborate the existence of three distinct groups of biblical text. First, there is the Palestinian text; the great majority of the Qumran biblical material belongs to this textual family. Moreover, the text of Samuel as used by the Chronicler (shortly after 400 B.C.), Josephus' Bible (the first century A.D.), and the Samaritan Pentateuch (the second-first centuries B.C.) are each also a part of the same textual tradition. Cross maintains that this textual tradition was preserved in Palestine, and thus named the "Palestinian text."

Second, we have the Egyptian text. A number of fragments from Cave IV (e.g. 4QJer[b], 4QEx[a]) present an affinity in text-type to the Septuagint, on the one hand, but, on the other hand, scarcely betray features of the Proto-Masoretic text, though bearing resemblance to the Palestinian text in certain ways. Cross attempts to explain these intriguing facts by locating this textual tradition in Alexandria, Egypt, where the Septuagint was produced. The "Egyptian" text perhaps branched off from the Old Palestinian family in the fifth or fourth century B.C.

Third, Cross asserts the existence of the Babylonian text. It is the direct parent text of the rabbinic *textus receptus,* which, in his opinion, was preserved by the Babylonian Jews independently of the other two textual families. It was brought back to Judaea when the Jews returned to the home land. Whereas "genuine exemplars of the Babylonian text-form at Qumran are exceedingly rare, and late in date,"[6] the biblical manuscripts left in the Judaean caves by Bar-Kosiba and his people are solely of the official rabbinic scripture. The *textus receptus,* therefore, must have been established in Palestine during the first century A.D. Cross also suggests that the Babylonian origin of Hillel, a most influential rabbi of this period, could be understood as "a reason for the unexpected rabbinic rejection of the Palestinian in favor of the Babylonian."[7]

With amazement, Cross points out the fact that the Pharisaic scribes adopted one particular local textual tradition without "wholesale revision and emendation nor by eclectic or conflicting recensional procedures"; this procedure stands in contrast to the case of the Septuagint or the New Testament.[8] As a result, all other texts differing from the accepted version seem to have been officially purged. Such rabbinic measures as well as the catastrophe of the war with Rome drastically reduced the number of Old Testament manuscripts. In this manner, the supremacy of the Masoretic text became firmly established. We may summarize this theory with the following diagram:

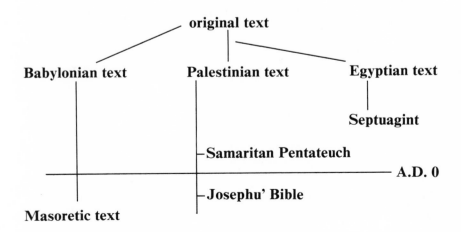

Cross' scholarly endeavor merits great acclaim both for the clear analysis of the extremely complicated textual data and the resulting ingenious theory. Of interest, as S. Talmon points out, is that this theory offers "a new synthesis" of the earlier rival views of de Lagarde and Kahle.[9] Cross, on the one hand, accepts the notion of the solidification of the textual traditions, an idea akin to the Lagardian approach, and, on the other hand, acknowledges the existence of variegated textual strands, which is Kahle's contention. Cross, however, explicitly rejects Kahle's theory of the "vulgar texts"; the terms "standard" and "vulgar" are anacronistic, since there was no standard until at least the close of the first century A.D. Qumran left no trace of attempting to stabilize the text.

The Cross theory, nonetheless, cannot escape scholarly criticism. First, critics object to the idea of the localization of the textual traditions. D. Barthélemy indicates that the scarcity of information with regard to literary activities among the Jews both in Babylonia and Egypt prevents us from drawing a clear-cut geographical picture of textual growth as does Cross.[10] It is likely that some books of the Septuagint (e.g., sections of Samuel and Kings, Ecclesiastes, and Esther) were not translated in Egypt, and also that the Psalms was rendered into Greek in Palestine, as H. J. Venetz and others contend.[11] If so, the parent Hebrew text of the Septuagint cannot be automatically characterized as Egyptian. E. Tov states that "the Septuagint does not reflect any Hebrew text which was characteristic of Egypt."[12] In locating the Proto-Masoretic text in Babylon, Cross does so, as G. Howard puts it, "by the process of elimination,"[13] i.e., after Palestine and Egypt, Babylon is the only place left to consider.

The second main criticism of Cross' theory concerns his assessment of textual types. "This is more or less a matter of personal judgment" (Barthélemy). Cross, in fact, relies often on very small fragments and also on a reconstruction of the Hebrew original from Greek and Syriac texts.

Third, Cross' theory seems to fall short of exhausting the multiplicity of textual traditions which somehow existed for almost two centuries within one tightly knit community at Qumran. The text of the incomplete, second Isaiah scroll (lQIs[b]) is virtually identical with the Masoretic text. A fragment of Jer-

emiah from Cave IV (4QJer[b]) shows a closeness with the Septuagint, and a fragment of Exodus written in paleo-Hebrew
script (the script derived from the old pre-exilic Hebrew script)
from Cave IV (4QpaleoEx[m]) and a text of Numbers from the
same cave (4QNum[b]) are similar to the Samaritan Pentateuch.
Many other biblical texts from Qumran are independent of these
three textual types. Such an enormous complexity inexorably
frustrates any neat categorization.

It seems, therefore, to be rather difficult to remain strictly
with the theory of three local texts. E. Tov says, "The Masoretic
text, the Septuagint, and the Samaritan Pentateuch, which traditionally have been presented as the only three textual recensions of the biblical text, represent, in fact, but three of these
many texts." These many texts "relate to each other in an intri-
cate web of agreements, disagreements and unique readings."[14]

Textual Complexity

S. Talmon, consequently, offers an alternative view: "It
appears that the extant text-type must be viewed as the remains
of a yet more variegated transmission of the Bible text in the
preceding centuries, rather than as witnesses to solely three
archetypes." The textual locale can be sought in the "isolated
socio-religious communities in Palestine" itself and not necessarily inside or outside of Palestine.[15] The textual diversity at
Qumran might have stemmed from the fact that the sectarians
must have come from many different parts of Palestine. In fact,
Philo and Josephus inform us that the Essenes were living in
various distinct villages and towns.

Talmon's view is in need of further clarification particularly
as to the nature of the "isolated socio-religious communities in
Palestine" where the local texts were supposedly preserved. Yet
he seems to be quite right when he says that "Qumran literati
considered biblical literature a living matter, and participated in
the ongoing process of its creation." In this sense, they were
"biblical Israel," unlike the Pharisaic rabbis who consciously
closed the biblical writings.[16]

Then in what way does the "biblical Israel" aid us in reading the Old Testament passages? Do the Qumran manuscripts

provide textual variants that might improve our biblical text? Let us next examine salient examples.

2. Textual Variants

Exodus

Monsignor P. W. Skehan published a preliminary report about a fragmentary portion of the Exodus scroll from Qumran Cave IV (4QEx[Q]).[17] According to him, the extant text which includes Exodus 6:25 to 37:15 represents the Samaritan recension. That is, the manuscript contains textual variants which agree with the Samaritan Pentateuch. As we have previously stated, this is the textual group which Cross calls "the Palestinian text." As for the script of the text, "it is now by far the fullest example we have, and a very fine one, of a quite regular Paleo-Hebrew bookhand,"[18] though not identical with the Samaritan script. The Paleo-Hebrew script of the Samaritan Pentateuch was once considered to be a sign of antiquity, but the discovery of the Qumran manuscripts altered this view. This archaic script was evidently revived during the last two centuries B.C., keeping abreast with the Jewish nationalism of those days.

Of considerable interest is a fragment of 4QEx[a] which Cross reports to belong to the Egyptian tradition reflected in the Septuagint, though at points it appears to offer a more consistent form of that tradition than the Septuagint itself.[19] For example, he adduces that there are four of the six variants found in the first five verses of the text (Ex 1:1–5) which ally themselves with the Septuagint against the Masoretic text, whereas only "one probably agrees with the Masoretic text against the Septuagint."[20]

It follows that there is a considerable amount of textual diversity at Qumran; the same cave, for instance, yielded the texts from one biblical book which represent the two different textual types, the Palestinian and the Egyptian. Further clarification of the whole question should await the event of the full publication of the material from Cave IV.

Leviticus

The textual variety at Qumran is attested to also by the Leviticus scroll from Cave XI (llQLev). According to D. N. Freedman's report,[21] the extant scroll includes the portion beginning with chapter fourteen through seventeen, written in the Paleo-Hebrew script. This is perhaps the oldest surviving text of Leviticus, dated the late second or the early first century B.C., when the Hebrew text was yet to be stabilized. Freedman counts thirty-nine textual variants compared with the Masoretic text, the Samaritan Pentateuch, and the Septuagint. Out of this number, only seven readings are unique to llQLev, and they are either trivial or inferior. Overall, "its affinities are predominantly with the Masoretic text and even slightly more with the Samaritan text."[22] Freedman therefore calls it a type of "proto-Samaritan" text.[23]

Deuteronomy

According to Cross, Cave IV yielded fourteen fragments of Deuteronomy.[24] One which contains the ending of chapter 32 was published by Monsignor Skehan (4QDeut^q).[25] Verse 43 of this manuscript compares in an interesting way with the Masoretic text which is somewhat corrupt here.

MT: Acclaim (or rejoice for/with) his people O nations,
   for he will avenge the blood of his servants,
   he will take vengeance on his enemies
   and will cleanse his land (of) his people.

4QDeut^q: Rejoice, O heavens, with him,
   and bow down to him, all angels,
   for he will avenge the blood of his sons,
   and will take vengeance on his enemies,
   and to his adversaries he will avenge
   and will cleanse the land of his people.

The Qumran text is supported by the Septuagint which runs:

Rejoice, O heavens, with him,
and let all the sons of God worship him;

rejoice, O gentiles, with his people,
and let all the angels of God strengthen themselves for him;
for he will avenge the blood of his sons,
and will take vengeance and recompense justice to the enemies,
and he will recompense those who hate,
and the Lord will cleanse the land of his people.

On the basis of this collation, Skehan attempts to reconstruct the original text:

Rejoice, O heavens, with him;
and ascribe might to him, all sons of God;
for he will avenge the blood of his sons,
and will cleanse the land of his people.

This evidence, though a small fragment, indicates, as we have observed in the Exodus fragment, the existence of some biblical texts which concur with the Septuagint. It helps in our probe into the original state of the text.

Samuel

The fragments of the Samuel scroll from Cave IV (4QSam,[a,b,c]) provide us with another set of intriguing textual variants. Cross dates 4QSam[a] to the first century B.C., and 4QSam[b] to the second century B.C. According to his analysis, the latter (along with 4QJer[a]) presents "clear exemplars of the most archaic hand at Qumran."[26] A preliminary report of 4QSam[c] was made by E.C. Ulrich; it consists of fourteen small fragments dating from the first century B.C.[27] All of these fragments came from a single continuous scroll of 1 and 2 Samuel. This indicates, as had been thought, that the present two books of Samuel constituted originally one volume.

Of significance in regard to the textual type of these manuscripts is that it appears to belong to the category of the Hebrew text from which the Septuagint was translated. After examining the texts which were found in a deteriorating and fragmented condition, Cross concludes that 4QSam[a] "diverged radically from the Masoretic text, and while following a reconstruction of the Septuagint recension (B), represented chiefly by Codex Vati-

canus, it included a number of additions."[28] Let us consider 1
Samuel 1:22 as an example:

> MT: But Hannah did not go up, for she said to her husband,
> "As soon as the child is weaned, I will bring him, that
> he may appear before Yahweh, and abide there
> forever."

> LXX: But Hannah did not go up with him, for she said to her
> husband, "(I will not go up) until the child goes up
> when I have weaned him and he will appear before the
> Lord and abide there forever."

> 4QSam[a]: But Hannah did not go up with him, for she said to her
> husband, "I will not go up until the child goes up when
> I have weaned him that he may appear before Yahweh,
> and abide before Yahweh there forever. And I shall
> make him a Nazirite forever all the days of his life."

Here the Qumran text presents not only its affinity to the Septuagint text but also the unique information that Samuel was a
Nazirite. The biblical story corroborates the accuracy of this
statement.

4QSam[b] agrees with the Septuagint and differs from the
Masoretic text thirteen times, while the opposite case occurs
only four times (three cases are in doubt).

An interesting variant is found in 1 Samuel 21:5, where we
read Ahimelech's answer to David who requested bread for his
men. The Masoretic text runs: "And the priest answered David,
and said, 'I have no common bread at hand, but there is holy
bread. If only the young men have kept themselves from
women.'" Both 4QSam[b] and the Septuagint add "then they may
eat of it,"[29] thereby completing the sentence.

According to Ulrich's comparative study,[30] 4QSam[c] offers
an interesting case: eleven times it differs from the Masoretic
text and follows the Old Greek text (recognizable through the
Codex Vaticanus), while the latter two agree with each other
seven times over and against the former. The Septuagint, however, concurs with the Masoretic text twenty-one times and with

4QSam^c six times. This peculiar fact seems to confirm D. Barthélemy's theory that 2 Samuel 11–24 of the old Septuagint was revised to conform with the Masoretic type of Hebrew text (the so-called Kaige recension).[31]

Furthermore, Ulrich counts seven readings in 4QSam^a superior to the Masoretic text, while only one of the latter is better. According to him, in the case of 4QSam^c there are as many as thirty-one superior readings (including twelve reconstructed ones); the Masoretic text, by contrast, affords seventeen (including four reconstructed readings in 4QSam^c) superior readings.[32]

In 2 Samuel 14:30, for example, the Masoretic text (= Aramaic and Syriac versions) has: "And he (Absalom) said to his servants, 'See, Joab's field is next to mine, and he has barley there; go and set it on fire.' So Absalom's servants set the field on fire." But 4QSam^c and the Septuagint add one more sentence at the end: "And the servants of Absalom set the field on fire; and the servants of Joab came to him with their clothes rent, and they said to him, 'The servants of Absalom have set the field on fire.'" Since these two portions end commonly with the same Hebrew words for "the field on fire," the copyist of the Masoretic text most likely omitted accidentally the latter passage and moved on to the next verse.[33] The Qumran text and the Greek translation (its parent Hebrew text) retain the original text.

In his doctoral dissertation published in 1978, Ulrich undertook a thorough investigation of the relationship between 4QSam^a and the texts of the Masoretes, the Septuagint, and the Bible which Josephus apparently made use of.[34] The conclusion he reached is that 4QSam^a represents a textual tradition of the Book of Samuel which the Chronicler used in his work and from which the Old Greek translation was made in Egypt. He cites forty-two cases where 4QSam^a and the Chronicler agree over and against the Masoretic text, and one hundred and forty-four readings where 4QSam^a and the Old Greek text agree against the Masoretic text.[35]

A complex sequence of recensional activity on the Old Greek version followed; the famous recension done by Lucian (the presbyter who became a martyr in the early fourth century A.D.) was commonly used in those days, and it reflects earlier revisions (the much debated proto-Lucian recension)[36] which

enabled it to conform to the 4QSam text group. Ulrich is also
convinced that Josephus employed a Bible of the 4QSam tradition when he wrote *the Jewish Antiquities.*

Ulrich's work is laudable; he successfully established the
textual affinity of 4QSam[a] and the Greek version. This appears
to lend support to his mentor's (F. M. Cross) local text theory.
The Samuel scroll from Cave IV indeed augmented the importance of the Septuagint for textual reconstruction.

E. Tov, however, criticizes Ulrich, pointing out that the
ratio of congruencies to incongruencies among the texts of
4QSam[a], the Greek, and the Masoretes may not be as high as he
claims it to be; it depends upon the restoration, reconstruction,
and evaluation of the texts. Tov, on his part, still favors the view
that 4QSam and the Septuagint should be regarded as mutually
independent, despite frequent accordance.[37] Thus scholarly
debate goes on. A complete publication of the material from
Cave IV will help to clarify many of these complex questions.

Jeremiah

Like the Samuel fragments, some fractional manuscripts of
Jeremiah came from Cave IV.[38] They include two groups of text:
4QJer[q] contains 7:29–9:2; 9:7–14; 10:9–14; 11:3–6; 12:3–6;
12:13–16; 12:17–13:7; 14:4–7; 15:1–2; 17:8–26; 18:15–19:1;
22:4–16, and 4QJer[b] has 9:22–10:18; 43:3–9; 50:4–6. While the
text of 4QJer[a] agrees with the Masoretic text, 4QJer[b] supplies us
with a Hebrew text identical to the Hebrew text underlying the
Septuagint.

The Greek version of this prophetical book is reduced by
approximately one-seventh to one-eighth, and ordered somewhat differently from the Masoretic text. Scholars' views differ
as to whether the Greek version was based on a shorter and possibly more pristine Hebrew text or caused instead by the translator's attempt to abbreviate the Hebrew text.[39]

4QJer[b] evidently attests to the existence of a shorter Hebrew
text. F. M. Cross indicates that in chapter ten "the Septuagint
omits no fewer than four verses" from the Masoretic Hebrew
text "and shifts the order of a fifth. The Qumran Jeremiah
(4QJer[b]) omits the four verses and shifts the order in identical

fashion."[40] Let us examine next 43:4–6 briefly. The Masoretic text says:

> And Johanan *the son of Kareah* and all the commanders of the forces and all the people did not obey the voice of Yahweh to stay in the land of Judah. But Johanan *the son of Kareah* and all the commanders of forces took all the remnant of Judah who had returned *from all the nations to which they had driven* in order to live in the land of Judah, the men, the women, the children, the daughters of the king, and all the people whom Nebuzaradan *the captain of the guard* had left with Gedaliah the son of Ahikam, *son of Shaphan,* and Jeremiah the prophet and Baruch the son of Neriah.

The italicized words are missing in 4QJer[b] and in the Septuagint. The Masoretic Jeremiah contains many instances of secondary expansion and later revisions, as exemplified in the above passage; names are often given in full, sometimes with titles, and explanatory phrases are added. The Jeremiah Septuagint, by contrast, betrays very few traces of such.[41]

4QJer[b] and the Qumran Samuel fragments certainly enhance the importance of the Septuagint. It is not "just a translation" or simply an example of ancient exegesis and editorial reworking, but is instead a valuable bit of textual evidence useful in recovering a more accurate and original Hebrew text.

Moreover, as E. Tov rightly points out, "the Septuagint and 4QJer[b] reflect not a different textual form (recension) of Jeremiah, but an earlier edition of the book. The first, short edition, preserved in Qumran and in the Septuagint, has been expanded to the form now found in the second edition (the Masoretic text)."[42] The discovery at Qumran, however small and fragmentary it may appear, sheds a valuable light on the textual evolvement both in Hebrew and in Greek.

Isaiah

In contrast to the variegated textual evidence we have observed thus far, the complete scroll of Isaiah from Cave I (1QIs[a]) demonstrates a remarkable consonance with the Masoretic text. (1QIs[b] is even closer; as B. J. Roberts says, its "deviations are not in any way greater or more significant than those in the Masoretic tradition itself."[43]) The textual differences between the two are often simply orthographic. In his thorough study of lQIs[a], E. Kutscher makes the observation: "It is not merely that scribal errors abound in all of them (lQIs[a], the Samaritan Pentateuch and the Septuagint), but that they all underwent conscious editing. . . . It is indeed paradoxical to find chronologically later manuscripts (those of the Masoretic type) to be superior to a far earlier manuscript (lQIs[a])."[44] lQIs[a] is dated, based on archaeological and paleographical evidence, to the late second century B.C. According to Kutscher's analysis, the language and orthography of the Qumran Isaiah scroll bear the mark of extensive influence of the language commonly spoken in Palestine in those days. The Masoretic text, however, retained the older textual tradition unaffected by changing linguistic developments.

Kutscher's theory has been criticized for its "prejudiced confidence in the Masoretic text," as J. Hoegenhaven puts it. The Qumran scribe may well have preserved an older textual tradition. Hoegenhaven contends, "One may object that the distinction between a poor manuscript and an accurate copy of a poor manuscript seems to be of little importance, but the point is that we cannot without solid concrete reasons declare that an individual manuscript is 'poor' only because it contains a number of secondary readings. We can only assign to it a certain contrast with less reliable tradition."[45]

There are, in fact, instances of readings seemingly different from, and even superior to, the Masoretic text. Since we have a publication of the entire text,[46] let us examine these variants in the following passages:

In the Masoretic text of Isaiah 3:24 we read:

> And there will be:
> instead of perfume, there will be rottenness,
> and instead of a girdle, a rope,
> and instead of well-set hair, a baldness,
> and instead of a festive garment, a girdle of sack cloth,
> for instead of beauty.

lQIs[a] adds at the very end "shame," thereby completing the last parallel. This addition is adopted by the *Revised Standard Version* and contemporary commentators.[47]

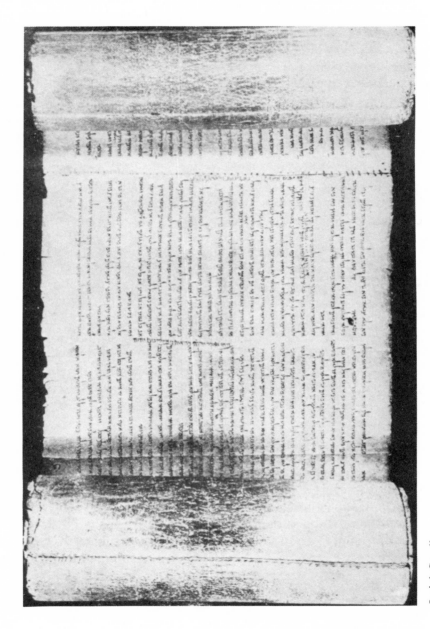

Isaiah Scroll

In the well-known passages consisting of Isaiah's prophecy of Immanuel (7:14), the Masoretic text has:

> Therefore the Lord himself will give you a sign.
> Behold, the young maiden shall conceive
> and bear a son and shall call his name Immanuel.

A textual variant of lQIs[a] in the last sentence can be taken as either "and his name shall be called Immanuel" or "and he shall call his name Immanuel." Modern translators and commentators follow the Masoretic text. Ancient versions, however, offer some variations—the Septuagint: "you shall call. . . ." (the Masoretic vowel pointings, in fact, seem to suggest that the subject is in the second person and female, though scholars still opt to consider it as the feminine third person by regarding it as a dialectical form[48]); and the Vulgate: "he will be called. . . ."

W. H. Brownlee takes "his name" as the subject in the lQIsa[a] sentence by speculating that the Qumran scribe altered the sentence because of the influence of 9:5 (9:6 in English versions) which says: "He (or impersonally, "they") shall call his name Wonderful Counselor, Mighty God, Everlasting Father, Prince of Peace." Thus in lQIs[a], "his name shall be called. . . ." (The ancient versions in Greek, Syriac, and Latin also have the passive voice here.)[49] If we follow Brownlee's interpretation, the Qumran rendering sets a clearer focus on the child as a sign of God's salvation.

If the sentence is to be rendered "he shall call his name Immanuel," however, it can mean either the child will name himself or one (an impersonal rendering) shall name the child. The child is again emphasized by the former translation. The latter finds an interesting correspondence in Matthew 1:23 where Isaiah 7:14 is quoted. Matthew reads: "They will call his name Immanuel." In both we see an impersonal subject.[50] Is this a sheer coincidence? Or did Matthew's Bible belong to the identical textual family with lQIs[a]?

In 11:6, famous as a messianic passage, lQIs[a] provides us with a better text. The Masoretic text runs thus:

> Wolf shall live with sheep,

and leopard shall lie down with kid,
and calf and lion and fatling together,
and a little child shall lead them.

lQIs[a] has: "and calf and lion shall be fattened together." This rendering is stylistically superior to the Masoretic counterpart; it completes the pattern (two subjects with one predicate) in each of the four sentences in this verse. The "fatling" of the Masoretic text occurs elsewhere in the Old Testament, but not its verb (as in lQIs[a]). The Peshitta supports lQIs[a], while the Targum agrees with the Masoretic text. The Septuagint seems to conflate both: "the calf and bull and lion shall feed together."

In the second half of verse four of chapter fourteen, there is a difficult word, *mad[e]hebah* in the Masoretic text.

How the oppressor ended;
Mad[e]hebah ended.

The King James Version puts it "the golden city"; this rendering relates the word with *zahab* (gold), the interchange of *d* and *z* due to Aramaic influence. This interpretation is accepted by some modern scholars such as H. Orlinsky.[51]

lQIs[a] has *mar[e]hebah* meaning "oppression," "turmoil," or "arrogance," which forms a good parallel to the previous line. The ancient versions (in Greek and Syriac) and modern translations adopt this rendering. The difference between these two Hebrew words lies in just one letter: *d* or *r*. In ancient Hebrew paleography, these two letters look very similar, which caused a scribal error.

The switching of these two letters also occurs in other places. For example, in 33:8b:

MT: Covenant is broken, cities reject, none regards.

lQIs[a]: Covenant is broken, testimonies despised,
     none regards.

Here the Qumran text provides a better text.[52]

In the Masoretic text of 14:30, a change of the subject disrupts the parallelism.

And the first-born of the poor will feed,
and the needy will lie down securely,
but I will kill your root with famine,
and he will slay your remnant.

In 1QIs[a] the subject of the last line is the first person singular: "I will slay your remnant," thereby creating a parallel and making the context smooth. Modern translators adopt this reading.

Another example of a superior reading supplied by 1QIs[a] is found in 21:8a. Here the Masoretic text has:

And a lion cried:
"Upon a watchtower, Lord,
I stand always by day,
and at my post I am stationed the whole night."

But why "a lion"? In lieu of "lion," 1QIs[a] has "the watchman," which makes perfect sense in the passage. The resemblance of the spelling of these two Hebrew words ('ryh—lion; hr'h—the watchman) apparently caused confusion on the part of the scribe.

The Masoretic text in 37:27–28 is corrupt.

And their inhabitants, short of hand (= feeble)
are dismayed and ashamed,
and are (like) plants of the field,
and green grass, grass of the roofs,
and a field before it rises (or before standing corn),
I know your sitting down and your going out and
your coming in,
and your raging against me.

The fifth line makes little sense. 1QIs[a] substitutes: "which is blighted before the east wind." This solves the problem. The Hebrew word for "blighted" is also used in the parallel passage in 2 Kings 19:26b.

In the sixth line, 1QIs[a] adds "your rising up," thereby again completing a parallelism:

I know your rising up and sitting down,
and your going out and your coming in.

Modern translators generally follow lQIsᵃ in 40:6, the beginning of Second Isaiah's prophecy.

MT: A voice said, "Cry."
And he said, "What shall I cry?"

lQIsᵃ: A voice said: "Cry."
And I said, "What shall I cry?"

While in the Qumran text, the dialogue occurs between God and the prophet, the voices are not identified in the Masoretic text (heavenly council?[53]). The reading of lQIsᵃ enjoys also the support by the Septuagint and the Vulgate.

In the following passages, too, lQIsᵃ receives both ancient and modern support.

49:17 in MT: Your sons hasten.
Those who tear you down
and those who destroy you
will go forth from you.

lQIsᵃ: Your builders hasten.
Those who demolish you
and those who destroy you
will go forth from you.

49:24 in MT: Can the booty be taken from the mighty
and the captives of the righteous be rescued?

lQIsᵃ: Can the booty be taken from the mighty?
Can the captives of a tyrant be rescued?

51:19 in MT: These two happened to you.
Who will pity you?
Devastation and destruction,
famine and sword.
How will I comfort you?

lQIsᵃ: These two happened to you.
      Who will pity you?
      Devastation and destruction,
      famine and sword.
      Who will comfort you?

60:19a in MT: The sun shall not be light to you any more by
      day,
      and the moon shall not shine brightness to you.

lQIsᵃ: The sun shall not be to you any more light by
      day,
      and the moon shall not shine brightness to you
      by night.

In 51:5, there is an interesting difference between the Masoretic text and lQIsᵃ.

MT: My vindication is near.
    My salvation has gone forth.
    And my arms will rule the peoples.
    Far shores wait for me,
    and for my arm they hope.

lQIsᵃ: My vindication is near.
    My salvation has gone forth.
    And his arms will rule the peoples.
    Far shores wait for him,
    and for his arm they hope.

No ancient version supports the third person singular pronoun as in this Qumran text, and modern translations all follow the Masoretic text. But who is the "he" referred to in lines 3–5? According to D. Barthélemy, the Qumran reading was original but the Masoretes later deliberately altered it to avoid a messianic association.[54] W. H. Brownlee also detects here messianic implication but disagrees with Barthélemy by insisting that it was a Qumran scribe who changed the text so as to assimilate the passage with the messianic Servant Songs.[55]

A similar variant is also found in 46:10b, where we read in the scroll: " . . . my counsel shall stand, and he (MT: "I") shall accomplish all my purpose." Here "my counsel" appears to be personalized. Again the translators of both ancient and modern times agree with the Masoretic text.

Likewise in 62:11 Brownlee attempts to point out another messianic reference.[56] The Masoretic text runs thus:

> Behold, Yahweh has proclaimed to the end of the earth.
> Say to the daughters of Zion,
> "Behold, your salvation comes;
> behold, his reward is with him,
> and his recompense before him."

1QIs[a] adds at the end of the first line "him," which is done in Hebrew simply by appending one stroke (*waw,* indicating the W sound) to *hshmy'* (proclaim). Thus the sentence comes to mean that God has proclaimed him (the Servant), God's salvation. Brownlee's suggestion is intriguing, but is also uncertain.

According to Brownlee, 1QIs[a] provides another messianic passage at the beginning of 53:11a. We read in the Masoretic text: "Out of the travail of his soul, he will see (and) be satisfied. . . ." In this text, the object of "he will see" is not mentioned. 1QIs[a] supplies here "light," i.e., "he will see light." This addition also occurs in 1QIs[b] and the Septuagint, and is accepted by modern scholars. Brownlee, drawing on Job 3:16, 20; 33:28–30, suggests a Job-like figure of a messianic servant whose resurrection is hinted at here. This paragraph (vv. 10–12) is extremely difficult to interpret. Some scholars (e.g., S. Mowinckel,[57] C. R. North,[58] etc.) are willing to accept it as a reference to the servant's resurrection, whereas others hesitate (e.g., C. Westermann[59]) or deny it altogether (e.g., J. Lindblom[60] and H. M. Orlinsky[61]).

The Habakkuk Commentary

The Qumran texts of the Minor Prophets, except for Habakkuk, which have been published thus far are unfortunately very fragmentary. But they belong to a textual tradition close to the Masoretic text. Some small portions of Hosea,[62]

Micah,[63] Zechariah,[64] Nahum,[65] and Zephaniah[66] all confirm this fact.

The sectarian commentary on the Book of Habakkuk from Cave I (lQpHab) contains the first two chapters of this prophetical book. The third and last chapter consists of a psalm entitled "the prayer of Habakkuk." Despite the absence of this chapter in this scroll, scholars, by and large, recognize the book's unity. In fact, a fragmented Greek scroll of the Minor Prophets, a possession of Jewish rebels during their second revolt against Rome (A.D. 132–135), was discovered at Naḥar Ḥever and was published by D. Barthélemy. It includes Habakkuk 3:9–15 as well as a few passages from the previous two chapters.

The variants found in the Habakkuk scroll are many but often orthographical. There are, however, a few passages which show important differences. An example of superior reading is afforded in 1:17:

MT: Shall he therefore empty his net and always slaughter nations? He will not be compassionate.

lQpHab: Therefore, he will draw his net always to slaughter nations and will not be compassionate.

Ancient versions also have "net" as does the Masoretic text. The interrogative form is employed only by the Masoretic text and the Targum, and not by lQpHab, the Septuagint, the Peshitta, and the Vulgate.

In 2:16a, the Masoretic text reads:

you will be sated with shame rather than glory.
Drink, you, too, and show your foreskin.

lQpHab, however, has in the second line: "Drink, you, too, and stagger." This seems to be a better reading, and modern translations (excepting the Jerusalem Bible) follow it. The Septuagint says here: "Heart, shake and quake." Other ancient versions, except for the Targum (= MT), also intimate the idea expressed in lQpHab.

Incidentally, it is interesting to note that the Qumran commentator applied the above passage to the Wicked Priest and denounced him because he "did not circumcise the foreskin of his heart and walked in the way of drunkenness to quench his thirst" (Col 11, lines 13–14). This condemning statement indicates that the commentator took the biblical passage not only as he had it ("walked in the ways of drunkenness" for "stagger," *hr'l* in Hebrew) but also as the Masoretes had it ("did not circumcise the foreskin") for the Hebrew word *'rl,* "circumcised," which is the root form of *h'rl,* "show one's skin." The solution eludes us as to whether this occurred simply by coincidence, because he knew the other reading, or as a result of the Targumic influence.[67]

The Qumran Habakkuk commentary, at any rate, represents a type of biblical interpretation characteristic to the Qumran sect. This hermeneutic method, moreover, finds a parallel in the New Testament. We will discuss this question in the next chapter.

Qumran Psalm Scroll

The discovery of the manuscripts of Psalms (11QPs[a] and 11QPs[b]—both of which belong to the identical textual type)[68] provide us with a variety of information of considerable significance with regard to the biblical Psalms and Jewish worship around the time of Jesus. The larger Psalm scroll (11QPs[a]) contains passages from forty-one Psalms, all of which are from the fourth and fifth books of the biblical Psalter. The order of these Psalms, however, is different from that of our Bible. Another interesting fact in this scroll is that seven non-biblical Psalms, including a prose apropos of David, are interspersed toward the end of the work.

These peculiarities prompted scholars like S. Talmon and M. H. Goshen-Gottstein[69] to maintain that this scroll was a collection of Psalms for liturgy at Qumran rather than a variant canon which J. A. Sanders and Y. Yadin (the editors of the texts) assume it to be. Talmon and Goshen-Gottstein underscore their contentions by noting that the occasions of some of these Psalms are said to be offerings of daily, sabbath, new moon, Day of Atonement, and intercessary prayer; this fact would indicate that this collection "admirably fits a synagogue Psalter, an incipient prayerbook."[70] Furthermore, the solar calendar, typical of the Essenes, is mentioned.

All of these Psalms, including the non-biblical ones, are assumed to be Davidic; the Davidic authorship legitimates their authenticity and authority. In fact, it is stated in column twenty-seven that David wrote 3,600 Psalms and 450 songs "through prophecy" given by God. Sanders is convinced that this authority signifies the scroll's canonical status, though it is in the stage of "an open-ended canon."[71]

As P. W. Skehan says,[72] however, Sanders' synonymous use of the terms "authoritative" and "canonical" is confusing. There appears to have been no such "canon"—no closed list of sacred books at Qumran. In Skehan's opinion, it is "a collection of Pss. 101–150 with liturgical regroupings and 'library edition' expansions."[73] He adroitly explains that it was derived from the standard text of one hundred and fifty Psalms which had by then already been established.[74]

F. M. Cross dates the biblical (canonical) Psalms to the Persian period and the collection represented by 11QPs^a (but rejected by the Pharisaic rabbis) to the Greek period.[75] In fact, Skehan has shown that the author of Jubilees (2:3) quoted a line from col. 26 of 11QPs^a.[76] This fact indicates that the material of this scroll was known during the second century B.C.

What kind of material then is unique to this scroll? This is the question we will now pursue briefly.

Non-Biblical Psalms

The scroll includes not only the biblical Psalms but also seven non-biblical Psalms, namely those which the Pharisaic rabbis in Palestine either rejected or did not have. For example, Ps. 151 is, as Sanders describes it, "a poetic midrash on 1 Samuel 16:1–13." It relates "a story of the humble shepherd David assuming the rule of Israel."[77]

This Psalm has been preserved in Greek, Syriac, and Latin. And now we have it in Hebrew, though it is unlikely that these other ancient versions were translated directly from it. The last couple of lines in 11QPs^a column 28 clearly indicate the beginning of another poem, continuing the theme with respect to

David. The Greek version apparently combined the two (Ps 151A and B) and does not present a meaningful context. As for other ancient versions, it is not yet determined whether they depended on the Septuagint or the common Hebrew recension.[78]

Textual Variants in the Qumran Psalm Scroll

As far as the text of the biblical Psalms from Qumran Cave XI is concerned, the variants it presents are chiefly orthographic and not vitally significant. There are, however, some noteworthy differences.

In Ps. 129:3 the Masoretic text runs:

The plowers plowed upon my back;
they made long their furrows.

11QPs[a] preserves only the first line, which says: "Upon my back, the wicked plowed." The Masoretic text perhaps is the original reading, but the Qumran text spells out the intention of the passage. The Septuagint has "the sinner," which suggests that the Hebrew text which the Greek translator used agreed with the Qumran text. M. Dahood comments that "the meaning of the (agricultural) metaphor had been blurred by the time of the Septuagint and 11QPs[a]."[79] Recent translators and commentators follow the Masoretic reading.

In 135:21, the Qumran scroll seems to provide a better reading:

MT: Bless Yahweh from Zion,
   he who dwells in Jerusalem, Hallelujah.

11QPs[a]: May Yahweh bless you from Zion,
   he who dwells in Jerusalem, Hallelujah.

H.-J. Kraus renders "Yahweh in Zion" by changing the letter *m* to *b* before the word Zion, thus "in" rather than "from."[80] Taking the m-enclitic, Dahood puts it "Yahweh of Zion."[81] The Revised Standard Version and the new translation published by the Jewish Publication Society of America adopt the Masoretic reading, while the New English Bible and the New American Bible prefer the Qumran text.

The most significant variation is found in Psalm 145. 11QPs[a] preserves only verses 1–7 and 13–21. These passages generally agree with the Masoretic text, but there are three notable differences. First, in verse five the Qumran Psalm completes what is anticipated to be a parallelism:

> MT: Of the glorious splendor of your majesty
>   and the works of your wonder I will meditate.

> 11QPs[a]: Of the splendor of glory of your majesty
>   they will speak;
>   about your wonder I will meditate.

The Greek and Syriac versions agree with the first half of the Qumran reading but differ in the second half ("they recont"). Many modern English translations follow the Masoretic text, however.

The second variant is significant in that every verse is followed by "Blessed be Yahweh, and blessed be his name forever." This antiphonal response heightens its effect for liturgical use. Curiously, no ancient version has such an arrangement. Did the Qumran choir add it?

This Psalm is followed by some statement in the manuscript, but it has unfortunately been lost except for a few words: "This is a memorial. . . ." This reference was most likely made in regard to some specific use in liturgy. But it is now beyond our reach even to speculate what kind of liturgy it would have been.

The third variant is also noteworthy. This Psalm is acrostic (i.e., each verse begins with a letter of the Hebrew alphabet and is arranged in alphabetical order), but the verse which supposedly begins with *nun* (after v. 13) is missing. The Qumran manuscript supplies it: "God is faithful in his words and gracious in all his deeds." This sentence is preserved in the Greek and Syriac versions as well. Modern English Bibles, except for the New English Bible, include it. This verse, however, just might be a later insertion, for there is an identical line in verse seventeen, and it is only this additional verse which has God as the subject, while Yahweh is used in other verses.[82]

The Qumran Targum of Job

When Aramaic became the official language under the Persian empire, it also began to be used widely by the Jews. These Aramaic-speaking Jews gradually lost their knowledge of Hebrew. For example, when Ezra read the Torah to the returned exiles in Jerusalem, teachers of the law were obliged to translate it into Aramaic (Neh 8:8). Aramaic versions of the Hebrew scripture became a practical necessity for personal use as well as public reading in the synagogues after a long process of literary development. Thus the so-called Palestinian and Babylonian Targums were eventually born. They were, however, not direct translations, but were paraphrases with explanatory and homiletical intentions.

The Qumran Caves IV and XI have yielded the earliest known Targums of Leviticus (4QtgLev) and Job (4QtgJob and 11QtgJob). The first two from Cave IV are fragmentary, but the last one from Cave XI still retains the form of a scroll. llQtgJob, however, contains unfortunately only fifteen percent of the original scroll: it ranges from 17:14 to 42:11, of which chapter 37 to 42:11 remains well preserved while the rest is badly damaged.[83]

Features of the Qumran Job Targum

Unlike later Targums, llQtgJob is a more literal translation, and its Hebrew original was generally close to the Masoretic text with only eighteen cases of minor differences.[84] Furthermore, the Masoretic order of the book is also corroborated by this Targum. For example, Elihu's speech, which is considered to be a later addition, is preserved in the traditional place (chaps. 32–37).

Curiously, however, this Qumran Targum stops at 42:11, leaving the rest of the column blank. Does this indicate that the translator's Hebrew original did not have the traditional climactic ending—the restoration of Job's enormous prosperity, his beautiful children, and his longevity (42:12–17)? Or did the ascetic Qumran scribe deliberately delete this portion?

It is also interesting to compare this ending with that of the Septuagint Job. After 42:17 the latter adds a paragraph relating

the line of Job's descendants and states that this reference is
quoted from "the Syriac book." F. M. Cross suggests that this
Syriac book might be none other than our Targum of Job and
that the same Targum, moreover, was the Targum which the
Rabbi Gamaliel I (St. Paul's teacher, according to Acts 22:3)
condemned (mentioned in the Babylonian Talmud, Shabbat
115a and the Jerusalem Talmud, Shabbat 16a).[85] These sugges-
tions are intriguing possibilities, but there is nothing more to
substantiate them.

Though generally faithful to the Hebrew text, the translator
deviates from it on a few occasions. In most cases he attempts
to smooth out the context by changing words, and in some
instances betrays his religious sentiment and views. Perhaps the
most striking example of this is found in his rendering of 42:6.
The Hebrew text says: "Therefore I (Job) abhor and repent in
dust and ashes," while 11QtgJob puts it: "Therefore I am poured
out and fall to pieces, and I become dust and ashes."[86] Here the
Job of the Hebrew Bible is a penitent sinner, whereas the Job of
the Qumran Targum is a suffering man who is perfect and needs
no self-abhorrence! Furthermore, in the latter half of verse nine
of the same chapter, the Masoretic text ("And Yahweh lifted up
the face of Job"—the Revised Standard Version: "The Lord
accepted Job's prayer") is rendered as "God listened to Job's
voice and forgave them (Job's friends) their sins on account of
him." The pious' prayer is able to induce divine forgiveness of
the others' sins. (It is interesting to note that the Septuagint also
has in this passage: "And he [God] pardoned their sin through
Job.")

Such a lofty picture of Job echoes in the rendering of 32:13
as well. The Qumran Targum has Elihu saying: "But God will
condemn us (Job's friends)" by changing the Hebrew text which
runs: "Let God rebuke him (Job)." These renderings reveal a
high esteem for Job's piety among some circles of the Jews of
the last post-exilic period.[87]

Provenance of Qumran Job Targum

When was a Targumic version such as this produced?
According to the modern editors of this Targum, it was copied
in the early part of the first century A.D., and the original work

was produced perhaps in the latter half of the second century B.C.[88] As a Targum it is early, indeed. J. Fitzmyer remarks: "This Targum may even antedate the time when the Book of Job came to be regarded as canonical, though its status as such does not seem to have been much contested."[89]

In the editors' opinion, this Targum was composed in Palestine. Its linguistic features, however, do not seem to corroborate this judgment. A thorough analysis by T. Muraoka has elucidated that (1) the language of our Targum belongs to the period between the time of the Aramaic preserved in the Hebrew Bible (Gen 31:47; Jer 10:11; Ezra 4:8–6:18; 7:12–26; Dan 2:4b–7:28) and the Aramaic of the Genesis Apocryphon; (2) it is far closer to the former than the latter; (3) it was "most probably preserved in the East between 250 and 150 B.C."[90]

This theory of the eastern origin may be further supported by the fact that this document contains a few Persian words but no Greek words. Also, the rabbinic Targum of Job (considered to be of Palestinian origin) is not related to it.[91] So, then, we may be able to presume that llQtgJob presents an exemplar of the Targum of Mesopotamian Jewry and is not a product of the Essenes at Qumran (unless we follow Murphy-O'Connor's theory that the sectarians were recent returnees from Mesopotamia).

We may also be justified in asserting that the non-expanded Aramaic versions of the Hebrew Bible (e.g., those close to the Hebrew text), such as 11QtgJob, were used by Jews outside their homeland for their private reading. C. Rabin even surmises that "such translations provided a pattern for the Onqelos-type targums."[92] The discovery of the old Targum at Qumran thus sheds valuable light on the early stage of the targumic tradition in Judaism.

The language of this Targum, according to Muraoka, was not the Aramaic spoken in Palestine. But as scholars universally recognize, the language of the Genesis Apocryphon represents the Aramaic used in Palestine. Let us then consider next the linguistic situation of Palestine around the turn of the century B.C. to A.D., including the language spoken by Jesus; here again the discoveries in the Judaean wilderness contribute greatly to our knowledge.

3. The Language of Palestine

Scholars once assumed that Aramaic was the common language used in Palestine during the last centuries B.C. and the earliest centuries A.D. Aramaic had become a *lingua franca* in the ancient Near East from about the eighth century B.C.[93] Hebrew had become a dead language following the exile, and the Hebrew of the Mishnah was, after all, an artificial language employed only by Aramaic-speaking rabbis. The evidence adduced in support of this view has included the Aramaic portions of Ezra and Daniel, the Aramaic quotations in the New Testament (e.g. "Abba"—"father," in Mk 14:36; Gal 4:6; Rom 8:15; "Talitha cumi"—"little girl, get up!" in Mk 5:41; "Eloi, Eloi, lama sabach-thani"—"My God, my God, why did you forsake me?" in Mk 15:34; "Maranatha"—"the Lord comes," in 1 Cor 16:22; "Ephatha"—"be opened!" in Mk 7:34),[94] Aramaic influence on the New Testament syntax,[95] the Aramaic original of Josephus' *Jewish War* (cf. *War,* 1:3), the Targums and some other rabbinic writings (such as Megillat Ta'anit).

This theory, however, has been seriously challenged. M. H. Segal has forcefully contended that Mishnaic Hebrew was not an Aramaicized scholarly jargon but indeed a spoken language which was born out of the peculiar dialectical condition of the post-exilic period. He, however, has consented to the traditional view that Jesus spoke Aramaic.[96] H. Birkeland has advanced arguments in his monograph that Jesus' Aramaic words in the Gospels were quoted precisely because they were exceptional; that is, Jesus used Aramaic "a few times" but originally spoke Hebrew, which was translated into Greek.[97] According to Birkeland, the language of the common people in Palestine at the time of Jesus was Hebrew.

A great majority of contemporary scholars seem to take the "revisionist theory,"[98] that is, while Jesus usually spoke Aramaic, Hebrew was indeed used by the Jews of those days. This view is predicated particularly upon the recently discovered documents from the Judaean wilderness. The Aramaic finds, in fact, constitute a major portion of the extant Aramaic corpus from that period.

Aramaic Evidence

The Genesis Apocryphon provides us with a good example of what Kutscher calls "Judaean Aramaic." According to him, the language of this manuscript belongs to a transitional stage between biblical Aramaic and a later Aramaic dialect. It betrays much evidence of Palestinian Aramaic and only a trace of eastern Aramaic. He states: "The Genesis Apocryphon is also important in Jewish language history as evidence that there was in pre-Mishnaic times a Palestinian Jewish Aramaic literature."[99] In addition to this scroll and other Aramaic fragments from Qumran (Prayer of Nabonidus, Description of New Jerusalem, Testament of Levi, Enoch, Pseudo-Daniel, Targums of Leviticus and Job), the letters of Bar-Kosiba and his people, as well as numerous ossuary inscriptions and funerary epigraphs in Aramaic,[100] are indicative of the spoken Aramaic of Judaea of the initial two centuries A.D.[101] Furthermore, in his well-known study of Aramaic influence on the Greek of the Gospels and Acts, M. Black tenders a convincing argument that the sayings of Jesus, in particular, were originally in Aramaic.[102]

Consequently, J. C. Greenfield accurately states in his review of Black's book, "Properly speaking, this (Qumran Aramaic) is the only literary Aramaic that we have that is contemporaneous with the Gospels and Acts and theoretically it is with the Aramaic of the Qumran finds that one should begin the examination of a possible Aramaic approach."[103] Agreeing with Greenfield's view, Fitzmyer has pointed out several instances of literary parallels between the Aramaic documents from Qumran and the New Testament.

In Luke 6:7 ("And the scribes and the Pharisees watched him, to see whether he [Jesus] would heal on the sabbath, so that they might find an accusation against him"), the Greek grammatical construction for "find an accusation" *(heurôsin katērein)* is unusual. But as the Genesis Apocryphon 21:13 attests, the Aramaic word *'ashtah* means both "to find" and "to be able." If there is an Aramaic influence in the use here of *heurein* ("to find"), the sentence means: "so that they might be able to accuse him"; thereby the problem is solved.[104]

Another example is found in Matthew 7:6: "Do not give dogs what is holy; and do not throw your pearls before swine. . . ." Here a "ring" (*q'dāshā'* in Aramaic) might have been mistaken for "what is holy (*q'dûshāh* in Aramaic). In fact, the Job Targum from Qumran has a sentence which has this word, ring: "And they gave him, each one a lamb and a ring of gold" (38:8). Thus in Matthew 7:6, the parallelism of "ring" and "pearl" is established.[105]

The Qumran Targum of Job contains the absolute use of "Lord" *(mārā')* as a title for God.[106] Thus, we now know that the New Testament use of "Lord" is rooted in the Palestinian Jewish tradition rather than in the Hellenistic milieu as scholars used to allege.[107]

Fitzmyer has also pointed out the occurrence of "son of God" and "son of the Most High" applied to "some human being in the apocalyptic setting" (though not a messianic figure) of a Pseudo-Daniel text from Cave IV (4QpsDan Aᵃ); these phrases are also used in Luke 1:32 and 35 in reference to Jesus.[108] Fitzmyer has further called our attention to the phrase, "among men of good will," which is found both in a fragmentary manuscript containing the vision of Amram and also in Luke 2:14.[109]

These examples might suggest that some pre-Lukan Jewish source was utilized by Luke for his infancy narrative, as R. E. Brown says that "the Greek of the infancy narrative is more Semiticized than the Greek of the most of the Gospel"[110] of Luke. A number of scholars even postulate that this Jewish source stemmed from the followers of John the Baptizer, though this theory is still uncertain.[111]

Another instance of a correspondence between the Qumran Aramaic documents and the New Testament is found in the references to healing patients through the laying on of hands (the Genesis Apocryphon 20:22 and 29; Mk 5:23; 6:5; 7:32; 8:23–25; 16:18; Lk 4:40, 13:13; Acts 9:12, 17–18; 28:8). As D. Flusser has indicated, the passage in the Genesis Apocryphon is the first reference to this practice ever found in a Jewish source; neither the Old Testament nor any rabbinic literature mentions it.[112]

These examples which we have observed well illustrate the Aramaic background of some of the New Testament portions, and that the Qumran documents provide us with cogent sources for the purpose of clarification.[113]

Hebrew Evidence

The language of the majority of the non-biblical manuscripts from the Qumran caves, however, is the Hebrew of the late post-exilic era. (The language of the Copper Scroll is different; it represents the oldest extant instance of Mishnaic Hebrew.) As many scholars have noted, this fact might very well have had to do with the Maccabean nationalism which effected a revival of the traditional Hebrew. Fitzmyer calls it a "neo-classical Hebrew."[114] It was presumably at the time of the rise of the Qumran sect. C. Rabin has made an interesting suggestion that the sectarian condemnation of the "halting" (lQH 4:16–17), "uncircumcised" (lQH 2:18–19), and "blasphemous" (CD 5:11–12) language of their opponents was referring to none other than the Mishnaic Hebrew which the Pharisees spoke.[115] If so, Mishnaic Hebrew was used in Judaea (except for Qumran) as an ordinary language.

We should also note some rabbinic comments made in the second century A.D. Rabbi Meir said: "Everyone who is settled in the land of Israel and speaks the sacred language (Mishnaic Hebrew?) . . . is assured that he is a son of the age to come" (J. Sheqalim, 3c). Rabbi Judah the Prince even demanded: "Why the Syriac language (i.e., Aramaic) in the land of Israel? Either the sacred language or the Greek language!" (B. Baba Qamma 82b–83a; B. Sota 49b). These words seem to witness to Hebrew as a vernacular falling into disuse.

Palestine around the time of Jesus was, consequently, in a multi-lingual state. According to Rabin's linguistic map of Palestine, "in Jerusalem and Judaea Mishnaic Hebrew was still the ruling language, and Aramaic took the second place"; and in the coastal plain and Galilee, "Aramaic and possibly Greek were the dominant languages spoken by people from all classes, while Hebrew mainly functioned as a literary language."[116] But after the fall of Jerusalem in A.D. 70, the center of learning moved to Galilee and Mishnaic Hebrew became simply a scholarly language. Aramaic and Greek, and then Latin, came to be used widely in Palestine.

Greek Evidence

Greek evidence is extensive.[117] Long before the conquest of the Near East by Alexander the Great in the fourth century B.C., Hellenistic influence reached Palestine.[118] The Hellenization of his conquered lands rapidly progressed, particularly in urban areas. Greek became the common language in political, commercial, and literary activities as well as in daily conversation among the educated. The Jews, needless to say, were in the midst of this overwhelming tide. Thus the Septuagint was produced.

There are Greek manuscripts from Qumran (4QLxxLev[a, b], 4QLXXNum, 7Q1 and 2) and also from Muraba'at. The Greek fragments of the Minor Prophets from Wadi Khabra, according to D. Barthélemy (the publisher of the text), represent a recension of the Greek translation of the Hebrew text, predicated upon rabbinic interpretative principles in Palestine during the first century A.D. This theory has gained wide acceptance among scholars. This evidence well attests to the fact that the traditional Jewish groups like the Pharisees and the Essenes, as well as the militant nationalists, included members who read the scripture in Greek. And it was most likely their first language.

Greek is also the language of some of the Old Testament apocrypha, the New Testament, and Josephus' works. Josephus, in fact, stated: "For our people (the Jews) do not favor those persons who have mastered the speech of many nations, or who adorn their style with smoothness of diction, because they consider that not only is such skill common to ordinary freemen but that even slaves who so choose may acquire it. But they give a credit for wisdom to those alone who have an exact knowledge of the law and who are capable of interpreting the meaning of the Holy Scriptures" (*Ant.* 20:264).[119] He wrote his first book, *The Jewish War,* "in his native tongue" (*War* 1:3), which is most likely Aramaic, and he admitted that he had help in rewriting it in Greek for his Roman readers (*Against Apion* 1:50). In a recent study of Josephus, T. Rajak has reached the conclusion that "it is quite safe to take Josephus' works, starting with the first, the *War,* as his own, and to treat him exactly the same way as we do other ancient writers. It is as well to dispel all fantastic notions of ghost writers at this early stage."[120]

In the third century A.D., there was at least one Greek-speaking synagogue in Palestine.[121] J. N. Svenster states in his investigation about the use of Greek by the Palestinian populace during the initial centuries A.D.: "So diverse literary and archaeological data from different centuries agree in their testimonial to a knowledge of Greek in broad layers of the Jewish population in Palestine."[122] The Jewish Christians of the first century A.D. "were on the whole in a better position to hear and speak Greek," for the Christian message was delivered not only to Jews but also to Gentiles.[123]

While Greek remained the language of the eastern Roman empire, Latin was a negligible factor in Palestine, where only on milestones, tiles, funerary inscriptions on Roman soldiers' graves, and the like is there any trace of Latin found.

Consequently, as Rabin describes, the Palestine of those days was "a country of many languages."[124] Incidentally, it is interesting to note that according to John 19:20 (not mentioned in the Synoptic Gospels), the title on Jesus' cross was written "in Hebrew, in Latin, and in Greek." (It is not determined what this "Hebrew" indicates: Hebrew, Mishnaic Hebrew, or Aramaic.)

Language of the Early Christians

The foregoing consideration leads us to assume that Jesus most likely spoke at least three languages: Hebrew, Aramaic, and Greek; he read the Hebrew scripture, engaged in dispute with scribes in Mishnaic Hebrew, taught the crowd in Aramaic, and conversed with the Romans in Greek. (Although Latin was the Romans' language, Greek was still used as a common means of communication at that time.)[125] Of these three languages, Aramaic must have been used by Jesus most often.

More than likely the immediate disciples of Jesus were Aramaic-speaking Jews who also possessed a working knowledge of Greek. But Greek-speaking followers were not at all far behind them. Explaining this historical fact, M. Hengel says: "One striking phenomenon here, which they (modern scholars) often ignore, is the fact that the message of the crucified and risen Messiah, Jesus of Nazareth, also found its way particularly to Greek-speaking Jews a few years, and perhaps only months, after the resurrection event which formed the foundation of the community. These Jews came from a wide variety of places in the Diaspora and settled in Jerusalem."[126]

This situation seems to find its reflection in Acts 6:1–7, which refers to a tension between the *hellenistai* and the *hebraioi,* both of the Jerusalem Christian community. (The tension was caused by a discrepancy over the daily provision for the widows.) As many contemporary scholars concur, the former denotes Jews who spoke only Greek, while the latter denotes Jews who used both Greek and Aramaic (or Hebrew).[127] To solve this problem, they elected seven respected men. Interestingly, their names were all Greek. Although many Jews had Greek names in those days, the fact that the seventh person was identified as a proselyte suggests that the other six were Jewish.

With regard to the identity of the *hellenistai,* a minority opinion is voiced by a renowned New Testament scholar, O. Cullmann. Capitalizing on apparent linkage between the Qumran literature and the Fourth Gospel which shows particular concern with the Hellenists, he insists that there is a close connection between the Essenes and the Hellenists. (Both of these groups, for instance, opposed temple worship. We will discuss this question in the following chapter.)[128] This suggestion, however, is untenable; the Qumran sectarians could not have had anything to do with those he defines as the "Hellenists," i.e., those who "live according to the Greek manner." Nonetheless, it seems quite possible that some of the sectarians might have joined the young Christian community after the Roman destruction of Qumran in A.D. 68, because these two groups show numerous common features. This is our subject for discussion in the ensuing chapter. How do the Judaean discoveries help in our understanding of this question?

4

The Significance of the Judaean Finds for New Testament Studies

What was the historical and religious milieu of the origin of Christianity? How did the ritual of baptism come to exist? Was there any specific Jewish liturgical practice which could have perhaps constituted the background of the Lord's Supper? What were the Jewish antecedents of some of the paramount theological features of the New Testament such as messianism, eschatology, and apocalypticism? Was the way the New Testament writers interpreted the Old Testament totally unique or were there parallels at that time? Various questions such as these are of profound significance to our understanding of the New Testament; nonetheless, they have, by and large, been shrouded in ambiguity.

The finds from the Judaean wilderness, particularly from Qumran, have shed invaluable light on these vital problems surrounding Judaism and Christianity around the time of Jesus and his early followers. In what ways then does the recent information about Judaea enrich our knowledge of this subject? This is the question we will pursue in this chapter. It seems appropriate, as we embark upon our task, to focus our attention first on John the Baptizer, a colossal figure standing at the threshold of the commencement of Christianity.

1. The Qumran Sect, John, and Christians

(1) Baptism in Judaism

What was the origin of Christian baptism? Did John the Baptizer initiate this rite? It has been long known that ancient rabbis offered baptism for those who wished to practice Judaism. According to rabbinic laws, in order for non-observant Jewish persons to be admitted into the religious community, they were required to be circumcised and baptized and to offer sacrifices. (The practice of offering sacrifices was discontinued after the destruction of the temple.) Upon entering the fellowship, the rite of washing with water was performed according to the law of Levitical purification (cf. Lev 11–15 and Num 19).

Proselyte Baptism

It is said in Mishnah: "The school of Shammai says: If a man becomes a proselyte on the day before Passover, he may immerse himself and consume his Passover-offering in the evening" (Pesahim 8:8).[1] Shammai was a great rabbi of the first century B.C. The school he established rivaled the school of Hillel during the ensuing century (cf. also the Talmud Kerithoth 81a). The basic intention of this baptismal practice was, therefore, purification and initiation.[2]

Some scholars (W. H. Brownlee, J. Jeremias, H. H. Rowley, etc.) suggest that John's baptism originated with this rabbinic proselyte baptism.[3] A direct relationship between them is far from obvious, however. Scholars like C. H. H. Scobie,[4] for instance, reject any link between the two, because of scanty evidence of the baptism of proselytes before A.D. 70. R. Schütz also indicates the difference by underscoring that the proselyte baptism was hardly the "baptism of repentance for the forgiveness of sins" performed by John.[5] John's baptism was eminently eschatological and messianic as well and was vitally connected with the person of John, for it was called "the baptism of John" (Acts 18:25; 19:3).

Qumran Baptism

More than a century earlier, however, the Qumran Essenes were observing a lustral rite through immersion. Josephus briefly mentioned this Essene practice (*War* 2:129, 138). In the ruined community center of Qumran, an elaborate water system which includes several reservoirs has been unearthed. In contemporary scholars' views, some of these cisterns had been utilized by the sectarians for the sake of ritual bathing.[6]

Some of the Qumran documents also refer to the sectarian observance of such a ritual. In the Manual of Discipline 5:13f., we read:

> (The wicked) shall not go into the water to touch the purification of the holy ones, for they shall not be purified unless they turn from their wickedness. For uncleanness is in all those who transgress His (God's) word.

As stated here, one's repentance and total acceptance of the Qumran sect's precepts were fundamental prerequisites for partaking in the water purification ceremony of the community. The word "purification *(tohorah)*" specifically indicates this ritual.[7] It was a privilege of membership to be able to participate, and offenders of this community rule lost their rights as members (see 1QS 6:22, 25; 7:3, 16, 19; 8:17; CD 9:21, 23). Sins constituting a violation of this ordinance, in fact, could not be cleansed away by even the lustral water. It says in the Manual of Discipline 3:4–8:

> He shall not be cleansed by atonement, nor purified by all the waters of purification, nor sanctified by seas and rivers, nor purified by all the waters of washing. Unclean, unclean shall he be, as long as he scorns the laws of God without being corrected by the community of His council. For by the spirit of the council of truth concerning the ways of man shall all of his sins be atoned so that he may see the light of life. And by the holy spirit of the community, in His truth, cleansed from all his sins, and by the spirit of uprightness and humility, shall his iniquity be atoned. And by the humility of his soul toward all the precepts of God shall his flesh be cleansed so that he may be sprinkled with waters of purification and sanctified in the waters of lustration.

No ritual could absolve one's sins, according to the Qumran sect. What then would? Only the holy spirit of the community could atone for a person's iniquities when the laws were obeyed with a contrite heart. As B. E. Thiering points out,[8] this paragraph refers to two different kinds of sin, each requiring separate cleansing: (1) the inner moral sin is to be expiated only by the holy spirit abiding in the community, and (2) the outer ritual defilement of the flesh, resulting from the inner sin, can be washed away by the water of lustral rite.

Josephus' information seems to confirm further this understanding of the Qumran ritual. He says in the *Antiquities* 18:117f. that the Essenes must receive baptism "not to gain pardon for whatever they committed, but as a consecration of the body, implying that the soul was already thoroughly cleansed by right behavior." Though Josephus' language is general and Hellenistic (for the sake of his Roman readers), he propounds here the Essene idea that the inner self is cleansed only by the observance of the laws and not by water, while the outer (bodily) defilement can be purified by water.

To sum up: the lustral ritual of immersion in water constituted an important religious activity regularly performed by Essene community members. They believed in a baptism of water and also of the spirit, the latter providing the former with a foundation; that is to say, the ritual purity derived from the members' absolute obedience to the laws. Total devotion to the laws, according to their conviction, was also an unmitigated necessity in the face of the imminent eschaton (see, for example, 1QS 8:12–16). The Qumran baptism was, therefore, an eschatological liturgy—a ritual occasion involving the final outpouring of the holy spirit.

(2) John the Baptizer and the Qumran Sect

Proximity of John and the Sect
The foregoing consideration not only reveals the existence of Jewish antecedents of the practice of baptism but also suggests a series of intriguing parallels between the lustral rite at Qumran and the baptismal ministry of John the Baptizer. First, both the Qumran sect and John practiced their cleansing rituals in the same geographical area, the Judean wilderness.[9] Second, they were contemporaries of each other. John was active during the twenties, when the sect was still in full swing (archaeological Phase II, according to de Vaux).

The third point of resemblance concerns the Baptizer's background. According to Luke 1:5,[10] his father was "a priest named Zechariah of the division of Abijah," the eighth of twenty-four ancient priestly orders, and his mother was also of priestly descent. Although Luke fails to mention that John too was a priest, his description of John's priestly lineage corresponds to the priestly emphasis of the Qumran sect.

Furthermore, Luke records the words of the angel Gabriel: "He (John) will drink no wine or strong drink, and he will be filled with the Holy Spirit even from his mother's womb" (1:15), thereby suggesting that he was a Nazirite (cf. Num 6; Jud 13:4–5; 1 Sam 1:11; Acts 18:18; 21:20–30). Likewise, the Qumran sectarians consecrated themselves (in a priestly blessing which reads: "May He consecrate *(nazar)* you to the Holy of Holies" in 1QSb 4:28), and did not drink fermented wine *(yayin)* but had unfermented or slightly fermented grape juice *(tîrōsh).*[11] Both John and the sectarians were highly ascetic, although there is no explicit statement that calls either of them Nazirite.

The possibility has also been suggested that after the death of his parents (for they were old when he was born), John was reared by the Essenes at Qumran. Luke states that he "grew and became strong in spirit, and he was in the wilderness till the day of his manifestation to Israel (i.e., until his public ministry)" (1:80). Josephus mentioned the Essene practice of adopting "other men's children, while yet pliable and docile, (to) regard them as their kin and mould them with their principles" (*War* 2:120). After John had grown, he became an independent preacher of baptism. As Luke 3:2 puts it, "The word of God came to John"; that is, it came in the manner of God's call to prophets in the Old Testament (e.g., Is 38:4; Jer 1:1; 13:3; etc.). The Essene upbringing of John is possible but not certain; it is, as Fitzmyer says, "a plausible hypothesis—which cannot be proved or disproved."[12]

Shortly after the discovery of the first scrolls, some people even suggested that not only John but also Jesus spent his younger days at Qumran, for it says in the Gospels that he was tempted and baptized in that vicinity. This is totally speculative, since we know virtually nothing of the years, thirty in all, before his public ministry began.

Fourth, John's message bears striking resemblance to that of the scrolls. According to the Synoptic Gospels, John was "proclaiming a baptism of repentance for the forgiveness of sins" (Mk 1:4; Lk 3:3). This phrase is missing in Matthew, but the identical tenet is found in Matthew 3:2, 6, 11. Matthew, in consonance with his major theme of the kingdom of heaven, cites the nearness of the kingdom rather than the forgiveness of sins as the reason for repentance. As Acts 13:24 indicates, such an understanding of John was commonly entertained by early Christians. The Gospels' information concerning the Baptizer was theologically oriented; that, however, does not necessarily mean that it was lacking in historicity. For the sectarians, too, the turning away from all sin toward God was a cardinal teaching (1QS 5:1, 14; 6:15; etc.). They called themselves "penitents of sin" (1QH 2:9; 6:6; CD 2:5).

The Q source in Matthew and Luke tells us of the Baptizer's preaching of imminent divine judgment with fire (Mt 3:7–12; Lk 3:7–9). Some of the Qumran scrolls also declare the identical message: the whole world, including the abyss and excluding the penitents, will be consumed by a catastrophic fire (1QH 3:28–33; 6:18; 1QS 2:7–8; CD 2:5–6).[13]

Of further interest is that, according to Matthew 3:7, John addressed this diatribe specifically to "many of the Pharisees and Sadducees" (Luke 3:7 says simply "the crowd"),[14] calling them a "brood of vipers." R. H. Gundry suspects that they came to John to make "critical observations" and not to seek repentance.[15] As we have noted in Chapter Two, the sectarians at Qumran raised violent criticisms of the religious and political establishment in Jerusalem, which must have included the Sadducees and the Pharisees. Their foes were called "serpent's venom" in 1QH 5:10 and 27f.[16] We may detect here common adversaries of John and the sect.

John's baptism was not a means for obtaining forgiveness of sins but rather purification of persons who had already repented. At this point, John and the sect agree (see Josephus' information about the Essene baptism which we cited previously).

Furthermore, Matthew 3:11 and Luke 3:16 record John's preaching of the baptism of spirit and fire which would be given by "one who is coming" and "mightier than" he.[17] Scholars often take "spirit" and "fire" to be opposites, one generating salvation and the other judgment. It is true that fire is used as a symbol of divine judgment in the Bible (e.g., Amos 7:4; Jer 21:12; Ez 39:6; Ps 89:46; Mt 18:8–9; 2 Pet 3:7; Rev 20:9–15). But it also serves as a metaphor of purification (Zech 13:9; Mal 3:2–3; 1 Cor 3:15; 1 Pet 1:7; etc.) through refinement (Num 31:23). Therefore, even if the word "fire" may primarily connote judgment in these passages in Matthew and Luke, the latter meaning, with its suggestion of eschatological purification by the holy spirit,[18] should not be overlooked.

As already observed, the sectarians participated in the rite of purification with water for cleansing outward sins and by the holy spirit for inner and deeper ones (1QS 3:4–8). Moreover, there is a reference to the spiritual refining by fire alongside purification by water and the spirit in 1QS 4:20f.:

> And then God will cleanse by His truth all the works of man, and will *refine* for Himself the frame of man, in order to destroy every spirit of iniquity from within his flesh, and will purify him by the spirit of holiness from all evil deeds. He will sprinkle upon him a spirit of truth like water of purification from all abomination and falsehood.

The Hebrew word used here for "refine" *(zgg)* occurs also in the Hymn Scroll 5:16, which praises the divine work involving refining of the psalmist (the Teacher of Righteousness) by fire.

The last major feature common to both John the Baptizer and the Qumran sect is their fervent eschatological messianism. Just as the sectarians expected the imminent arrival of the messiahs at the end of time (1QS 9:10–11; 4QBless 1:3–4; CD 12:23; 20:1; etc.), John declared, according to all four Gospel writers (Mk 1:7; Mt 3:11; Lk 3:16; Acts 13:25; Jn 1:27), that the coming messiah was "mightier than" himself.

From the foregoing observation, it is clear that the Qumran sect and John the Baptizer must have belonged to the same religious milieu. This fact has prompted many modern scholars to identify John as an Essene (at least a one-time Essene).[19] Nonetheless, a direct and mechanical identification between the two seems impossible to make, for there are several undismissable differences as well. More recent scholarly opinion tends to be more cautious.

Differences between John and the Sect

First of all, there is no direct and explicit evidence of a connection. John did not create such an exclusive and sacerdotal community as the Qumran sect; he urged everyone, religious or secular, learned or unlearned, to repent and be baptized. The difference in their costumes well illustrates this fact. John was wearing "a garment of camel's hair and a leather girdle around his waist" (Mt 3:4; Mk 1:6), the clothing which intends to identify him as Elijah (2 Kings 1:8; cf. Mt 17:12f.; Mk 9:12f.). The sectarians, however, were garbed in priestly white. John showed no sign of disturbance by any possible physical contact with those who were deemed by the law of purity as unclean, whereas the people of Qumran made every effort to avoid such association.

Third, John's baptism, unlike the Qumran daily lustration, was performed once in a person's lifetime. This difference stemmed from the fact that the Qumran rite was intended to achieve Levitical purity, while for John the baptism was decidedly a proleptic experience of divine judgment and forgiveness at the end of history.

Scholars also have pointed out the fact that there were a number of smaller pious groups which practiced baptism in Palestine and Syria around the time of Jesus, such as the Hemerobaptists, the Nazoreans, the Ebionites, the Elkasaites, and the Mandaeans.[20] For example, Ebionites, according to Epiphanius (c. 315–403), the Bishop of Salamis, "had a baptism of initiation besides the daily ritual bath" (*Panarion* 30, 16), the observance redolent of the Qumran praxis.[21] These sects were Jewish-Christian groups often influenced in various ways by Gnosticism. Josephus also mentioned Bannus, a hermit who was "using frequent ablutions of cold water, by day and night, for purity's sake" (*Life* 11).

All in all, we may conclude that the Qumran sectarians belief and practice afford the closest parallel to John's baptism yet known. Clearly in both the Qumran sect and John, the lustral immersion in living water is an experience of receiving the eschatological outpouring of the holy spirit.

(3) The Disciples of John and Christians

As W. Wink states in his study of John the Baptizer, the early "church stood at the center of John's movement from the very beginning and became its one truly great survivor and heir."[22] This fact is made clear as the Gospel writers tell us that Jesus was baptized by John, an important witness to Jesus the Christ. After John's execution, his disciples buried him and "told Jesus" (Mt 14:12)—i.e., they reported to him. This brief sentence in Matthew suggests that John's disciples turned to follow Jesus, though their exact number eludes us. In fact, according to John 1:35–40, two of the Baptizer's adherents became the first disciples of Jesus; one of them was Andrew, who, in turn, brought his brother, Simon Peter, to Jesus. The close contact between the Baptizer's group and the early Christians is also mentioned in John 3:22–26 and 10:40–42.

As widely acknowledged by scholars, the community of the Fourth Evangelist was still trying to win the Baptizer's followers over to Christianity. The Gospel, as a matter of fact, reveals various features similar to the Dead Sea Scrolls. (This question will be discussed later.) Modern scholars, therefore, have noted a probable connection: the Essenes—John the Baptizer and his disciples—the Christian community of the Fourth Gospel writer.[23]

Furthermore, it is extremely intriguing that Luke mentions a group of approximately a dozen disciples of the Baptizer in Ephesus,[24] where the Fourth Gospel was most likely written. This is also the locale of the Christians to whom the Letters to the Ephesians and to the Colossians were addressed; both of these letters clearly betray features parallel to the Qumran scrolls. (We will mention this question later.)

We may conclude, therefore, that the Qumran sect influenced the early Christians in various ways, notably through John the Baptizer and his disciples. The Christian group, however, was unique in that they found the awaited messiah in Jesus, while the other two were left open-ended. The Qumran sectarians were highly ascetic, withdrawn in the wilderness.

Jesus and his followers, by contrast, were active openly; they did not hesitate to mingle with ordinary people, including even those who were social outcasts. The great joy of the arrival of the Messiah overwhelmed eschatological anxiety: "Can the wedding guests fast while the bridegroom is with them?" (Mk 2:19).

2. *Use of Scripture*

(1) The "Way" in the Wilderness
John the Baptizer, as all four Gospel writers attest, was a witness to the arrival of the long-awaited Christ. To prove it, they commonly cite Isaiah 40:3. The Masoretic text runs:

> A voice cries:
> "In the wilderness prepare the way of Yahweh,
> level in the wasteland the highway for our God."

The quotation in the Gospels (Mt 3:3; Mk 1:3; Lk 3:4; Jn 1:23), at variance with the Hebrew text, agree with the Greek version (the Septuagint) at the first line: "The voice of one crying in the wilderness, 'Prepare. . . .'"

Interestingly, the Manual of Discipline from the Qumran Cave I also quotes the same passage of Isaiah. We read in the column 8, lines 13–16:

> And when there becomes the community in Israel according to these rules, they shall separate themselves from the midst of the habitation of perverse men to go into the wilderness to prepare there the way of Him (God), as it is written: "In the wilderness prepare the way of. . . . (Yahweh). Level in the wasteland a highway for our God." This is the study of the Law (which) He commanded by the hand of Moses, so as to do according to all that is revealed from time to time, and according to that which the prophets revealed through His holy spirit.

Both the Gospel paragraphs and the Qumran portion are important, as each proclaims the most vital concern of the respective groups: the former—the legitimacy of the voice ushering in the Messiah; the latter—the valid reason for their existence in the wilderness. The Gospel writers, by connecting the "voice" with "the wilderness," intend to drive home the contention that the Baptizer was none other than a voice of witness. (John 1:23 lays particular emphasis on this point: "I [John] am the voice. . . .") In the Qumran text, however, the "voice" is not quoted because it carries no prophetic significance.

The Gospel texts also underscore the message: "prepare the way" (for the imminent coming of the messianic kingdom). This way is to be prepared not just in the wilderness but in the whole world. By contrast, in the Qumran text, as in the Masoretic text, the "way" is unequivocally said to be prepared exclusively "in the wilderness"—that is, in the place where the sectarians have their home in the Judaean wilderness. The "way" means to both the Essenes and the Christians the way of salvation. But for the former it signifies the study and practice of the Law, while for the latter it represents the salvation provided by Christ.

Though we see here an interesting parallel between these two texts in their use of the Old Testament, we must note a significant difference of theological intention between them. Both of the texts recognize the Old Testament as having vital prophetic value; however, they differ widely in their interpretation of its prophetic implication. This fact is quite evident not just in this particular case but also in the numerous other places throughout the Qumran literature and the New Testament. There are many quotations and allusions from the Old Testament in both of these writings, for their authors firmly believe that each of their groups has fulfilled scripture. How then do they claim to have fulfilled scripture? In what manner do they interpret scripture? Let us examine this matter further.

(2) Pesher

Though in the Qumran literature there is no rigid system of interpreting scripture, the type of exegesis which is most prevalent and characteristic in the documents is called *pesher* (a Hebrew word meaning "interpretation").[25] The word occurs regularly in expository compositions such as the Commentary on Habakkuk. It also occurs in about fifteen other pesher works (which exist in fragmentary condition; these works include commentaries on Old Testament books such as Isaiah, Micah,

Hosea, Zephaniah, Nahum, and Psalms). In addition to such commentaries running section by section on an individual biblical book, they also provide a series of interpretative comments on passages selected from various parts of scripture concerning a certain theme (e.g., 4QF1, 11QMelch, etc.). J. Carmignac calls the former the "continuous pesher" and the latter the "thematic pesher."[26]

The pesher usually assumes a fixed literary form with slight variations: a biblical quotation is followed by a formula including the word *pesher* which commences a paragraph of interpretation. For example, in the beginning of column eight of the Habakkuk Commentary, after citing Habakkuk 2:4b ("But the righteous shall live by faith"), it says: "The interpretation *(pesher)* of this concerns all those who observe the Law in the House of Judah, whom God will deliver from the House of Judgment because of their affliction and their faithfulness to the Teacher of Righteousness."

In this interpretation, the prophetic words of Habakkuk (probably the early sixth century B.C.) are lifted out of the original context and applied in the author's immediate situation. Thus, "the righteous" (the righteous Israel in the Habakkuk context) is used in reference specifically to the Qumran sect itself, which would be delivered from its foes in Jerusalem (in Habakkuk, the Babylonians). What the prophet meant by "faith," i.e., faithfulness to the Mosaic Law, is converted and used to indicate the sectarians' loyalty to their leader, the Teacher of Righteousness.

Nature of Pesher

In addition to such isolation and contemporalization of scriptural passages, the pesher exhibits the third significant characteristic—an apocalyptic orientation. The Habakkuk Commentary 7:1–5 proffers a lucid demonstration of this feature. The pesher of this portion concerns Habakkuk 2:1–2, and it says:

And God told Habakkuk to write down that which was to come in the final generation. But of the consummation of time He did not let him know. And as for that which He said:

"That he who reads may read quickly" (Hab 2:2), the interpretation of this concerns the Teacher of Righteousness to
whom God had let know all the mysteries of the words of His
servants the Prophets.

According to the Qumran exegetes, the Old Testament
prophets, including Habakkuk, did not fully comprehend the
whole thrust of their own prophetic utterances. But now in these
last days, say these exegetes, the Teacher of Righteousness is
able to make the prophetic interpretation explicit, because God
has revealed to the Teacher all mysteries. These mysteries, as far
as the Qumran theologians are concerned, pertain to things
which will happen at the imminently approaching end of the
world. In this light, consequently, scripture is understood and
scrutinized.

Belief and interpretative practice such as this are a typically
apocalyptic phenomenon. Often in apocalyptic literature, certain individuals are said to have received a special revelation
from God in regard to matters of the consummation of the
world, the arena of a dramatic war between powers of good and
evil. It is interesting to note that in the Book of Daniel, which is
the only apocalyptic book in the Old Testament, the Aramaic
cognate of the Hebrew *pshr* occurs a little more than thirty times
in reference to Daniel's interpretation of dreams.[27] Daniel is
given the special privilege of being able to interpret dreams
through which divine mysteries regarding the course of history
are predicted and explained.

Both in Daniel and in the Qumran pesher literature, the
Aramaic word *raz* is used to signify this important concept of
"mystery," which we will discuss later. The role of the Teacher
of Righteousness, in a way, corresponds to that of Daniel, as
both are considered the inspired expositors of the revealed mysteries of the final time.[28] Daniel, for example, reinterprets Jeremiah's prophecy of the seventy-year exile (Jer 25:11) to mean
seventy weeks of years (i.e., 490 years which ranges from the
time of the exile to approximately the author's time, i.e., the second century B.C.) before the end of history (Dan 9:24–27). In a
similar manner, the Teacher explains various Old Testament

prophetic passages by reapplying them to the situation of his day which he believes stands on the threshold of the new world of God. Both Daniel and the Teacher claim to disclose a hidden meaning in the scriptures through divine inspiration, and both attempt to explicate their contemporary conditions with that inspired wisdom so as to encourage their readers (followers) to hold to their beliefs.[29]

Methods of Pesher

With such a conviction, the Qumran expositor scrutinizes the biblical text. As we have already observed, the passages he cites are wrested from their original context to fit the sectarian contentions.[30] Some key words and phrases provide him with clues to deciphering the hidden sense of the passages. A few examples follow.

The Habakkuk Commentary 4:9ff. deals with Habakkuk 1:11: "Then the wind changed and passed, and it made its power its god." The Masoretic text is not clear; the Revised Standard Version puts it: "Then they sweep by like the wind and go on, guilty men, whose own might is their god." In the Habakkuk context, the passage refers to the violent Chaldeans, but in the Qumran Commentary it is applied to the *"Kittim"* (presumably the Romans), aggressors when the sect was in existence. Then in the ensuing explanatory paragraph, the rulers of the Kittim are called the "House of guilt" *(bêt ashmāh)*. This expression stems from *āshēm* (guilt), a word occurring in the Masoretic text but not in the Qumran quotation. Such a different reading of a word as this occasions a radical reinterpretation of the text by the Qumran expositor.[31]

At the beginning of the eleventh column of the Commentary, Habakkuk 2:15 is cited and construed. There is an orthographical variant in the quotation, which prompts a significant sectarian statement: "Woe to him who makes his neighbors drink in order to gaze on the festivals *(mw'dyhm)*." The Masoretic text says at the end of the verse: "in order to gaze on their pudenda *(m'wryhm)*." The difference in the spelling between these two words involves (1) a switching of the letters *waw* (w) and *ain* ('), and (2) an exchange of *resh* (r) for *daleth* (d). Such orthographical variations are often found in the Qumran manuscripts.

But these changes are vital to the meaning of the passage. By using the word "festivals," the expositor relates the verse to an incident involving the persecution of the Teacher of Righteousness by the Wicked Priest during "the festival of rest, the Day of Atonement" (lines 6–7). Furthermore, as D. Patte indicates,[32] the Qumran commentator not only changes the word but also divides the word so that the specific festival, the Day of Atonement, may be alluded to. That is to say, *mw'dyhm* ("festivals") is separated into two parts: *mw'd* ("festival") and *yhm* (an abbreviation of *ywm hkpwrym* ("the day of Atonement")).

Pesher and Midrash

The Qumran expositors did not have a monopoly on such expository devices; ancient rabbis also employed them. They produced the massive interpretative works on scripture called Midrash. The purpose of Midrash was to give the Jewish general populace moral and religious instructions based on scripture, rather than to pursue a purely scholarly scrutiny of the biblical text. Explaining the fundamental nature of Midrash, A. Wright says, "Rabbinic midrash is homiletic reflection on the Bible, which seeks to apply a given text of the past to present circumstances."[33] Likewise, R. Bloch states in her well-known article concerning Midrash that contemporarization is the essence of the midrashic procedure.[34] Midrash is predicated upon the belief that scripture as God's word must be relevant to people of all times, and, therefore, is open to new understanding in all new situations. Midrash intends not only to examine the biblical text but to adapt it to the present.

"Pesher" is, in fact, juxtaposed with "midrash" in 4QFlorilegium 1:14 and 19. The verb form *drsh* ("to seek" or "to investigate") occurs often in the Qumran documents. Furthermore, even without the word pesher, the expository use of scriptural passages identical to pesher is found in many places of the sectarians' literature. In the Damascus Document 6:3ff., for example, Numbers 21:18 is cited: "the well which the princes dug, which the nobles of the people delved with the scepter." (The Masoretic text agrees with the Qumran text.) This is part

of the ancient workers' song (the Song of the Well) which is
quoted here to indicate a well in the desert provided by God for
Israel. A reinterpretation by the sectarian author runs as follows:
"The well is the Law, and those who dug it are the converts of
Israel (i.e., the sectarians). . . and the scepter is the investigator
(dôrēsh) of the Law (i.e., the Teacher of Righteousness)." The
Hebrew word for scepter, $m^e\hbar\hat{o}q\bar{e}q$, can mean "leader," "law-
giver," as well as "scepter."

Is pesher then a part of the rabbinic tradition of Midrash?
Or do they differ totally from each other? Some scholars have
contended that pesher belonged to a sub-genre of the early Jewish hermeneutical tradition. L. Silberman, for example, sees no
fundamental difference between them, at least in their literary
form. Yet he reckons the fact that pesher is distinctive in its
eschatological contemporarization.[35] Hence he states: "This suggests that the Midrashim are farther removed from Daniel than
is the Pesher. It may well be that the latter lies athwart a line of
development leading from the midrashic presuppositions
already at work in Daniel to the formal structure of the
Petirah."[36]

W. H. Brownlee, classifying pesher in the category of the
traditional Midrash, uses the expression "pesher midrash," as
though placed side by side with the other two divisions of rabbinic Midrash: Midrash Halakha and Midrash Haggadah.[37] Midrash Halakha deals with the legal, ritual, and doctrinal parts of
scripture for the purpose of giving instruction in the proper
application of scriptural laws in daily life, while Midrash Haggadah is more homiletical, dealing with that which the Halakha
does not deal with (i.e., non-legal parts of scripture such as narratives, poems, etc.). A. Wright also views the pesher as close to
the midrashic tradition and calls it "an haggadic midrash."[38]

However, other scholars underscore pesher's difference
from rabbinic midrash. L. H. Schiffman points out what he considers to be an essential difference between these two interpretative methods. He says that Midrash "brings testimony from
another biblical passage to confirm its suggestion," whereas
pesher "gives no such supporting evidence."[39] J. Neusner also
indicates that pesher's form (i.e., citation of the text—the pesher

of "this is that . . .") is unrelated and completely unlike the forms of Pharisaic-rabbinic midrash.[40] We should also note that Midrash lacks an apocalyptic overtone, which is, by contrast, of basic importance to the Qumran scriptural interpretation.

D. Patte seems right when he says that at Qumran, a clear demarcation between the halakhic and haggadic uses of scripture does not seem to be tenable.[41] It is rather futile for us to attempt to define and neatly classify the genre of pesher as compared with rabbinic literature (which comes a little later than the Qumran writings).[42] The ancient scriptural expositors at Qumran (the Teacher of Righteousness in particular)[43] do not seem to have been especially enthused about establishing a school of hermeneutical methodology as an academic subject. But they had one vital concern: scriptural utterances should be fulfilled through the sect which would be led by the Teacher at the imminent coming of the end of time. It was, they firmly believed, their crucial task to clarify and witness to that fulfillment.

(3) Scriptural Interpretation at Qumran and in the New Testament

As the foregoing consideration elucidates, the Qumran documents provide us with hitherto unavailable evidence of a pre-rabbinic period of ancient Jewish interpretative activities. They are of enormous value, furthermore, since they afford an intriguing precedent for the New Testament use of the Old Testament. Here again we are able to observe peculiar similarities between the Dead Sea Scrolls and the New Testament.

A comparison of these two groups of literature is far from facile; it involves difficult problems of great complexity. For instance, it is impossible for now to determine exactly the Old Testament text of the earliest Christians as well as that of the sectarians.[44] According to R. H. Pfeiffer, eighty percent of the Old Testament quotations in the New Testament are from the Septuagint.[45] The next question is: What recension or edition of the Septuagint is used? And what about the remaining twenty percent of Old Testament quotations? As we have discussed in the previous chapter, there were no standard texts in Hebrew, Aramaic, and Greek in the first century A.D.

Another formidable problem concerns the precise assessment of the manner in which the New Testament writers cite and allude to Old Testament passages. They sometimes seem to exercise a literary freedom, while at other times their quotations agree strictly with the Septuagint text known to us. For example, according to E. E. Ellis' study, fifty-one of Paul's citations are in virtual or absolute agreement with the Septuagint, with twenty-two of these differing with the Hebrew. In four passages, Paul follows the Hebrew against the Septuagint. And thirty-eight times he diverges from both.[46] This list evinces Paul's reliance on the Septuagint, yet not solely; the variance with the Greek is, in fact, considerable as well. In explaining this complex fact, Ellis writes: "He quoted from his memory in accordance with literary custom or for an exegetical purpose, rather than as a result of 'memory lapse.'"[47]

Let us proceed in our discussion of the "literary custom" and "exegetical purpose" (in Ellis' words) in the early Christian use of the Old Testament in comparison with the Qumran sectarian method.

Quotation Formulae

First, the literary custom. In his thorough study of Old Testament quotations in the Qumran literature and in the New Testament, J. A. Fitzmyer amasses literary formulae common to both.[48] The examples are as follows:

"For it is written" (1QS 5:15; CD 11:18, 20)—(Mt 2:5; 4:6, 10; 26:31; Lk 4:10; Acts 1:20; 23:5; Rom 12:19; 14:11; 1 Cor 1:19; 3:19; 15:45; Gal 3:10; 4:27).

"As it is written" (1QS 5:17; 8:14; CD 7:19; 4QF1 1:12)—(Mk 7:6; 2:23; Lk 3:4; Acts 15:15; Rom 1:17 and fifteen times more in the Pauline corpus; Jn 6:31; 12:14).

"As it is written in the Book of . . ." (4QF1 1:2; 11QMelch 9–10)—(Acts 7:42; see also Mk 1:2; Lk 2:23; Acts 13:33; 1 Cor 9:9; 14:21).

"As it is written in the book of Isaiah the prophet" (4QF1 1:15)—"As it is written in the Book of the words of Isaiah the prophet" (Lk 3:4).

"These are the ones about whom it is written" (4QF1 1:16)—"This is he about whom it is written" (Mt 11:10; Lk 7:27).

"And is it not written that . . .?" (CD 9:5)—"Is it not written . . .?" (Mk 11:17; Jn 10:34).

"As it (or he) said" (CD 7:9, 14, 16; 20:16)—(Lk 2:24; Jn 7:38; Rom 4:18; Heb 3:7; 4:3).

"As (or about) . . . God said . . ." (CD 6:13; 8:9; 9:7)—(Mt 15:4; Acts 7:6, 7).

"As (a particular Old Testament person) said . . ." (CD 5:8; 6:8; 8:14; 19:26)—(Acts 2:25; 3:21; Rom 10:19, 20).

The literary formulae expressing the idea of fulfillment which are characteristically used numerous times in the New Testament are lacking exact counterparts in the Qumran documents. This is contrary to our expectation, since this religious notion is of utmost importance in both groups of literature. Nonetheless, parlance such as "when the word will come (i.e., takes place, comes true) which is written . . ." in the Damascus Document (7:10; 19:7) and "this is the time which is written . . ." (1:13) indicates clearly a message about the fulfillment of scriptural passages. The former phrase, in fact, parallels "then shall come to pass the word that is written. . . ." in 1 Corinthians 15:54.

As Fitzmyer points out, the lack of the fulfillment formulae in the Qumran literature stems from the sectarian "forward look"—the end is imminent but has not yet come. By contrast, the New Testament writers hold "a backward glance"—the fulfillment by Christ has already been completed.[49]

The foregoing comparison demonstrates not only literary expressions strikingly similar in both the Qumran and the Christian writings but also the consonant interpretative stance. There are many instances of expository citation of Old Testament passages in the New Testament which are peculiarly redolent of the Qumran pesher. The New Testament has, however, neither the word *pesher* (its Greek equivalent) nor the literary form exactly identical to the Qumran model. Scholars consequently tend to be more cautious in saying that the New Testament contains a "pesher-type" exegesis.

Scriptural Interpretation in Matthew

A scholar like B. Lindars discerns "a typical example of pesher adaptation" in Matthew 2:6 where Micah 5:1 is quoted (no parallels in other Gospels).[50] Mt 2:6:

> And you, Bethlehem, the land of Judah,
> are by no means least among the rulers of Judah;
> for from you shall come a ruler
> who will govern my people Israel.

This passage in the original context is a promise that after the exile future salvation will come through a Davidic king from Bethlehem. Micah says that though Bethlehem of Ephratha (= LXX)[51] is small among Judah's clans, yet from thence will a messianic ruler come (LXX: "You are few in number among the thousands of Judah, yet . . ."). Matthew's text by contrast, strikes an emphatically positive note: "by no means least." Another alteration, "the rulers of Judah" for "Judah's clans," (based on a variant reading in the Hebrew text) underscores the unique importance of the messianic authority as against other ruling powers (such as the one in Jerusalem).

Matthew's quotation is taken not only from Micah 5:1 but also from 2 Samuel 5:2, which reads in the latter half: "and the Lord said to you (David), 'You shall be shepherd of my people Israel, and you shall be prince over Israel.'" Matthew thus cites two different passages from the Old Testament by wresting them from their original contexts and connecting (or conflating) them to the theme of the Davidic Messiah from Bethlehem, in order to assert the legitimacy of the messiahship of Jesus. According to Matthew, the passages of Micah and 2 Samuel are fulfilled by Jesus the Christ. Such a literary and theological use of Old Testament passages comports very well with the Qumran pesher.

There are many other instances of such interpretative citations of Old Testament portions in Matthew, the writing which quotes and makes allusions decidedly more than any other book of the New Testament. By comparing the pesher of the Habakkuk Commentary and the Old Testament quotations of the First

Gospel, K. Stendahl in his well-known book, *The School of St. Matthew and Its Use of the Old Testament,* advances the theory that Matthew's Gospel is a product of a "school" which practiced a pesher-type exegesis in the same way as the sectarians did at Qumran. Jesus was in fact a rabbi, and his style of rabbinic teaching bequeathed an indelible pattern in the early Christian community. Following the selfsame model, Matthew's church engaged itself in an intensive interpretative activity using the Old Testament; its expository citations of Old Testament passages with the special type of introductory formulae were precisely the fruits of that endeavor.

Brilliant though the scholarship demonstrated in this study is, Stendahl's insistence of the existence of the "Matthean School" seems to be in want of convincing proof, which has invited various scholarly criticisms.[52] Perhaps he draws too close a parallel between the Qumran pesher and the Matthean treatment of the Old Testament. The First Gospel must have been written with pronounced missionary zeal, rather than as an outcome of a scholarly, detailed study and interpretation of the texts themselves. Nonetheless, it may very well be recognized that Matthew's church immersed itself in investigating the Old Testament by employing a method very similar to the pesher in order to prove that Jesus of Nazareth was indeed the long-awaited Messiah.

Another noteworthy instance of a parallel between the Qumran and the Gospels' use of the Old Testament is found in their reference to the prohibition of polygamy.[53] In Damascus Document 4:20f., in support of monogamy, Genesis 1:27 ("Male and female created He them") is quoted. The author calls it the "principle of nature." Likewise, according to Mark 10:6 (= Mt 19:4), Jesus cites the identical passage from Genesis, underscoring the oneness of a married couple. In order to reinforce the point, he also quotes Genesis 2:24 ("Therefore a man leaves his father and his mother and cleaves to his wife, and they become one flesh") and declares that monogamy is the rule "from the beginning of creation." In both, the theological basis for monogamous marriage is exactly identical: the principle of a nature created by God.

Divorce Law

It is also instructive to compare the teachings of marriage and divorce in the Gospels, the Qumran scrolls, and the rabbinic literature. As for divorce, the school of Shammai was opposed to it, except in the case of the wife's unchastity. This view was held on the basis of Deuteronomy 24:1 ("If she finds no favor in his [her husband's] eyes because he has found some indecency in her"). The rival school of Hillel, by contrast, allowed for divorce "if even she spoiled a dish for him" (Mishnah Gittin 10:9). This position was predicated upon the identical passage of Deuteronomy. The great rabbi Akiba said, as the above-mentioned Mishnaic paragraph records, that a husband could divorce his wife "even if he found another fairer than she," because the Deuteronomy passage says: "if she finds no favor in his eyes."

The Temple Scroll 57:17–19 proscribes both polygamy and divorce. Referring to the king, it is stated: "Also he shall not take in addition to her another wife, for she alone shall be with him all the days of her life."[54] Likewise, Mark 10:6 expressly forbids divorce, whereas its parallel passage in Matthew approves divorce but only on the ground of "unchastity *(porneia)*" (see also Mt. 5:32). The latter, therefore, concurs with the strict teaching of Shammai.

The Hebrew equivalent of *porneia* (unchastity, immorality) is *zenûth* (the Septuagint consistently translates it so). *Zenûth* is counted as the first of the three cardinal snares ("the three nets of Belial") in the Damascus Document 4:17 (the other two being wealth and the defilement of the sanctuary). The author of this document then denounces the sect's foes by saying that they "have been caught by *zenûth* in two things, by marrying two women in their lifetime" (4:20f.). C. Rabin takes this immorality as a reference specifically to incestuous marriage, and also because the ancient rabbis understood *zonah* (unchaste woman) in Leviticus 21:7 to be a woman who has broken the laws forbidding incest.[55]

If that is the case, viewing the rigor with which monogamy was commonly held to in the Qumran literature and the Gospels, the only condition for divorce which Matthew mentions in 19:9, "except for unchastity," may very well refer to the case of incest.[56] A husband had to even keep an unfaithful wife (as long as she did not commit incest) just as the prophet Hosea did at God's bidding. Such an extremely strict teaching concerning the indissolubility of marriage led to the disciples' negative response: "If such is the case of a man with his wife, it is not expedient to marry" (Mt 19:10). Mark, who makes no mention of that condition, does not report these words of the disciples. The disciples' comment has, in fact, puzzled modern interpreters,[57] but such Qumran and rabbinic references seem to provide fresh insight into the paragraph in Matthew.

Sabbath Law

A law concerning the Sabbath purveys another halakhic case which illustrates a diametrical difference between the Essenes and Jesus. In the Damascus Document 11:14, there is a prohibition against rescuing a young domestic animal that might fall into a pit on the Sabbath, since such a rescue is considered to be work. By contrast, Jesus insists: "If one of you has a sheep and it falls on the Sabbath into a pit, will he not lay hold of it and lift it out? Of how much more value is a man than a sheep! So it is lawful to do good on the Sabbath" (Mt 12:11–12; cf. Lk 14:5).

Earlier rabbinic regulation directs the feeding of the animal to keep it alive until it can be removed after the Sabbath (T. Shabbat 14:3). But a later ruling allows indirect assistance enabling the unfortunate animal to extricate itself.[58] In general, the Essene rules are often stricter than the rabbinic laws. Uniquely, Jesus exercises great freedom; he is, as he says, "lord of the Sabbath" (Mt 12:8; Mk 2:28). In such a halakhic aspect as well, the discoveries of these old manuscripts enrich our understanding of ancient Jewish and early Christian teachings.

Example from the Pauline Corpus

(i) Righteousness through Faith

Let us discuss next an example of theological importance from St. Paul's letters. Here again the Judaean finds have made a considerable contribution. In Galatians 3:6–14, the apostle puts forth one of his major themes, that of righteousness through faith, by appealing to the exemplar Abraham, the father of faith (Gen 15:6; 12:3; 18:18) and also by citing Habakkuk Commentary 2:4 to support his contention. (As we have mentioned previously, the Habakkuk Commentary sets forth the sectarian interpretation of this passage.)

Since no one can abide by all the laws, Paul argues, no one can be justified before God by the law. (This assertion is based on Deuteronomy 27:26.) But "Christ redeemed us from the curse of the law, having become a curse for us—for it is written, 'Cursed be every one who hangs on a tree'" (Gal 3:13). This last quotation which the apostle makes is taken from Deuteronomy 21:23.[59]

This type of logical deployment is not a modern one but rather a traditional Jewish one similar to that found in Qumran and rabbinic argumentation. In Paul's writing, the "curse" of the law and the "curse" of Christ do not have the same meaning. However, "curse" functions as a keyword connecting two different passages from Deuteronomy, and it is used as a term demonstrating the significance of Christ's redemptive death. Consequently, Paul's basic message is: faith in Christ brings a blessing, while works of the law yield a curse.[60] To prove and give authority to his point, several passages are quoted from the Old Testament, taken out of context, placed in concatenation, and applied to a specific situation (the eschatological event of Christ's redemption). This whole process of Paul's use of the Old Testament is in consonance with the Qumran exegetical model.[61]

(ii) Crucifixion

Deuteronomy 21:23, which Paul cites in this paragraph (Gal 3:13), plays an important role further at Qumran and in Christianity. As scholars unanimously agree, the pesher on Nahum (4QpNah) concerns the incident where Alexander Jannaeus (the high priest during 103-76 B.C.) crucified and slaughtered Jews whom he considered to be his enemies—those who had previously invited the Seleucid king Demetrius III (who reigned 95–88 B.C.) to fight with Jannaeus. Demetrius' name, in fact, appears in 4QNahum fragments 3–4, column 1, line 2.[62]

In lines 6–8, we read: "The interpretation of it (Nahum 2:13a) concerns the lion of wrath [. . .] death on the seekers of smooth things, whom he hanged living men [on the tree, as this is the law] in Israel as of old, for of one hanged alive on the tree [. . .]" The "lion of wrath" alludes to Alexander Jannaeus, who crucified the "seekers of the smooth things" (identified as the Pharisees). The reconstruction of the second lacuna: "on the tree as this is the law" is proposed by Y. Yadin.[63] He suggests that this law refers to Deuteronomy 21:22–23.

Reinforcing this view, Yadin adduces evidence from the Temple Scroll, column 64, lines 6–13. This passage ordains that the death penalty shall be carried out by "suspending" the convict alive for the charge of treason on the basis of Deuteronomy 21:22–23.

What we have here is a pre-Christian halakhic interpretation of Deuteronomy 21:22–23 (crucifixion in the form of a hanging on a tree). Such a Jewish halakhic background lies behind New Testament phrases concerning Jesus' crucifixion like "hanging on a tree" in Acts 5:30; 10:39; 1 Peter 2:24.[64] Indeed, Jesus was crucified on the tree, being "accursed by God and men" (11QTemple 64:12), for he was willing to "become a curse for us" (Gal 3:13). At Qumran the Law is the vehicle for salvation, whereas in Paul's belief, Christ's death is the means for redemption. "Christ redeemed us (especially Jewish Christians, in context) from the curse of the law" (3:13).

Example from Hebrews

For another example of a parallel between the Qumran scrolls and the New Testament in their use of the Old Testament, let us look at the Letter to the Hebrews. This New Testament writing contains close to one hundred instances of quotations and allusions from the Old Testament. The author exercises a great amount of freedom in his treatment of these Old Testament passages and betrays a Qumran pesher style of interpretation.

(i) Use of Psalm 8

In chapter two from verse six onward, for instance, the author contends that Jesus is superior to the angels, employing

Psalm 8:5–7, as a basis for this contention. The quotation from Psalm 8 agrees with the Septuagint, which is a literal translation of the Hebrew original. The first line of verse 5, however, is missing in the New Testament portion.[65] This passage from Psalms refers to human beings in the order of things in the creation. But the author of Hebrews applies it to Jesus. "The son of man" in Psalm 8:5, indicating human beings ("man" and "son of man" form a synonymous parallel, a feature very common in Hebrew poetry), provides the author with a cogent indicator for the Christological reinterpretation.[66] (This Psalm is applied to Jesus also in Mt 21:16; 1 Cor 15:27; Eph 1:22.)

Our writer, therefore, takes the original wording—"You (God) made him (man) a little lower than *elōhîm* (which could mean God, gods, or angels; the Septuagint: angels)"—to mean that God made Jesus lower than the angels. This was done just for "a little while" (i.e., in a temporal sense, not in terms of status as in the Old Testament) to allow for Jesus' vicarious death (Heb 2:9). Because of this, the author contends further that we see Christ "crowned with glory and honors" (Ps 8:6). He then interprets the passage, "You put all things under his (human) feet" (Ps 8:7b) in the eschatological perspective, because, he admits, "as it is, we do not yet see everything in subjection to him (Jesus Christ)" (Heb 2:8).[67]

Such a use of the Old Testament text belongs to the same hermeneutical category as the pesher which we have been discussing.[68] Vital to the Christian author is the witness to Christ; Old Testament passages are to be read in a Christological light. They are sometimes allegorized and at other times taken as a source foreshadowing Christ.

(ii) Typology

It has often been suggested that the allegorical interpretation of scripture by Philo, the Jewish philosopher in Alexandria (c. 20- A.D. 50), proffers a helpful background for Hebrews' use of the Old Testament.[69] Philo, for example, allegorizes Melchizedek as human reason rising in divine intoxication to God. He does this by etymologizing the name Melch-zedek ("king of righteousness") and the title "king of Salem" ("king of peace")

(*Lequm Allegoria* III, 25, 79). The identical etymologization occurs in Hebrews 7:2.

From Philo's writing, however, typological exegesis is totally missing. A typology is an understanding of the history of salvation where persons, events, and institutions are believed to be divinely ordained in such a way that they correspond to their counterparts. For instance, Paul calls Christ the second and last Adam (Rom 5:12–17; 1 Cor 15:45–47), and likewise Melchizedek foreshadows Christ, according to the Letter to the Hebrews. Such a view, where a type anticipates an antitype in history, is different from an allegory which is not based on the historical process.

In Hebrews, the correspondence between Old Testament types and promises and the New Testament claims of fulfillment is a fundamental exegetical pattern. God's plan of salvation in history—whose consummation was thought to be soon—constituted a vital part of the faith of the author and other writers of the New Testament.[70] On this point, too, the approach to scripture on the part of the New Testament Christians and the Qumran sectarians was in congruity.

(iii) Addressee of the Letter to the Hebrews

The Letter to the Hebrews not only affords us evidence of the Qumran style of scriptural interpretation, it also intimates a possible intriguing connection with the Qumran sect. Y. Yadin has suggested that this letter was addressed to a group of Jews who were converted to Christianity from the Qumran sect.[71]

The letter asserts Jesus' superiority to the prophets (1:1–2), to the angels (1:3–2:18), to Moses (3:1–4:13), and to the Aaronite priesthood (4:14–10:18). The last point is exceedingly important as attested to by the number of passages devoted to the subject; it underscores (1) that Jesus is a high priest, (2) that his priesthood is superior to that of Aaron, and (3) that he is a royal priest, i.e., both a royal and a priestly Messiah.

This contention would seem to be especially pertinent to readers with an Essene background. As the phrase in 1QS 9:11 ("until the coming of a prophet and of the messiahs from Aaron and Israel") well indicates,[72] the sectarians believed in the emergence of the prophet, the priestly messiah and the royal (lay) messiah at the end of time. The prophet was to be a "prophet like Moses" as mentioned in Deuteronomy 18:15 ("The Lord your God will raise up for you a prophet like me [Moses] from among you, from your brethren; to him you shall be obedient"). The Qumran document furnishes no further information about this figure. As for the two messiahs, we learn that the royal or lay messiah stands subordinate to the priestly messiah (cf. 1QSa 2:11ff.). This hierarchy is certainly consonant with the basic priestly orientation of the Qumran sect itself. The author of Hebrews emphatically declares that Jesus Christ is superior to each of these three offices.

In order to reinforce the distinctive contention of Christ's ascendancy over the Aaronite priesthood, the author calls Christ "a high priest forever after the order of Melchizedek" (5:6, 10; 6:20; 7:11, 15, 17). Melchizedek is, according to Genesis 14:18–20, the priest-king of Salem (identified with Jerusalem in Ps 76:2; Genesis Apocryphon 22:18, etc.) who blessed Abraham and received from him in return a tithe. The figure is, furthermore, donned with a messianic character in Psalm 11:4 ("You—messianic ruler—are a priest forever after the order of Melchizedek").[73]

(iv) Melchizedek

At Qumran, Melchizedek obtained unique messianic stature. The thirteen Hebrew fragments from Cave XI (11QMelch) contain a thematic pesher of several passages from Leviticus, Deuteronomy, Psalms, and Isaiah, the major subject of which concerns the eschatological salvation by the hand of Melchizedek; his expiation will be executed on behalf of "the men of the lot of Melchizedek" (2:8), i.e., the sectarians, and his vengeance against Belial, the evil power (line 13).[74] Melchizedek is described as a heavenly redeemer.[75] He is called *elōhîm* (heavenly being) in 2:10 and "king" (2:15–16).[76] He functions as an eschatological judge.

The Qumran Melchizedek fragments and Hebrews, therefore, are in striking agreement on Melchizedek as the heavenly messianic figure, the high priest who presides over the celestial court. He is "without father or mother or genealogy, and has neither beginning of days nor end of life" (Heb 7:3). Being such, he is superior to Abraham, Levi, and Aaron. (Note in Genesis 14 that Melchizedek receives a tithe from Abraham, Levi's ancestor. In Psalm 110:4 he is called "a priest forever.")

The Qumran Melchizedek documents do not provide any further elaboration on the Old Testament Melchizedek. Hebrews, however, interprets him as a figure foreshadowing Jesus Christ. He is the heavenly redeemer, ruler, final judge, and perfect and eternal high priest. The author of Hebrews adds a description which finds no counterpart in the Qumran text: Melchizedek's "resembling the Son of God" (7:3). This phrase underscores the superiority of Christ over Melchizedek; the latter is after all a prototype of the former. In such a manner, the author establishes the absolute ascendancy of Christ.

Such unique Christology as expounded in Hebrews, consequently, can be properly understood in the light of the Qumran Melchizedek text. Before the Qumran discovery, scholars had sought background material for the Melchizedek Christology in sources such as the writings of Philo. We realize now, however, that the Qumran manuscripts provide us with the major background source.

"Son of Man"

The foregoing observation regarding Hebrews and the Qumran Melchizedek fragments further leads us to a couple of significant concepts in the New Testament. The first concerns the "Son of Man," a term which often occurs in the New Testament, referring to Jesus. Scholars have been investigating intensively this peculiar phrase. Where is its provenance? What does it mean?

There is no known instance of "son of man" as a title for an apocalyptic messiah in pre-Christian Judaism.[77] It is not absolutely clear whether it originated with Jesus himself or with the early Christians. Many scholars opt for the latter, contending that the notion of Jesus as the Son of Man accrued from the pesher-type interpretative activities of the early church.[78] That is to say, the Christian interpreters of the Old Testament applied to Jesus the vision mentioned in Daniel 7:9–14 which describes the son of man (probably the archangel Michael mentioned in Daniel 10:13 and 12:1[79]) receiving "dominion and glory and kingdom" (see Mt 25:31; Mk 13:26; 14:62; Rev 14:14; etc.). This interpretation seems to have been further reinforced by the use of Psalm 8 (as we have mentioned previously) and Psalm 110. These Psalms include God's words regarding the kingly messiah ("a priest forever according to the order of Melchizedek" who "sits at the right hand" of God). On the basis of these scriptural passages, early Christians described Jesus as the apocalyptic Messiah—the eschatological redeemer, the suffering Messiah, the glorified ruler, the judge with divine authority, and the eternal and perfect high priest.

If such is the case with the New Testament concept of the Son of Man, then this figure resembles the Qumran Melchizedek considerably. The correspondence is seen not only in terms of the image, functions, and attributes, but also in more detailed description such as a destruction of the evil ones with fire (Mt 13:42; 11QMelch 3:7) and a sounding of the trumpet (Mt 24:31; 11QMelch 2:25).[80] Consequently, we have in the Qumran Melchizedek documents possible background material for the long-sought New Testament Son of Man.

Light vs. Darkness

The Qumran Melchizedek documents shed light on another important concept found in some of the New Testament writings. It concerns a dualistic scheme of thought. Melchizedek (identified with Michael, the guardian angel, who is perhaps "the Son of Man" in Daniel 7) represents the "Prince of Light" as opposed to Melchiresh, the Prince of Darkness. Such an apocalyptic figure of evil is mentioned also in a fragment from Cave IV (4QpsDanA[a] = 4Q246). It is dated to the last third of the first century B.C.[81] The content pertains to the end of the world when the evil power represented by one called "son of God," "son of the Most High" (it is not clear whether he calls himself so or other people do so) will dominate. The travail will last "some years" until "the people of God shall rise." Because of its poorly preserved condition, it is far from facile to obtain an accurate meaning from it, but D. Flusser seems to be correct in his interpretation of this "son" as being an antichrist like "the man of lawlessness, the son of perdition" who "proclaims himself to be God" mentioned in 2 Thessalonians 2:1–12. He is the antichrist.

The Qumran fragment is of great significance because it contains the pre-Christian reference to the "Son of God" and the antichrist figure.

As has been well known, the Qumran sect embraced such an apocalyptic dualism, which finds its expression in many places throughout the Dead Sea Scrolls; the world is an arena of a fierce conflict between the spirit of truth and falsehood and between the sons of light and the sons of darkness. History, as the sectarians see it, is rapidly approaching its end which is to be consummated in a final battle resulting in the ultimate victory of the forces of goodness. The War Scroll deals with this theme. The same type of dualism is found as well in other Jewish literature from the intertestamental period, such as First Enoch and the Testaments of the Twelve Patriarchs, among others.

Scholars have long contended that there has been an influence of Zoroastrianism on Jewish apocalyptic dualism. Zoroastrianism is an ancient Persian religion which preaches the final victory of the god of Light, Ahura Mazda, over the prince of Darkness, Ahriman; history is a process involving long and truculent battles between these two powers. If the Qumran sect indeed comprises a group of recent returnees from Babylon (as we discussed in Chapter Two), it is very likely that the sectarian teachings were affected by Zoroastrian ideas.

Be that as it may, both Zoroastrian and Jewish dualism are highly ethical in nature. It is particularly so in the Qumran dualism. According to the Qumran belief, God has predestined a "lot" for every person, good and evil. The sectarians, by remaining loyal, preserve their righteous lot against the outside world, a world which is destined to the lot of Belial (Satan) and will meet with the Day of Vengeance. Nonetheless, there is a certain amount of individual freedom; one can choose whether or not to enter the sect and whether or not to stay with it.[82] Repentance is a prerequisite for forgiveness and cleansing. Though righteousness is given by God, one must also earn it through observing the rightly interpreted (i.e., the sectarians') Law.[83] Then, do divine predestination and human free will contradict each other? E. H. Merill answers this question in this way: "The very fact that a man joined the Community proved that he was one of the predestined. He did not do so to become one of the Elect; he did so because he was one of the Elect. Predestination did not contradict free will; it provided the rationale as to why men chose 'freely' as they did."[84]

Such ethical and theological dualism plays a significant role particularly in the Johannine writings as well (also in Gal 5:16–23; Eph 6:10–12; etc.).[85] The Fourth Gospel writer emphatically tells us that Jesus came from "above" to the "world below" as "the light" to "overcome the darkness" (1:4f., 9; 3:31) and was thus raised to the "heaven" (2:13f.). As such he is "the truth" and "the light" over and against "falsehood" and "death" (14:6). Everyone should choose to "love" light and "hate" darkness (3:19). God sends "the spirit of Truth, the Paraclete" to aid the sons of righteousness (14:16f., 26; 15:26).[86] The sectarian literature likewise refers to two spirits of truth and falsehood and exhorts the sons of righteousness to walk in the way of light. By contrast, the sons of perversity are under the rule of the angel of darkness (1QS 3:18–24).

The whole pattern of thought and vocabulary is common to both John and Qumran. The root of John's dualistic theological scheme must be Jewish apocalypticism as typically attested to in the Dead Sea Scrolls. It has much less of relationship with the Hellenistic sources, nor does it occur in the Old Testament. Another point should be noted here: both Qumran and John are decidedly concerned with their present struggle with the forces of evil. John states, for example, "One not believing has already judged" (3:18). In this sense, their eschatology is not simply futuristic as found in other apocalyptic books. In this sense again, their dualism is not essentially cosmological but ethical. This close parallel reinforces the possibility of the Qumran-John connection. Nevertheless, the evidence falls short of allowing us to draw a direct line between the two. A vital difference between them is that the Qumran theology has a community orientation (or restriction), John a Christological direction.

3. Temple Theology

Symbolic Temple at Qumran

A distinctive theological idea expressed in the Dead Sea Scrolls is the concept of the community as a symbolic temple.[87]

It is of great significance that this symbolism is found uniquely both in the scrolls and in the New Testament. We read in the Manual of Disciple 9:3–6:

> When these things come to pass in Israel, according to all these rules for a foundation of the holy spirit, for eternal truth, to expiate the guilt of sin and faithlessness of wickedness and for favor for the land more than the flesh of burnt offering and the fats of sacrifice and an offering of the lips for the law as a pleasant fragrance of righteousness and perfection of way was a willing gift of an acceptable offering; at that time, the men of the community shall be set apart, a house of Aaron to be united as a holy of holies, and a house of community for Israel, those who walk in perfection.

In this passage and also in 5:5–6 and 8:4–10, the following crucial assertions are made:[88] (1) the community is analogically conceived as a temple where divine truth is reposed; (2) this symbolic temple consists of the priests ("the house of Aaron") and lay members ("Israel"), corresponding to the holy of holies and the rest of the holy precinct of the temple of Jerusalem; (3) the sacrificial cult offered in this "community-temple" manifests the correct interpretation and observance of the divine Law, as opposed to the act of offering sacrificial animals as performed in the Jerusalem temple. The life obedient to the Law is, symbolically, a temple liturgy. (In the Damascus Document 11:18–21, prayer is said to be the equivalent of an offering and more acceptable than an unlawful sacrifice. "Offering of the lips" in the Manual of Disciple 9:5 means prayer.) Therefore, burnt offerings were not performed at Qumran.[89]

The fundamental reason for their developing such a symbolic notion is that they adjudged the people in charge of the Jerusalem temple as being religiously and morally corrupt for not observing the Law in the same way as the sectarians. As a result, the temple itself was considered defiled. It is stated unequivocally in the Damascus Document 20:22f. that "Israel sinned and made the temple unclean." This prompted them to depart from Jerusalem to establish their own community at Qumran. Their community, accordingly, was built upon a new covenant with God; it was believed to be a decisive part of the divine plan of salvation at the finale of history. As against the old and impure temple, the covenant community represented a pure, new, and eschatological temple.

This "community-temple," the Qumran sect insisted, was not only set apart from defilement but was also established for the purpose of obtaining atonement for the sinful land. The sect, in other words, was a salvific agent for the ushering in of a pure, new and final world. The sectarians believed in Ezekiel's prophecy which predicted that the living water from the temple would transform a barren wilderness and the dead sea into a paradise (Ez 47:1–12). That is the very reason why they founded their community on the shore of the Dead Sea in the Judaean wilderness. They were there fervently anticipating the opportunity for eyewitnessing and participating in the eschatological transformation of the world.

Symbolic Temple in the New Testament

A striking fact is that except for the New Testament, no such symbolic interpretation of the temple is detected in ancient Jewish writings or in the Old Testament. Nor is it found in any Hellenistic sources. In Paul's letters to the Corinthians, the Christian community is described as a temple. Paul writes: "Do you not know that you are God's temple and that God's spirit dwells in you?" (1 Cor 3:16). In 2 Corinthians 6:14–17 he states:

> Do not be misyoked with unbelievers. For what fellowship have righteousness and iniquity? Or what communion has light with darkness? What accord has Christ with Belial? Or what lot has a believer with an unbeliever? What agreement has the temple of God with idols? For we are the temple of the living God; as God said, "I will live in them and move among them, and I will be their God, and they shall be my people. Therefore, come out from there, and separate yourselves from them, says the Lord, and touch nothing unclean. . . ."

Both of these passages refer to the indwelling of the holy spirit, which makes the "Christian temple" holy. The concept of the holy spirit abiding with the sect is also underscored at Qumran. The latter text presents an even more compelling proximity to Qumran theological ideas: an essential conflict between believers and unbelievers, righteousness and iniquity, darkness and light, Christ and Belial, and God's temple and idols. God's people are strongly urged to separate themselves from the unclean world. Believers have no common "lot" with unbelievers. All these teachings using even the same vocabulary are typically stressed at Qumran. (One can list numerous citations here—for example, 1QS 1:9–11; 2:16f.; etc.) The concatenation of several passages from the Old Testament is also quite characteristic in the Qumran documents (e.g. 4QTestimonia).

The correspondence between this paragraph and Qumran theology is thus overwhelming. In addition to this fact, because 2 Corinthians 6:14–7:1 interrupts the flow of the context of the letter, modern scholars such as J. A. Fitzmyer are of the opinion that this portion is "a Christian reworking of an Essene paragraph which has been introduced into the Pauline letter."[90]

In Ephesians 2:20–22, the Christians are also called a "holy temple in the Lord" and a "dwelling place of God in the spirit." This reference is made in the context of a message of reconciliation through Christ's redemption, as it is said, "You are no longer strangers and sojourners, but are fellow citizens with the saints and members of the household of God" (v. 19). Here we notice a difference between the Christian use of the temple symbolism and that of the Qumran Essenes. For the latter, the symbolic temple consists only of the "saints," an often used designation for angels as well as for the sectarians themselves. For the former, in sharp contrast, the symbolic temple was composed by and for every person by virtue of Christ's sacrifice. Each person, therefore, could become a "fellow citizen" with the angels.

The temple symbolism is by no means confined within the Pauline and Deutero-Pauline epistles. In 1 Timothy 3:15, the church is called "God's house (i.e., temple), the pillar and foundation of the truth." Needless to say, the temple here refers to the Christian community rather than a physical building. The phrase, "the pillar and foundation of the truth," occurs nowhere else in the New Testament. In the Manual of Discipline 5:5f., however, we have an interesting parallel:

> In order to lay a foundation of truth for Israel, for the community of the eternal covenant, to make atonement for all

who are volunteers for the sanctuary in Aaron and a house of truth in Israel. . . .

The basic agreement found in these two passages is: (1) that both the church and the Qumran community are said to be God's temple in a metaphorical sense, and (2) that they both are claimed as the foundation for truth.

It is also intriguing that the next verse (3:16) in the Timothy text mentions the greatness of the mystery of the Christian faith. In the New Testament the word *mysterion* (mystery) often refers to the gospel revealed by Christ (e.g. Mk 4:11; Rom 16:25f.; 1 Cor 2:7; Col 1:26f.). In the Qumran Scrolls, the mystery occurs many times, denoting God's ineffable works in nature (1QH 1:11, etc.) and history, in particular, his plan for the final days (1QS 4:18; 1QpHab 7:14; 1QM 3:9; etc.). Just as the Christian mystery is revealed by Christ to his followers, the Qumran mystery is divulged to the sectarians, especially to the Teacher of Righteousness (1QpHab 7:4, etc.). (We will discuss the question of "mystery" in Chapter Five.) In both, the symbolic temple is the place where the eschatological revelation of God's mystery takes place.

Another instance of the Christian temple symbolism is found in 1 Peter 2:5, where the Christians are admonished to be "like living stones built into a spiritual house, to be a holy priesthood, to offer spiritual sacrifices acceptable to God through Jesus Christ." As the Christians are fashioned into a spiritual temple, "he (God) built for them in Israel a firmly established house (i.e., sect)" (CD 3:19).

Here again, however, we have a Christian elaboration of this symbolic theme. Each Christian is termed a "living stone" in the analogy of Christ who is "the living stone, rejected by men but in God's sight chosen and precious" (v. 4). By adhering to Christ (the cornerstone), the Christians (the stones) are built into the living temple. The metaphor of Christians being living stones is found only in this passage in the New Testament. In the Manual of Discipline 8:7, the sect is called "the tried wall, the precious cornerstone." A similarity in image, though not quite identical, can be noted here. The stone metaphor in these passages is taken from Isaiah 28:16 and Psalm 118:22.

The notion of Christians as a "holy priesthood" is mentioned here and only here in the entire New Testament. It is based on Exodus 19:6, which states that Israel is "a kingdom of priests and a holy nation." At Qumran, however, the distinction between the priestly group and the lay element is maintained clearly, though the Levitical purity is required of every member.

Spiritual Sacrifices

Our passage from 1 Peter also enjoins the Christians to "offer spiritual sacrifices," that is, a life totally dedicated to God incorporating purity of the soul, obedience to the truth, a sincere love of the brethren, a witness to God's work, good works, forbearance, prayer, humility, and so on. By offering such "spiritual sacrifices," the Christians can truly be "living stones" just as is Christ, the "chosen and precious living stone." Because such spiritual sacrifices are offered, the Christians form a "spiritual temple."[91]

At Qumran, too, as we have already indicated, a life wholly dedicated to God was conceived as a sacrificial offering. There is, however, a vital difference between the two: in Christianity, "the spiritual sacrifice" was accomplished "through Jesus Christ," whereas in Essenism it was performed through rigid observance of the Law. The process of conceptualization was identical, but the content and goal were different from each other.

Structures of the Symbolic Temple

Another intriguing instance of comparability is found in a fragment of a sectarian commentary on Isaiah 54:11–12, which describes the rebuilding of Jerusalem following the Babylonian exile. The restored city is to be constructed with various precious stones. In this document (4QpIs^d, fragment 1), the sectarian interpreter applies the prophecy to the sect: the new Jerusalem represents their community as the jeweled parts of the city correspond to the various groups within the community (i.e., the council of the community, the priests, the lay members, the congregation of his chosen one, and the twelve). Here we see a notion of the sect as the symbolic Jerusalem (the temple-city). The temple is not mentioned here, but this symbolism stands as a corollary of the temple symbolism. (In the Commentary on Micah from Cave I, the Teacher of Righteousness is said to be Jerusalem, "the high place of Judah.")

The imagery of these precious stones seems to derive from the jewels on Aaron's breastplate emblematizing the twelve tribes of Israel (Ex 28:17–20). The sectarian author understood this Isaiah passage not only in terms of the existing sect itself but also with reference to the entire Israel of the final days, the sect being her foundation.

A vision of the heavenly Jerusalem in Revelation provides a significant parallel to that found in the Qumran commentary on Isaiah, fragment d. Just as the future Jerusalem is described in the Isaiah commentary, so the heavenly Jerusalem in Revelation is also said to be constructed with precious stones (21:18–21). In this apocalyptic image, the number twelve plays an important role: there are twelve gates with the names of the twelve tribes of Israel inscribed on them (stems from Ezekiel 48:31–34); there are twelve angels at each gate, imagery perhaps inspired by Isaiah 62:6; and there are twelve foundations inscribed with the names of the twelve apostles.

The implication of this symbolic description is that the new Jerusalem is the dwelling place of the community of the faithful (as against the old unfaithful Jerusalem which is to be punished). The foundation of the community is the twelve apostles. Consequently, both in the Qumran fragment and the passage from Revelation, the future Jerusalem of Isaiah is interpreted in terms of the community of those with the true faith, that is, the true Israel, the true people of God.

Both the Qumran and Christian communities are said to be led by twelve men. In the Isaiah fragment, we read: "ALL YOUR PINACLES (Is 54:12a). Its interpretation concerns the twelve [men of the council of the community, who . . .][92] give light by the decision of the Urim and Thummin. . . ." In the Manual of Discipline 8:1, twelve perfect men and three priests are said to lead the sect.[93] In the War Scroll 2:1, too, twelve priests, twelve Levites, and the heads of the twelve tribes are mentioned.

Scholars like D. Flusser have maintained that the institution of the twelve disciples of Jesus not only corresponds to the twelve tribes of Israel (cf. Mt 19:28), but also reveals the influence of the Qumran sect. In his opinion, this Essene "ideology of the twelve" (as he calls it) derived through John the Baptizer. (Flusser holds the view that the Baptizer was not an Essene but was "spiritually related" to the sect.) The supremacy of twelve individuals, in fact, is attested to only in the Dead Sea Scrolls and in the New Testament.[94] Other scholars are skeptical regarding this possibility. W. Schmithals, for example, asserts that the notion of the important twelve individuals does not exist before Jesus' resurrection, and that it rather indicates a core Christian group existing during the time shortly after Easter.[95]

It seems more probable for us to assume that, in lieu of a Qumran influence on Jesus himself, the converts from the Baptizer's disciples (who were originally related to the Essenes, as we have discussed before) brought the notion to the very young Christian community.

As the foregoing observation indicates, many of the vitally significant theological ideas and terminologies of the Qumran Scrolls and the New Testament are so similar that one can scarcely discard a possible historical contact between the sect and the New Testament Christians. The temple symbolism—a theological expression of a basic self-understanding on the part of both of these groups—is a case in point.

Reasons for Temple Symbolism

As B. Gärtner points out, the temple symbolism is predicated upon three factors in both: (1) a criticism of the Jerusalem temple and its sacrifices; (2) a belief that the last days have begun; (3) a conviction of God's dwelling in themselves.[96] Prompted as they were by the same basic understanding, only these two religious bodies entertained a symbolic concept of a group as a temple. In view of these facts, G. Klinzing in his careful study of the subject matter has arrived at the conclusion that the Christian temple symbolism was undoubtedly derived from the Qumran community.[97] As Gärtner suggests, it is not unlikely that Jesus himself was aware of this principal Qumran tenet.[98]

These possibilities are most likely. Nevertheless, we are lacking decisive evidence to draw a direct connection between the Qumran and the Christian concepts of the temple and cult, for there are differences as well. The Qumran sect rejected the Jerusalem temple of its time because the sect condemned the officiating priests. This by no means meant that the sectarians repudiated wholly the temple itself or its cultic function and personnel. On the contrary, the harsher they denounced the Jerusalem religious establishment, the more ardent did they long for an ideal temple with rites performed therein in their purest form.

The Future Temple

The sectarians' claim of the ideal temple seems to have found its expression in the Temple Scroll.[99] This unique pseudepigraphic literature ordains the construction of a temple and the cultic furnishings therein with precise specifications and dimensions. The temple building is to be encircled by three concentric square courts. This structural plan is rather distinctive; it was never mentioned before nor was it actually built throughout biblical and Jewish history. The temple was supposedly always rectangular with two courtyards.

B. Z. Wacholder, who regards this scroll as the "sectarian Torah," goes so far as to say that the author vilifies not only his contemporary temple as being polluted but "even the temple erected by David and Solomon (as being) . . . an idolatrous structure. The square dimensions of the true temple are intended to contrast with the rectangular sanctuary erected by Solomon."[100] The square shape, according to him, derived from the square shape of the breastplate of Aaron the priest, with the twelve precious stones corresponding to the number of Israel's tribes.[101]

Y. Yadin, the editor of the scroll, indicates that the author apparently intended to present here the real and ideal temple and its cult. It is assumed to be a Torah, as the text is written in the form of a direct revelation from God (i.e., God's words are in the first person singular). Even if the document exhibits no particular polemical intention,[102] the sectarians at Qumran, by preserving such a heterodox "Torah," seem to demonstrate their opposition to the authorities in Jerusalem.

The scroll, however, distinguishes this temple from the final and eternal temple which God himself will build on "the Day of

Blessing" (see 11QTemple 29:7-10).[103] The author of the scroll purveys no further elaboration concerning this final temple of God, nor do the other Qumran writings supply us with much information.[104]

The New Testament yields no evidence that Jesus and the earliest Christians expected such a final and eternal temple to be built. Jesus was accused "falsely," according to Mark 14:58 and Matthew 26:61, of planning to destroy and rebuild the temple in three days (see also Mark 15:29). Whether Jesus actually stated this or not,[105] we do not know. But the temple referred to in this instance is symbolic of the Christian community, for the "three days" mentioned in this passage obviously refers to Jesus' resurrection and not to some final sequence of events ushering in the construction of an actual temple.[106] Furthermore, the Fourth Gospel writer adds an explanatory comment: "But he spoke of the temple of his body" (2:21). For Christians, the final and eternal temple is none other than a community of the faithful and not an actual temple building (the "temple not made by hand" as against the "temple made by hand" in Mark 14:58; the former replaces the latter).[107] For this reason, the early Christians did not take over the Jewish sacerdotal hierarchy; all Christians were even called "priests" (1 Peter 2:5; Rev 5:10). By contrast, at Qumran the priestly order and leadership were rigidly retained.

Luke tells us that the earliest Christians worshiped God at the Jerusalem temple (Lk 24:53; Acts 2:46; 3:1; 5:42). But as McKelvey puts it: "The apparent devotion of the first Christians to the temple of Jerusalem was a transitional phenomenon."[108] This shift was especially quickened by the addition to the Christian community of early Hellenistic Jewish Christians and Gentile Christians. Stephen's speech in Acts 7 indicates this; he states in the presence of the high priest that "the Most High does not dwell in houses made with hands" (v. 48).[109]

As the Christians departed from Judaism, the church as the body of Christ became the locus of their worship and fellowship. This happened because early Christians believed that the redemption of Jesus Christ replaced once and for all the temple and its sacrificial rites by fulfilling their meaning. In an apocalyptic vision of the Book of Revelation, the heavenly Jerusalem was described as being without the temple, because "its temple is the Lord God, the Almighty, and the Lamb" (21:22).

It is interesting to note that God and/or Jesus Christ are explicitly said to be the temple only in the Johannine writings (Jn 2:21 and Rev 21:22), while, as we have observed, particularly in the epistles in the New Testament, the community of the faithful represents the temple. The Qumran sect entertained the temple symbolism which corresponded to the latter, but it never conceived of a messiah as the temple. The Johannine temple symbolism is a uniquely Christian development.

For the sectarians, the central importance of the Law overwhelmed their messianic belief; their rigid devotion to the Law prompted their criticism of the contemporary Jerusalem temple, their symbolism of the community as the temple, and their expectation of the ideal temple. For the Christians, every aspect of their belief and life was predicated upon their faith in Jesus as the Messiah. The temple was thus replaced by the believing community, which was also the body of Christ.

The form of symbolic transference of the notion of the temple is identical in both groups, yet the content is totally different one from the other. It is quite likely that the earliest Christians (some of them, Essene converts) took over this symbolism to articulate the content of the Christian faith. The discovery of the Judaean documents thus enriches considerably our comprehension of important concepts and images of the New Testament Christians' fundamental self-understanding and self-expression.

Excursus: The Communal Meal at Qumran and the Last Supper

Qumran Communal Meal

The Manual of Discipline 6:2–8 ordains a communal meal which begins with a priest's blessing over the bread and wine. Likewise, the Rule of the Community 2:11–22 legislates the same meal where the members, led by the priest who is followed by the "messiah of Israel," sit according to rank. The blessing of the bread and wine is done again in the identical order of rank:

the priest, the messiah of Israel, and the remainder of the congregation.

There is no doubt that this meal constitutes an important part of the Qumran community life. Participation at the table comprises a privilege of full membership; condemned members (1QS 7:20) and newcomers (recent arrivals up to two years, according to 1QS 6:20f.) are excluded. Josephus mentions an Essene custom where the communal meal is held twice daily (*War* 2:133–138). According to him, the Essenes, after a purifying bath, "assemble in a private apartment into which none of the uninitiated is permitted to enter . . . as to some sacred shrine." They are seated in silence according to rank, and the meal begins and ends with the priest's prayer.[110]

Since no further detailed description of the meal is provided by either the Qumran sect or Josephus, its exact reconstruction is beyond our tether. Josephus' report appears to coincide basically with the sect's own description of the meal. Both emphasize the restrictive and communal nature of the meal, the rigidly ordered seating arrangement and procedures, and the priestly blessings. The Qumran material, however, makes no mention as to the immediate procedural sequence of the bathing and the meal, the silence during the meal, and whether or not all the meals are communal. Josephus, however, refers to the loaves and "one plate with a single course" of food for each participant but does not mention wine.[111]

A question emerges here: Was this meal an official cultic practice of the sect? Many scholars have considered it so. B. Gärtner, for example, views that it was meant to embody the priestly practice of the eating of sacrifices at the temple. Since the sectarians condemned the Jerusalem temple as being defiled, they, the symbolic temple, held the meal at Qumran, anticipating the perfected ritual of the heavenly temple.[112]

This is an interesting suggestion. But it has met with strong objections. L. H. Schiffman contends that there is no evidence that it was an institutionalized cult or liturgy. The priest's dominant role stemmed from his honored status rather than for any liturgical reason. The bread and wine do not necessarily indicate that it was a "eucharistic" meal. It was supposed to be pure because of the vigorous sectarian emphasis on purity laws.[113] There was no polemical intention attached to the meal either.

Rather than a cultic practice, J. Neusner points out, the meal at Qumran looks somewhat similar to the table fellowship of the Pharisees. Both were meant to be "appropriate undertakings to keep ritual purity and consume properly grown and tithed foods."[114] As such, the Qumran communal meal was not quite equivalent to the Christian Eucharist, though the approximation of the two has sometimes been suggested. Neusner writes:

> The Dead Sea sect's meal would have had some similarity to the Eucharist if it had included some sort of narrative about the Temple cult, or stories about how the sect replicates the holy Temple and eats at the table of God, how the founder of the community transferred the Temple's holiness out of unclean Jerusalem, and how the occasion calls to mind some holy event of the past. But we have no allusion to the inclusion of such mythic elements in the enactment of the community meal.[115]

The Lord's Supper

We should remember, however, that New Testament references to the Lord's Supper (Mk 14:22-25; Mt 26:26-29; Lk 22:15-20; 1 Cor 11:23-26) reflect liturgical embellishments of the post-Easter church based on the tradition it possessed.[116] It proffers the sacramental experience of Christ's sacrificing himself for others' sins. By receiving the wine, one enters a "new covenant" with God.

That these passages originated with the post-Easter Christian community does not mean that Jesus had no such meal before his arrest; there is no particular reason to doubt that. But the question here concerns the meal's exact nature and just when it was held. The Synoptic Gospel writers tell us that it was a Passover meal which was celebrated during the evening of the fourteenth of Nisan (Thursday), according to the Jewish calendar. But was it really lawful for the Jewish authorities to judge and convict a man on Passover? Was it possible actually for the many events (from the trials to the burial) to all take place on one day, Friday?

Moreover, according to the Fourth Gospel, the farewell meal was held "before the Passover feast" (13:1–2), and Jesus' trial before Pontius Pilate was on "the day of Preparation for the Passover" (19:14). In the official calendar then the Last Supper was not a Passover meal. St. Paul does not characterize it as a Passover meal either. Jesus died his sacrificial death at the very time when the paschal lambs were slaughtered. In other words, Jesus was the paschal lamb (see also 1 Cor 5:7; 1 Peter 1:19; Rev 5:6). John mentions also in 19:29 the hyssop which, according to Exodus 14:22, was used to dab the lintels of the Hebrew homes with blood from the sacrificial lamb at the first Passover in Egypt. Another Passover allusion to Jesus' crucifixion may be found in the reference to the incident that Jesus' leg bones were left unbroken. This corresponds to the law in Exodus 12:46 and Numbers 9:12 which state that the paschal lamb's bones should not be broken. R. Bultmann, therefore, concludes that John identifies the Last Supper not as a Passover meal but as an ordinary meal.[117] But if it was indeed a Passover meal, when was it held? Which report is more accurate, that of the Synoptic writers or that of John?[118]

To solve this peculiar conflict, evidence from Qumran has been adduced by some scholars. A. Jaubert's theory is best known. According to it, this vexing question can be best explained by postulating two different calendars: the lunar one currently adopted by the officials in Jerusalem and the solar one advocated by sectarians such as those at Qumran. (In Jaubert's opinion, the latter was the old priestly calendar, and the authors of Jubilees and I Enoch also followed this calendar.) So, the chronology of Jesus' last day would have been the following: Jesus celebrated Passover on Tuesday evening (the Eve of Passover according to the solar calendar) and died on Friday (the Eve of Passover according to the lunar calendar).[119]

This approach apparently smoothes out the problems well, yet it remains hypothetical. Besides, did Jesus really observe the sectarian calendar? There is no evidence that he did; the Synoptic writers never once hint that he disagreed with the official calendrical holidays.[120] A conclusive solution unfortunately eludes us at this point.

Whether it was a Passover meal or not, it was undoubtedly a communal meal centered around Jesus. (One might say that Christ was the host of the table.) He and his disciples most likely held such meals regularly. As many scholars indicate, the meals were conducted with a highly eschatological perspective.[121] Mark records Jesus as saying: "I shall not drink again of the fruit of the vine until that day when I drink it new in the kingdom of God" (parallel—Mt 26:29; Lk 22:16, 18; 1 Cor 11:26 has "until he comes"). We may very well call it an anticipatory messianic banquet. Participation in the imminent joyous world of God was experienced through the sharing in the communal meal. Such a paradisiac image is referred to also in Matthew 8:11 (= Luke 13:29), 22:1–10 (= Lk 14:15–24), Luke 22:30, and Revelation 19:9. (See also 1QH 6:14–17; 7:23–25; 8:20.)[122]

Such a characteristically eschatological nature of the meal of Jesus' group certainly corresponded to the Qumran communal meal described in the Rule of Community. Both shared the common quality of a proleptic messianic banquet of the community of the new covenant. It is indeed striking that future eschatological salvation was believed to have entered uniquely the present time by means of the Qumran sectarians and the New Testament Christians.[123] A vital difference between them, however, was that the Christian meal constituted a fellowship meal centered around Jesus Christ. The long-awaited Messiah was already there.

With such a Christ-centered eschatological hope, the early Christian church in Jerusalem, as Luke tells us in Acts 2:42–47, shared all things in common voluntarily, worshiped together at the temple, and participated in the common meals at members' homes. The "breaking of bread" mentioned in this paragraph (vv. 42 and 46) specifically refers to the Eucharist which they celebrated. (Note that "breaking of bread" is distinguished from "share meals" in v. 46.) J. Jeremias explains that the meals were not originally repetitions of the Last Supper, but of the daily table fellowship of the disciples with Jesus. "Only gradually, although indeed already in pre-Pauline times, was the early Christian celebration of meals linked with, and influenced by, the remembrance of the Last Supper."[124] This same meal was called *Agape* (feast of love) in Jude 12.

The Didache, the oldest church order written around the beginning of the second century A.D. in Syria, appears to attest to the practice of the eating of a common meal followed by the Eucharist.[125] As with the Qumran meal, the non-initiated (the unbaptized) were explicitly excluded (9:5). During the second century, however, the meal came to be separated from the Eucharist, thereby making the latter an independent liturgy of the Christian church.

To conclude, there is no evidence that the Qumran meal was a "cult" practice equivalent to the Eucharist. There is no polemical intention attached to it. The Agape meal of which the earliest Christians partook was a continuation of the common meal of Jesus and his disciples. It was an anticipatory messianic banquet for the people of the new covenant. In this respect, the communal meal at Qumran was identical with that practiced by the Christians. The Agape meal, however, demonstrated a singularly Christ-centered fellowship—a symbolic temple.

It is beyond our scope, at least for now, to determine exactly the date of the Last Supper. The calendrical evidence from Qumran falls short in aiding our attempt at this point. Whether the meal was a Passover meal or not, it became the historical root of the Christian Eucharist. There is no evidence to speculate otherwise.[126] In the post-Easter church, the eucharistic celebration was originally linked with the Agape meal, but later it became an independent liturgy constituting the heart of Christian worship.

Conclusion

The significance of the Qumran literature for our understanding of the New Testament can hardly be overestimated. In general, the Jewish roots of the New Testament writings have been appreciably demonstrated. Historically, the Qumran influence on the earliest stage of the Christian movement may be recognizable. John the Baptizer must have played an important role in the interlinkage between the two groups. Some Essenes, in fact, seem to have joined John's baptism "crusade" and then went on to become sympathizers (if not direct disciples) of Jesus' teachings. Unfortunately, however, decisive evidence which would serve as a connecting link is missing. A noted scholar of the Qumran Scrolls, G. Vermes, rightly states that the "Essene parentage of Christianity however still remains a distinct possibility and requires further examination. Nevertheless, it is not inappropriate to stress in advance that the emphasis laid on the punctilious observance of the Mosaic Law at Qumran contrasts so strongly with the peripheral importance given to it in the New Testament, that a linear descent of one to the other seems extremely unlikely."[127]

Sociologically speaking, both groups lived outside the established society and possessed intense eschatological beliefs. They formed their own fellowships. The sect at Qumran was totally an exclusive community, shunning contact with the outside world which it considered to be impure. S. R. Isenberg accurately says that "Qumran became a counter-culture, a counter-society with counter-institutions."[128] Because of the fierce criticisms of the political and religious authorities in Jerusalem, the sectarians embraced a distinctive notion of the temple: they themselves were a symbolic temple. They abandoned the contemporary temple of Jerusalem, not only insisting on the ideal temple and cultic observance therein, but also anticipating the perfect and final temple to be built by God himself in the near future. They believed, in addition, that membership in the sect itself provided a guarantee of eternal salvation.

The group following Jesus was, as G. Theissen puts it, "a movement of wandering charismatics" who relied on small groups of sympathizers in a variety of places.[129] These "homes" of the followers eventually grew into the more organized churches.[130] In contrast to the separatist group at Qumran totally dominated by adult males, the young Christian church comprised many people "of every age, of every rank, and of both sexes," as the Roman author Pliny the Younger (A.D. 61-c. 113) wrote to his emperor, Trajan (*Epistle* x, 96,9). They were, unlike the Qumran people, *in* the world, but, like the sectarians, *not of* the world. They were open to the whole world, as Jesus himself exemplified.

The Christian communities were, therefore, not exclusive; the sectarians were. Nonetheless, the Christians claimed to have an absolute monopoly regarding divine salvation through Jesus Christ. The Christ-centered fellowship was understood symbolically as the true temple. Such a symbolic idea of the temple (i.e., a group of people = the temple) is found only in the Dead Sea Scrolls and the New Testament. Unlike the sectarians, however, the early Christians entertained no plan of an ideal temple nor of the eternal future temple, for the church as Christ's body replaced the temple. In short, albeit an intriguing similarity in self-understanding as the symbolic temple, the decisive difference between these two groups rests in the fact that at Qumran everything hinged upon the Law, while in Christianity Christ was the all in all.

Following up on such a theological perspective, it should be noted that each group in its own way held to the conviction of itself as the true Israel, the authentic heir of God's chosen people at the end of history. This claim found its expression particularly in each group's use of the Hebrew scripture. What is at stake is, to borrow Isenberg's words, the "control of redemptive media based on a monopoly of exegetical authority."[131]

Here again the proximity between the two groups is too evident to be dismissed as accidental. The early Christian expositors of the Old Testament employed an interpretative method which resembles remarkably the pesher of the Qumran exegetes. It is eminently charismatic and apocalyptic. It underscored the prophetic character of the whole of the Old Testament; various scriptural passages were wrested from their original contexts for use in explaining and/or legitimizing the interpreters' beliefs and situation. The ultimate source of such an interpretation reposed with the Teacher of Righteousness at Qumran and with Jesus in the case of Christianity. In the latter, however, Jesus was not only the final interpreter but he himself was also the vital subject of prophecy.

All in all, the Qumran sect provides us with many significant parallels—closer than any other known Jewish group of that period—to the early Christian movement, including John the Baptizer and Jesus himself. Missing, however, is evidence to prove a direct contact between the two. Differences exist as well, and they ultimately reside in Jesus himself. The discoveries from Qumran, at any rate, contribute enormously to our understanding of the New Testament.

5

Mysticism at Qumran and in Rabbinic, Christian, and Gnostic Literature

1. Divine Mysteries

Esotericism, as we have noted more than once, constituted one of the basic characteristics of the Qumran sect. Applicants to the community were required to take an oath of absolute obedience to the rules of the sect, thereby abandoning the outside world (1QS 5:7–9; CD 15). That is, in fact, the only oath which the sectarians made; no other oaths were allowed. Their teachings were kept secret (1QS 4:6; 9:18; 10:24). Josephus confirms this in his statement that the Essenes reported "none of their secrets to others, even though tortured to death" (*War* 2:14).

Such strict secrecy apparently was motivated by the sectarians' desire to keep themselves pure (according to their interpretation of the Law) by avoiding contact with the outside world which they regarded as polluted. But no doubt their secrecy also derived from their conviction that God had revealed special mysteries only to them because of their purity and loyalty to the Law. Therefore, they cherished and safeguarded their special privilege as the possessors of divine secrets.

To refer to the divine secrets, the writers of the Qumran scrolls often used the word *raz*.[1] This word came from the ancient Persian language and was used by Jews from the very late post-exilic times onward.[2] It occurs in the Hebrew Bible only in the Book of Daniel (translated as *mysterion* in the Septuagint) to express the idea of God's concealed plans concerning the imminent end of the world. These plans were believed to have been unveiled to Daniel through divine inspiration.

In contrast to such an apocalyptic sense of *raz* in Daniel, in Ecclesiasticus the term was used in reference to wisdom; God supposedly revealed through wisdom the hidden truths of nature and of human actions (e.g., 1:30; 43:32). It was thought that divine secrets could be also ascertained through the studying of the ancient traditions (ch. 39).

In some of the pseudepigraphic literature as well, the notion of divine mysteries plays a significant role. Like Ecclesiasticus, I Enoch and II Baruch contain references to God's revelation of truth concealed in the cosmos as well as in human acts (including evil acts). Besides these two books, IV Ezra also talks about divine providence during the final period of history. In this respect, the authors of these three writings assumed for themselves Daniel's eschatological orientation regarding the notion of divine mystery.

The Qumran literature seems to include all of these ideas. The sectarian writers emphatically depicted the mysteries of divine providence in this world involving a series of clashes between the forces of light and darkness (1QS 3:20–23; 4:18; 11:3–5; 1QM 14:9). Their teachings purportedly embodied hidden truth revealed only to them by God while concealed from others (1QS 4:6; 9:18; 1QH 2:13; 7:27). A final judgment would be executed upon the wicked (1QM 3:9; 15; 16:11; 1QH 4:27), who were acting according to "the mysteries of sin" (1QH 5:36). The author of the Hymn Scroll (the Teacher of Righteousness?) praised the marvelous mysteries in the created world (1QH 1:1–21) and God's mysteries of salvation (8:4ff.; see also CD 3:18). He was guided by the "mysteries of His wisdom" (9:23). The Teacher perceived the divine disclosure of "all the mysteries of the words of his servants the prophets" (1QpHab 7:5), which concerned the end of history (7:8).

Nonetheless, there are some differences between the Qumran concept of *raz* and that of the Jewish literature mentioned earlier. R. E. Brown points out the differences in the following areas: (1) the Qumran authors mentioned cosmic mysteries less frequently ; (2) they did not describe elaborate visions as did the others; (3) there was no mention of wisdom as a personified agent of revelation at Qumran (where the agent was the holy spirit); (4) Qumran stood alone in pre-Christian literature with claims to possessing the mysteries of special interpretation of the Law.[3] This last-mentioned area was the most important and unique aspect of the Qumran theology of divine mysteries. It was based solely upon the inspirational exegesis of scripture. Qumran esotericism permitted no indulgence in any aberrant mystical experiences. Yet it was itself a mysticism prompted by an intense speculative exegesis of biblical passages.

It is interesting to note that in the Pauline and deutero-Pauline letters in the New Testament, the word *mysterion* (Greek equivalent of *raz*) occurs in a manner similar to that of mystery in the Qumran scrolls. (The word appears in the Pauline corpus more than twenty out of the total twenty-eight times in the New Testament.) In Romans 11:25, the ultimate salvation of Israel is said to be a mystery. Evil forces continue at work in the world until the second coming of Christ; this is also called a mystery (2 Thess 2:7). As we have observed, such an historical and eschatological usage of the concept of mystery is often found in the Qumran literature as well.

In Ephesians 5:23, marital love is said to be analogous to the relationship between Christ and the church. This analogy is supported with a quotation from Genesis 2:24: "For this reason a man shall leave his father and mother and be joined to his wife, and the two shall become one." The allegorical understanding of this Old Testament verse, with the subsequent analogy of love, is called "a great mystery." This is very much like Qumran pesher in which scriptural passages are believed to contain mysteries that can be understood only from a specific vantage point (in the Dead Sea Scrolls, from the vantage point of the sect itself; in the New Testament, from that of Christ and his followers).

That which is distinctive in the New Testament concept of mystery is its Christological connotation. St. Paul was writing to the Christians in Corinth about "God's wisdom in mystery" (1 Cor 2:7) which was prepared before the birth of the world and which up to that time had been concealed from the world (1 Cor 2:8; Eph 3:9; Col 1:26). The mystery of God is none other than Christ himself (Col 2:2), and the mystery of Christ comprises the redemption which he has accomplished (Col 1:26f.). Finally, because of Christ's salvation, the faithful will inherit God's kingdom, and a glorious transformation, rather than death, will take place (1 Cor 15:51ff.).

The fundamental pattern of this Christological notion of mystery, however, still resembles the Qumran theological scheme, if we bracket all references to Christ and his work. Both agree on the basic points: the pre-existence of divine mystery, its character of secrecy throughout the ages, and its final revelation to one particular group of people, the faithful (the Qumran sect or the church), according to God's special plan. Scholars have assumed that the New Testament concept of mystery derived from an ancient Near Eastern cult.[4] But the documents from Qumran suggest that it derived instead from Jewish roots.

2. Angelic Liturgy

As noted above, the Qumran mysticism was closely related to the interpretation of scripture. This observation leads us to an examination of a unique document from Cave IV. The document in question is usually called *The Songs of the Sabbath Sacrifices* (4QShir Shabb) and describes angelic liturgy. J. Strugnell published two fragments in 1959.[5] The remainder of the document, consisting of eight fragments, has been investigated by his student, Carol Newsom, for her doctoral thesis. It will be published soon in the Harvard Semitic Series.[6] In addition, twenty-five very small fragments containing the end of a scroll of this literature were found in Cave XI,[7] and a fragment was also discovered at Masada.[8]

They were apparently copied during the first century B.C. The researchers of this writing are of the opinion that it was composed by a sectarian author. The major reasons for this view are: (1) it shows a similarity to other Qumran documents (e.g., 4QBerakot, in particular); (2) it uses the heading "by a sage," a familiar phrase in the Qumran literature; (3) it follows the solar calendar which the sectarians vigorously observed. Strugnell is convinced that it demonstrates "the original theology of the sect."[9]

According to Newsom, the entire document comprises thirteen separate songs, each one for the purpose of celebrating the liturgy of the first thirteen respective Sabbaths of the year. Strugnell explains the standard literary form of these songs as follows:

> The first line of a typical section runs, "By a sage. The song of the Sabbath sacrifice for the seventh Sabbath on the 16th of the 2nd month. Praise God, all ye angels . . ." and then the *Maskil* (sage) exhorts the angels, under numerous names, to various forms of praise. These then are elements in the liturgy of the Sabbath offering, composed by a *Maskil* for every Sabbath of the year according to the Essene calendar; according to one's judgment on another disputed issue one will see in them songs which accompanied the sacrifice schematically performed at Qumran, or songs by which these sacrifices were spiritually replaced.[10]

The text pertains to the sacrificial rite for the Sabbath celebrated in the heavenly temple by the angels. It is, however, not a visionary presentation; there is no mention of a seer's journey through the heavens as described in the Enochian literature. Rather, it reflects the actual Sabbath liturgy of the Essenes—the sectarians believed that they shared the "lot" with the angels (1QS 11:7–8; 1QH 11:11); i.e., the angels and the sectarians worshiped God jointly. The angels are said in our text to serve as priests at the temple in heaven. They maintain perfect purity therein; likewise the sectarians observe vigorously the laws of Levitical purity—the sect considered itself to be a symbolic temple.

We read in the text that the heavenly temple enshrines seven sanctuaries, each of which has seven angelic priesthoods. (There seems to be no mention of seven heavens or seven separate temples. The notion of the multiplicity of heaven is often attested to in apocalyptic writings.) The description of the temple depends heavily on Ezekiel's vision of the future temple (Ezek 40–48) in terms of its image and vocabulary. Various parts of the temple are referred to, such as the walls, pillars, and so on, but no specifications regarding the actual size and measurements of the temple are given. Presented instead is a vague spatial arrangement. (Newsom notes that there is a fluctuation of image in the description.)

The text, therefore, is not intended to be a commentary on Ezekiel's chapters. The imagery and words of Ezekiel apparently inspired the author's speculative imagination to compose the angelic liturgy at the heavenly temple. The structural portions of the temple were mentioned not for the sake of offering a detailed blueprint but in order to summon the architectural parts to join the chorus in praise of God! This speculative understanding of the biblical passages created in the sectarian mind a mystical image of a celestial world. As L. H. Schiffman correctly points out, the mystical speculation at Qumran is predicated upon scriptural exegesis and contemplation.[11] This type of mysticism may be called "literary mysticism." This, as we will discuss further in the next section, seems to be a fundamental quality not only of Qumran esotericism but also of Jewish apocalypticism and some of later Jewish mystic literature.

Merkabah

In the text B of *The Songs of the Sabbath Sacrifices* which Strugnell has published, an eminent theme of the mystical speculation is that of the chariot-throne of God (*merkabah* in Hebrew) and stems from Ezekiel's vision of theophany (Ezekiel 1 and 10). It plays a central role in some apocalyptic books and later mystic texts as well. In chapter one of the Book of Ezekiel, we read that the prophet saw in a vision a divine chariot drawn by cherubim while he stayed with fellow exiles in Babylon. Above the firmament over the cherubim's heads, he also observed "an appearance like a sapphire stone; the likeness of a throne was a likeness as the appearance of a man on it" (1:26). This is indeed an exceptional instance of an actual, though cautiously indirect, description of God himself in the Old Testament. (The biblical authors consistently avoid mentioning direct human visual access to God.) In chapter ten, Ezekiel is said to have seen the same divine throne in a vision of the temple of Jerusalem, but here there is no mention of the appearance of God.

The author of our text from Qumran also narrates the scene of the angels who in a gentle singing voice are blessing "the figure of the chariot-throne above the firmament of the cherubim" (lines 3–4). Here we find one notable difference from the description in Ezekiel chapter one: the Qumran author makes no attempt to refer to God himself. Ezekiel's visionary image of God is found in indirect rhetoric: "a likeness as the appearance of a man." Yet to the sectarian, the reference is all too anthropomorphic, so in his account the cherubim are said to bless "the form of the chariot-throne." (The "form" [*tabnît* in Hebrew] occurs in Ezekiel 10:8.)

In the depiction of the movements of the chariot and the angels as well, there is a significant correspondence between Ezekiel's passages and the Qumran text. Ezekiel 1:19 states: "And in the going of the living beings, the wheels went beside them," and 10:16 says: "And in the going of the cherubim, the wheels went beside them." The Qumran text has in line four: "And in the going of the wheels back and forth, the holy angels go forth." Interestingly, the mythological "living beings" in Ezekiel 1:19 are called the cherubim in Ezekiel 10:16 and in the Qumran text. There is a fluidity of imagery as Ezekiel's living beings and cherubim are identified with angels. (In I Enoch 61:10 and 71:7 not only cherubim and seraphim but also "wheels [*ophanîm*] are called angels.) This presents an example of a development in angelology in post-exilic Judaism.

Another instance of the Qumran amplification of Ezekiel's passage is found in line five, which says: "And from between his glorious wheels *(galgalîm),* like the appearance of fire, are the spirits of the most holy. Round about are the appearance of streams of fire in the likeness of *hashmal.* . . ." In Ezekiel 1:4–5 we read: "A wind storm came from the north, a great cloud, and a fire flashing, and its brightness all around and out of its midst, like a gleam of *hashmal.* And from its midst came the likeness of four living beings." The similarity of vocabulary and imagery between these two passages is quite evident, though Ezekiel's sentences are extremely ambiguous.

"Hashmal" occurs only in Ezekiel 1:4, 27, and 8:2 in the Old Testament. Its exact meaning is uncertain; the Septuagint and the Vulgate translate it as "amber," and modern scholars surmise it to be an inlay of some kind of shiny metal (gold or brass).[12] As Strugnell suspects,[13] the clear meaning of the term had been lost by the time of the Qumran author, who perhaps took it to mean simply something very bright, as it is appositional to "the appearance of streams of fire." (Just as the "wheels"—ophanim and galgalim—became angels' names, hashmal also came to indicate a class of angels in later Jewish mysticism.)

At any rate, hashmal, the spectacular brilliance, is said to surround the most holy spirits. "The most holy spirits" apparently signifies the spirits of the angels, which replaces in our document Ezekiel's "stormwind and great cloud." This is also our sectarian author's interpretation of Ezekiel's text. "Wind" and "cloud" often accompany theophany in the Old Testament (wind—1 Kings 19:11; Job 38:1; 40:6; Zech 9:14; cloud—Ex 13:21; 19:10; 40:36f.). In the Qumran angelology, angels are servants of God like courtiers of the heavenly palace. As H. Ringgren says, "the angels seem to be—as in the Old Testament—God's heavenly courtiers rather than actual intermediary beings" at Qumran.[14]

Construing Ezekiel's passages further, our Qumran author writes in line six: "The spirit of the living God moves continuously with the glory of the wonderous chariots (chariot-thrones).[15] This description of the spirits obviously reflects the busy movements of the living beings, fire, and the wheels mentioned in chapters one and ten of Ezekiel. For example, it says in Ezekiel 1:13 that in the midst of the living beings there is something which looks like torches moving to and fro. The Qumran exegete reads it as the movements of the angels.

In line seven and eight, the angels' hallelujah chorus is mentioned: "And there is the still voice of blessing at the sound of their going. And they praise the Holy One as they return on their way. . . . The sound of jubilant rejoicing falls silent and there is a still voice of the blessing of the angels in all the camps of God." In Ezekiel there is no reference to the angelic chorus. It may be derived from the scene of theophany in the account of Isaiah's prophetic call recorded in Isaiah 6 where there is a description of seraphim flying and singing sanctus to the Lord of hosts. It is a common practice on the part of the Qumran authors, including the writer of this text, to conflate passages, words, and images found in various different portions of scripture.

The "still voice" of the angels is taken from 1 Kings 19:12, where Elijah is said to have heard God's "low still voice" at

Mount Sinai. The angels' songs in small tender voices during the liturgy in the seventh heaven are mentioned in II Enoch 20:4. Later Jewish mystical writings also refer to the still voice of angels singing.[16] So far as we know, our text from Qumran marks the first use of this description in Jewish or Christian writings.

The foregoing examination of *The Songs of the Sabbath Sacrifices* demonstrates that this literature represents a specimen of Qumran esotericism; it narrates angelic liturgy in heaven. The work sprang from a profoundly mystical interpretation of Ezekiel 1 and 10. It is by no means simply a rational product, but is a result of an intense search for the revelation of the divine mysteries concealed in scriptural passages. Only genuine inspiration, believed to be operative among the sectarians alone, could enable one to have a glimpse of the unfathomable world of God by going far beyond the plain sense of biblical words. Such a distinctive religious activity is what we have already termed "literary mysticism." It is not an unleashed indulgence in some aberrant experience, but is instead an esoteric speculation inspired by biblical words, phrases, sentences, and images. Unlike the pesher type of interpretation where, though esoteric in its essential nature, historical decipherment often plays a major role (e.g., the Wicked Priest, the Kittim, etc.), the scriptural exegesis operative in *The Songs of the Sabbath Sacrifices* is no longer concerned with the historical domain. It plays instead the tune of the ineffable; it echoes the tone of the celestial.

3. Knowledge

Esoteric Knowledge at Qumran

Through divine inspiration, according to the sectarian belief, one can obtain hidden knowledge concerning God's will and plans. An acquisition of such secret truth, moreover, sets one free from all the iniquities of this world as well as from falsehood. It, therefore, results in salvation. A "saved" person in turn has a deepened understanding of truth, having his mind enlightened through salvation. The notion of such a special kind of wisdom and knowledge, consequently, plays a vital role in Qumran theology. Words denoting it occur numerous times in the Dead

Sea Scrolls, although there is no uniform terminology for it.[17] The most significant word is *da'at* (knowledge), which is found often and most particularly in the Manual of Discipline and the Hymn Scroll.

According to the Manual, an applicant to the sect is required to be examined in regard to "his insight and his deeds according to the Law" (1QS 5:21). After his admission, he is educated and tested year by year according to his "understanding and the perfection of his conduct." He then may be either promoted or demoted (5:24). With such intense training, full-fledged members are called "those who know" (1QH 11:14). One who has achieved a high level of esoteric knowledge and ethical virtue is "a wise man *(maskîl)*." He must "teach all the sons of light concerning the nature of all the sons of man, all the spirits which they possess with their distinctive characters, their works with their classes, and the visitation for chastisement and the time of their reward." In short, he must instruct all about how God's providence operates in the world. The author of the Hymn Scroll (most likely the Teacher of Righteousness) declares himself: "I am a *maskîl;* I know you, O my God, because of the spirit which you have put in me" (1QH 12:11–12).

Particularly in the Hymn Scroll, we often encounter the literary form: "I know." The author says: "These things I know from your (God's) knowledge, for you have uncovered my ear to mysteries of wonder" (1:21; cf. 4:27f.). Because God exists, "I know that there is hope" (3:20; cf. 6:3; 9:14), and "I know that righteousness is not of man" (4:30). "I know that truth is [in] your (God's) mouth and in your hand righteousness" (11:7). "I know that man is not righteous except through you" (16:11). "I know that no riches equal your truth. . . . I know that you have chosen them (the sectarians) from all (people)" (15:22–23).

H. Ringgren, in explaining this literary form "I know . . ." says that "it was evidently a fixed formula in the cultic language to express assurance," and cites Psalm 20:6 ("I know that Yahweh will help His annointed"), 41:1 ("By this I know that Thou art pleased with me"), and other passages from the Old Testament. However, he goes on to say, "This original function had probably been forgotten when the Qumran psalms were written, but the formula was retained as a biblical expression—it is a well-known fact that the language of the Qumran writings is permeated with biblical expressions."[18] Ringgren is correct in positing that the "I know" form derived especially from the Old Testament Psalms, and we should also stress that it was employed not through a style of mechanical borrowing but through deep personal contemplation. The biblical expression triggered the Qumran poet's religious feelings and insight—his literary inspiration.

The above quotations from the Hymn Scroll also illuminate the nature and content of "knowledge." It involved intuitive acumen into God's mysteries concealed in human affairs, natural phenomena, and scriptural words, thereby transcending any cognitive or rational conceptions. Therefore, the author was able to say to God quite directly, "I know you," as cited before. This was indeed a simple yet most profound confession of an intimate communion with the ineffable God. God was the ultimate subject of this mystical knowledge.

The God whom the inspired one sought to know was not at all a static object of philosophical speculation; he was, just to the contrary, the one who initiated the "knowledge" relationship between himself and the human. The poet professed that God had "known him from the time of my (his) father" (9:30), and chastised him "in the mystery of your (God's) wisdom" (9:23). He "knows every scheme of action" (7:13). "You (God) are a father of all your sons of truth" (9:35). "Nothing can be known without your (God's) will" (10:9). He was the "God of knowledge" (1:26). This compact and essential attribute of God occurs also in the Manual of Discipline 3:15: "From the God of knowledge comes all that is and shall be."

Tradition of Mystical Wisdom

Such a heavy emphasis on "knowledge" at Qumran stood in the wisdom tradition of ancient Israel. The Book of Job contains repeated assertions that human intellect can scarcely fathom the profound laws of the created world and the divine way of handling human affairs. For example, we read in 11:6–7; "And he (God) would tell you (Job) the secrets of wisdom. . . . Can you find out the mystery of God or can you find out the limit of God?" In the midst of inexplicable suffering, Job bravely confesses: "I know that my vindicator lives; he shall stand on the dust at last" (19:25). The Book of Job does not provide the reader with any clear-cut theoretical answer as to why there is human suffering; it rather intends to drive home the instruction that the refusal of giving any cognitive solution itself would hopefully lead people to understanding more clearly the will of the ineffable God.

The mystical wisdom found itself in a far more developed form at Qumran than in the wisdom literature of the Old Testament. Many scholars have attempted to explain this development against the background of Jewish apocalypticism. The apocalyptic trend exercised a significant influence among the Jews, particularly during the last two or three centuries B.C. Its teaching hinged upon a revelation of divine hidden plans concerning the imminent catastrophic end of the world. The plans were purportedly unfolded through visions to only a few privileged individuals. These visionaries thus claimed that they possessed special knowledge as to when and how the cosmic consummation would come. They also asserted that they had special knowledge as to the divine judgment, where the righteous ones would be saved from the final disaster while the wicked would be condemned to eternal punishment.

Jewish apocalypticism was thus a form of an eschatological belief, but it was also literary esotericism. It inspired a number of books in which the visionaries utilized scriptural passages to elucidate their messages. As typically exemplified by the pesher of the Dead Sea Scrolls, the writers always attempted to supply new information which was supposedly concealed in the passages. In this manner, it was alleged, the original meaning of biblical statements would be manifested. I. Gruenwald explains it by saying: "The key note voiced throughout apocalypticism is that which transcends the biblical concept of knowledge."[19] As many scholars, including Gruenwald, contend, such a highly speculative "knowledge" was a stepping stone to an even more esoteric type of knowledge as seen in Gnosticism. Before we deal with Gnosticism, let us observe further Jewish mysticism.

4. Merkabah Mysticism

Mysticism in the Pharisaic-Rabbinic Tradition

Ancient rabbinic writings attest to the existence of a mystic trend in Judaism in the initial centuries of our era. But the written record is far from abundant, for the movement developed in very confined circles in Jewish tradition, and a majority of rabbis were extremely cautious about the esotericism. The rabbis forbade the general public from cultivating it. In the Mishnah, Hagigah 2:1, it says: "The forbidden degrees may not be expounded before three persons, nor the story of creation before two, nor (the chapter of) the chariot before one alone, unless he is a sage that understands his own knowledge. Whosoever gives his mind to four things, it were better for him if he had not come into the world—what is above? what is beneath? What was before time? And what will be hereafter?" "The forbidden degrees" refers to a law prohibiting incest in Leviticus 18:6. "The story of creation" is, of course, Genesis chapter one. "(The chapter of) the chariot" is Ezekiel chapter one.

The last two of those topics were popular subjects of speculative interpretation among the Jewish mystics of the early centuries A.D. As the foremost authority on Jewish mysticism, G. Scholem, has elucidated: "Palestine was the cradle of the movement, that much is certain. We also know the names of the most important representatives of mystical and theosophical thought among the teachers of the Mishnah. They belong to a group of the pupils of Johanan ben Zakkai, around the turn of the first century A.D."[20] Before the destruction of Jerusalem in A.D. 70, "an esoteric doctrine was already taught in Pharisaic circles"[21]

The origin of this mystical tradition is shrouded in ambiguity. But the discovery of the Qumran documents, particularly *The Songs of the Sabbath Sacrifices,* provides us with invaluable evidence that a mystic movement was quite operative among the Essenes as early as the first century B.C. It is most likely that they embraced the mysticism connected with the chariot-throne of God as a cherished subject of their esoteric teachings even before the establishment of the sect at Qumran in the second century B.C.

Mysticism in Apocalyptic Literature

(1) First Enoch

The oldest literary evidence of the throne mysticism is found in the First Book of Enoch, whose provenance must be in a circle close to the Qumran sect. Aramaic fragments of this book, in fact, were found at Qumran.[22] This literature is the oldest of the three pseudepigrapha attributed to Enoch, the seventh descendant of Adam and Eve in the Genesis story. The enigmatic passage in Genesis 5:24 ("Enoch walked with God. And he was not, for God took him") prompted various speculations, especially among the apocalyptists and mystics. Instead of dying, Enoch, it was believed, was taken by God to heaven and was able to see the scenes of heaven and learn about the secrets of the universe, the destinies of angels and peoples, good as well as wicked, the course of world history, and other subjects.

In chapter fourteen, Enoch's vision of his ascent to heaven is narrated. It is said that he was lifted up to heaven by clouds, and saw a house (the divine palace) built by crystal (Ezek 1:22). Upon entering the house, he was overwhelmed with terror. Then he saw another house which was "greater than the former, and everything was built with tongues of fire. And in every respect it excelled (the other)—in glory and great honor—to the extent that it is impossible for me to recount to you concerning its glory and greatness" (v. 16). Next he saw "a lofty throne—its appearance was like crystal and its wheels like the shining sun; and [I heard?] the voice of the cherubim; and from beneath the throne were issuing streams of flaming fire. And the Great Glory was sitting upon it—as for his gown, which was shining more brightly than the sun, it was whiter than any snow" (vv. 18–20).[23]

No explanation is needed to verify this visionary scene derived from Ezekiel chapter one. It resembles strikingly the heavenly scene described in the text B of *The Songs of the Sabbath Sacrifices* from Qumran. This chapter of I Enoch was, according to scholarly consensus, most likely written in the third century B.C. It is, therefore, the earliest known instance of throne mysticism. It contains the major components of the later Merkabah mysticism: the ascent of a seer to heaven, the celestial hosts, the two houses (one inside the other), the feeling of terror, a revelation of the hidden glory of God, his throne, and so on. I. Gruenwald, therefore, calls this vision "a model vision of Merkavah mysticism."[24] The central theme of the oldest Jewish mystical tradition involves a heavenly divine throne and a constellation of visionary images related thereto. Scholem unequivocally states: "No doubts are possible on this point: the earliest Jewish mysticism is throne mysticism."[25]

Another vision of the heavenly palace is described in chapter seventy-one. This chapter belongs to one independent section (chaps. 37–71) usually referred to as the Book of Similitudes, which, according to J. T. Milik, was composed in about A.D. 270. No manuscripts from this portion have been found at Qumran, and it contains passages regarding a messianic figure, "the Son of Man." Milik thinks, therefore, that it derived from a Christian world.[26] Yet other scholars maintain its Jewish origin from the first century B.C.[27]

In this chapter, we read again of Enoch's vision of his ascent to heaven, where he saw a spectacular sight of a divine palace being guarded by angels. That which is unique in this vision is the appearance of God called "the Head of Days." This is an exceptional reference in the known writings of throne mysticism.

(2) Second Enoch

The Second Book of Enoch also talks about Enoch's heavenly ascent in his vision. In this book, heaven is divided into seven layers. Only the longer text mentions the tenth heaven. (The book has been preserved in two different recensions: one is long and the other is short.) In the third heaven, for instance, paradise is said to be located. (Interestingly, the paradise of the third heaven is also mentioned in 2 Corinthians 12:2–4.) Enoch sees the divine throne in the seventh heaven; it is called "the many-eyed thrones." The expression "many-eyed" obviously came from the divine chariot in Ezekiel 1:18. Heavenly hosts of angels, cherubim and seraphim are perpetually serving God. Despite a terrible sense of fear, Enoch, encouraged by his guiding angels, sees from a distance God sitting on an exceedingly high throne. Heavenly beings, incessantly singing praises, are heard in every heaven (except in the fifth heaven, according to the longer text). This reminds us of the gentle voice of the angelic hymn in the Qumran *Songs of the Sabbath Sacrifices.*

The origin of the Second Book of Enoch is not certain. Many scholars believe that it was written in the first century A.D. It evidently inherited Merkabah mysticism from the Qumran document and I Enoch.

(3) The Apocalypse of Abraham

The Apocalypse of Abraham, which was composed perhaps sometime between A.D. 70 and the middle of the second century, relates Abraham's vision of the heavenly throne. In this literature, Abraham sees "under the fire a throne of fire and the many-eyed ones round about, reciting the song, under the throne four fiery living creatures, singing" (18:3). The scene further includes "behind the living creatures a chariot with fiery wheels. Each wheel was full of eyes round about. And above the wheels was the throne which I had seen" (18:12f).[28]

This visionary description is, needless to say, drawn on I Enoch. He mentions Abraham's ascent to heaven, his fear during the vision, the encouragement and guidance of an angel, God's mountain, heaven and hell, and the angels' worship of God. All of these are familiar subjects in I Enoch. A unique element in the Apocalypse of Abraham is a long hymn of Merkabah which the guiding angel tells Abraham to recite with him "without ceasing" (17:8–21). As Gruenwald says, it is "more like a liturgical hymn or sapiential psalm which recites the grace of God and His benevolence" and "has very little in common with the lyrical and numinous qualities" of the hymns of the later Merkabah mystic literature.[29]

(4) The Ascension of Isaiah

A vision of the heavenly throne is also narrated in the Ascension of Isaiah. With the help of an angel, Isaiah journeys through seven heavens. The heavens are said to become successively more glorious as he ascends from one to another. In each of the first five heavens, there is a throne in the midst, guarded by angels; these thrones are occupied by angels. Different scenery emerges as the visionary comes to the sixth heaven, where no throne is seen. Isaiah joins with the angels in singing the praise of God. Upon reaching the seventh, fear grips him. Jealous angels attempt to prevent him from entering, but God intercedes, permitting him entrance. A similar instance of an angel's negative action is also found in later writings of throne mysticism. The seventh heaven is the holiest; it is where God dwells. Isaiah, however, cannot see the Great Glory; he instead hears the voices of angels and the righteous singing hymns of praise. There is no mention of God's throne.

This book is Jewish in origin, but was revised by Christians in the second century A.D., as attested to by the reference to the descent and return of the Messiah to the seventh heaven.

(5) The Book of Revelation

A representative vision of the heavenly throne from early Christian literature is found in the Book of Revelation (written toward the end of the first century A.D.). At the beginning of chapter four, it is said that John the seer hears a voice "as a trumpet" inviting him to see "what needs to happen after these things," i.e., events at the final time (v. 1). This voice is identified with the voice he heard earlier (1:10), ushering in a visionary appearance of the risen Christ. The seer falls down from fear "like a dead man" (1:17), but Christ encourages him to write what he sees. Such a pattern of the seer's experiences of terror and encouragement is often found in visionary narratives.

In chapter four, we read that upon hearing the voice, John immediately goes into a trance. There is no hint of his heavenly ascent nor of an angelic guide. In this respect, it concurs with the Qumran *Songs of the Sabbath Sacrifices* and not with I Enoch and other Jewish apocalyptic and later mystic writings which narrate a visionary's journey guided by an angel. The same is the case concerning the number of heavens. The former intimates no more than one heaven, but the latter presents often elaborate descriptions of several layers of heavens.

The throne vision in Revelation, however, agrees with the latter group of Jewish writings in its direct reference to God: "One seated on the throne" (v. 2). Ezekiel uses an indirect manner of alluding to a divine presence on the throne, and the Qumran document has no mention of it. Our seer describes God "like the appearance of jasper and carnelian" (v. 3). Around the throne was a bow which shone, resembling an emerald. These precious stones are mentioned in Exodus 28:17–21, where they represent some of Israel's twelve tribes on the high priest's breastplate. These gems are also named in Ezekiel's reference to God's garden of Eden (Ezek 28:13). The "bow" must have derived from Ezekiel's vision of theophany, in which the brightness around the divine throne was like "the bow in the cloud in the day of rain" (1:28).

John's vision includes twenty-four elders, each sitting on a throne and wearing white garments and gold crowns on their head (v. 4). In A. Feuillet's opinion, they are saints, and the number twenty-four may have its origin in the twenty-four classes of priests mentioned in 1 Chronicles 24.[30] A little later in the vision, they throw their crowns before God's throne and fall down in front of God to worship him (v. 10; cf. 11:16ff.; 19:4). In chapter five, the elders sing a "new song" in praise of Christ, each holding a harp and golden bowls full of incense, which are considered to be "the prayer of the saints" (vv. 8ff.). It is a liturgical scene at the heavenly temple. As Gruenwald points out, the elders have priestly-angelic functions.[31] The reference to "a glass sea like crystal" in verse six symbolizes the bronze sea (a large vessel made of cast bronze) at Solomon's temple (1 Kings 7:23–26; 2 Kings 16:17).

"Four creatures full of eyes" are also seen "in the midst of the throne and around the throne" (v. 6). They are like a lion, an ox, a man, and a flying eagle, the same as those mentioned in Ezekiel 1:5–14. Ezekiel says that each creature has four wings (1:6), but our seer observes six on each; this is in consonance with the wings of the seraphim of Isaiah's vision at the Jerusalem temple (Is 6:2). They ceaselessly sing the sanctus day and night (v. 8).

Evidently, all of the imagery and motifs presented in John's vision of the heavenly throne in chapter four are derived from the Merkabah mystic tradition of ancient Judaism. J. M. Ford points out that this chapter contains no Christian element.[32] Ford's theory that Revelation chapters 4–11 originated in an oral form from the circle of John the Baptizer before Jesus' public ministry may be too hypothetical, but as for chapter four, it is reasonable to assume that it stands in the wake of Jewish Merkabah mysticism.

Ford says that the Merkabah vision does not seem to occur in Christian writings.[33] It is interesting to note that the Apocalypse of Paul, an important example of Christian apocalyptic literature from the early Christian era, draws from Revelation 4 a scene of a heaven in which St. Paul purportedly sees a vision. (His ascent to the third heaven mentioned in 2 Corinthians 12:2 precipitated later apocalyptic speculation. The Coptic manuscript of the Apocalypse of Paul found at Nag Hammadi, Egypt, describes Paul's ascent even to the tenth heaven. A reputable modern scholar, J. M. Bowker, goes so far as to suggest that Paul, a learned Pharisee before his conversion to Christianity, actually practiced Merkabah mysticism. His ascent to the third heaven and his visionary experience on the road to Damascus arose from a base of Merkabah contemplation.[34] This is an intriguing suggestion, but it is highly conjectural.) Paul is said to have heard the voices of the twenty-four elders as well as a great multitude of angels and cherubim glorifying God.[35] But no reference at all is made to a divine throne.

A little later Paul also sees in "the city of Christ" the heavenly Jerusalem, the "golden throne" at the several gates "with men on them who had golden diadems and gems," and also "between the twelve men, thrones set in another rank which appears to be of greater glory."[36] These thrones are for the pious Christians and do not constitute the divine throne. In explaining the lack of Merkabah vision in Christian writings, Ford correctly states: "The 'throne' in Christianity recedes to give place to the contemplation of the Lordship of Christ (cf. Acts 7:56). Paul does not boast of his ascent to the third heaven but of the power of Christ tabernacling over him in this weakness (2 Cor 12:9)."[37] One should remember also that in order to profess the Lordship of Christ, some earlier Christians at times use imagery common in Jewish throne mysticism as attested to in Revelation and the Apocalypse of Paul. As well, Merkabah mysticism was seemingly kept alive in Jewish and Christian apocalyptic literature.

Ezekiel the Tragedian
The use of the imagery and motifs of throne mysticism was of course not confined within the apocalyptic tradition. A Jewish

dramatist who lived in Alexandria, Egypt, during the second (or first) century B.C. provides a good example. He is usually called Ezekiel the Tragedian, for he wrote tragic dramas using Old Testament stories in Greek. His work, *The Exodus,* which depicted the history of the departure of Israel from Egypt, was known to some church fathers (Eusebius and Clement of Alexandria).[38]

In this poetic drama, it is said that in a dream Moses finds himself on Mount Sinai and sees a high throne reaching to the heavens. On the throne sits God in the form of a man of the noblest appearance, with a crown on his head and a scepter in his hand. He bestows on Moses the crown and the scepter and tells him to sit on the throne which he has vacated. As Moses takes the seat, the heavenly stars (no mention of angels) kneel before him. Here the author combines four motifs from the Old Testament. He harks back first to Exodus, which he uses as the dramatic setting; second to Ezekiel 1 in his description of theophany; third to Daniel 7 in reference to Moses' receiving the kingship from God; fourth to Genesis 37:9 (Joseph's dream) with regard to the stars' worshiping Moses.

It is striking that the scene implies Moses' deification. As W. Meeks has shown,[39] such a notion was evidently in existence in certain Jewish circles. It resembles, in a way, the archangel Metatron, who is said to be the transformed Enoch and possesses supreme authority accorded by God (as is referred to in the next section). He is called "Lesser Yahweh." A. F. Segal has investigated the belief in "Two Powers in heaven"; it was a belief apparently cherished by some Jews.[40] Such intermediaries as Adam, Moses, Enoch, Metatron, Melchizedek, Michael, and others came to be considered almost like another God. (Segal thinks that this was the background which allowed Christians to view Jesus Christ as the second person in the doctrine of the Trinity.)

The Babylonian Talmud Hagigah 15a records that Rabbi Aher (purportedly one of the four who entered heaven) is said to have declared: "Perhaps—God forfend!—there are two divinities!"[41] Other rabbis reacted negatively; the paragraph goes on to state that Metatron was punished with sixty fiery lashes, and Aher was accused of being a heretic.

Such a heretical notion was apparently in existence already in the time of Ezekiel the Tragedian. In the opinion of P. W. van der Horst, what our dramatist meant by Moses' taking over the divine throne is that "it is only in and through Moses that we can know God."[42] To underscore the view that Moses is God's vice-regent, the author made use of the Merkabah vision. Though he was not interested in Merkabah mysticism itself, he was quite aware of its significance and usefulness.

Yohanan ben Zakkai and His Disciples

The Talmudic literature also provides us with an interesting story pertaining to Merkabah mysticism. The Babylonian Talmud Hagigah 14b and the Jerusalem Talmud Hagigah 77a (and in shorter form in Tosephta Hagigah ii, 2 and Mekilta Mishpatim 21, 1) narrate that Rabbi Elazar ben Arakh asked his teacher Yohanan ben Zakkai about the Merkabah in Ezekiel 1. The disciple recited the passage and interpreted it. During the discourse, according to the portion in the Jerusalem Talmud, "fire came down from heaven and surrounded them, and the ministering angels were dancing in front of them as groomsmen rejoicing before the bridegroom." And "one angel was speaking from within the fire, saying: 'It is as you say, Rabbi Elazar ben Arakh, this is what the Ma'aseh Merkabah (the account of the chariot) is!'"

The parallel paragraph in the Babylonian Talmud says that the fire came down from heaven and surrounded all the trees in the field. The trees began to sing a song of praise. Then came the angel's voice of affirmation from the fire.[43] (Both of these versions came from a common older source. The shorter version of the story, found in Mekilta and Tosephta, seems to be older than the Talmudic parallels.[44])

This description may indicate that some mystic or ecstatic experience might have been involved during the discourse. It is, however, far from certain; there is no mention to the effect that these two rabbis ascended to heaven, and the story involves an exegesis of Ezekiel. It is literary mysticism. Besides, they are not popular heroes of later Jewish mystical writings either. But Rabbi Akiba is. The oft-quoted passage from the Babylonian Talmud Hagigah 14b tells us that four persons (Ben Azai, Ben Zoma, Aḥer, and Akiba—all rabbinic scholars from the second century A.D. in Palestine) entered paradise but Rabbi Akiba alone returned unharmed. This short anecdote intimates the mystical experience of these individuals. It also warns of the danger which such an esotericism might involve; proper understanding of esoteric experience and teachings would require supreme spiritual maturity.

The content of the discourse between Rabbis Elazar and Yohanan is not mentioned in the Talmud. As Gruenwald admits, "It is really very difficult to guess what the Merkavah speculation of the circle of Rabban Yohanan ben Zakkai was like."[45] Later Jewish legends customarily call this circle *"Yordey Merkabah,"* meaning "descenders of the Merkabah." It is "paradoxical," as Scholem says,[46] that the mystics are said to descend rather than ascend to higher spiritual realms, but *Yordey Merkabah* was a self-designation by the Jewish mystics.

According to Scholem, there were organized groups (schools) of mystics, who kept their most secret knowledge (gnosis) from the public lest they run into conflict with orthodox rabbinic Judaism.[47] Even "heretical Gnosis of a dualistic and antinomian character" undoubtedly existed on the fringe of Judaism during the early centuries A.D., and it was condemned by the traditional rabbis as a heresy *(minim)*.[48] Evidence of Merkabah mysticism is not extensive in early rabbinic Judaism; yet it did exist during the Tannaitic period.[49] Mystical speculation involving Merkabah is also attested to in rabbinic midrash from as early as the Tannaim. I. Chernus has collected many examples.[50]

However, D. J. Halperin in his detailed study of the Merkabah materials in the rabbinic literature[51] contends that the Merkabah expositions by the Tannaitic rabbis during the initial two centuries of our era involve neither ecstatic, mystical praxis nor secret teachings. They were instead the public exegesis of Ezekiel's vision, to which the people enthusiastically listened. But the popular enthusiasm provoked opposition and restriction by certain rabbis who acted out of the fear of ill effect on the general populace. Later in early medieval times, the mystic lore was embellished by the Amoraic scholars. Halperin suggests, moreover, that an ecstatic praxis and secret doctrine seemingly did exist among the Jews in Babylonia.

Though Halperin says that his conclusion does not discredit Scholem's view, he criticizes it for a lack of support from rabbinic sources.[52] His study deals neither with a group of esoteric writings generally called the Hekhalot literature nor with apocalyptic literature and Qumran documents. In his opinion, the rabbinic literature was not as close to these other literary deposits as Scholem assumes. Lacking rabbinic evidence from the earliest century of our era, it is extremely difficult to come up with a clear-cut picture; this issue is obviously in need of further investigation and possibly and hopefully new discoveries.

Finally, an observation should be noted here: as the studies by Scholem and Gruenwald clearly indicate, the early (pre-Hekhalot) written evidence for the throne mystical speculation comes mainly from some of the apocalyptic literature which does not seem to be of Pharisaic-rabbinic origin. Does this mean that throne mysticism was born and nourished in the milieu of the Essenes? This is at least an excellent possibility.

5. Hekhalot Literature

The Hekhalot literature signifies a group of Jewish writings which deal with esoteric subjects including Merkabah mysticism. The word *hekhalot* means "palaces," for visionaries purportedly visited heavenly structures. The literature is considered to have been written in the early medieval age, but as scholars acknowledge, its older material may very well go back to the time before the fall of Jerusalem in A.D. 70. It encompasses writings such as the Lesser Hekhalot, the Greater Hekhalot, Merkabah Rabbah, the Book of the Hekhalot (the same as III Enoch), the Treatise of the Hekhalot, and others.[53] All of these contain revelations apropos of the teaching of Merkabah, allegedly received and transmitted by Rabbi Akiba and Rabbi Ishmael, both well-known religious leaders and scholars who died about the time of the Second Revolt against Rome.

According to Scholem, the oldest of these books is the Lesser Hekhalot and then the Greater Hekhalot. Both of them are of supreme importance.[54] These books relate the visionaries' journey through the seven heavens, each of which has a palace. At the gate of every heaven, they are tested as to their worthiness; angels even attempt to prevent them from going further, with the intention of safeguarding the holiness of God. (There is also an element of jealousy on the part of the angels, given the mystic's privilege of being allowed to see the heavenly throne.) In the seventh heaven, God meets heavenly courtiers and the visionaries. Akiba and Ishmael, in fact, encounter God, despite their great fear. These are some of the distinctive features we have already noted in the throne visions in several samples of apocalyptic literature.

In the Greater Hekhalot it is said that Rabbi Akiba converses with God, who is called Zohararicl (meaning "God of the shining Light"). The throne is described to have been carried by the Living Creatures (cherubim, ophanium, and other beings) since the creation of the world. They bow down before God, an act which may well signify, as Gruenwald points out,[55] that when God is absent from the palace in the seventh heaven, he dwells in the eighth heaven (the throne is in the seventh). This speculation perhaps alludes to Ezekiel 1:22f. which specifies God as sitting above the cherubim. The heaven above the seventh, God's usual abode, certainly intends to get across symbolically the idea of his transcendence.

The angels are assigned to perform various tasks in this literature. They guard the heavens, prepare and administer the heavenly court, and conduct liturgies by singing hymns, offering prayers, and even dancing. They also guide and help the visionaries, and play the role of intercessor on behalf of humans. The angelic ritual is said to be observed when the people of Israel recite their prayer, thereby creating a correspondence between the heavenly and earthly divine services. This simultaneous worship is underscored in *The Songs of Sabbath Sacrifices.* The function of the angels is far more extensive than that of the angels described in the Qumran document, however.

The majesty of the heavenly palace and the importance of the angels are emphasized in the Book of the Hekhalot (often called the Third Book of Enoch). It contains Rabbi Ishmael's account of his journey to the heavens, which includes his visionary encounter with the chariot-throne of God, wonders of the highest heaven, and the archangel's revelation.

In the description of the throne vision, the Book of Ezekiel is extensively used. The vision is clearly identified as "the vision of the chariot" (1:1); the visionary (Ishmael) says that the guiding angel "presented me before the throne of glory so that I might behold the chariot" (1:5f.; see also 1:10, 12). "The fiery seraphim" are standing beside the chariot-throne (1:7; see also the description of ophanim, the wheels, in chapter 25; four creatures are mentioned as well in chapters 20–21). The hashmal and the river of fire are said to issue from beneath the throne of Glory (36:1f.). All of these passages are based on the Book of Ezekiel.

Angels also play an important role in this book. Thousands of them are said to serve various functions. The most significant of all is the archangel called Metatron. It says that God sends Metatron to help usher the rabbi into the seventh heaven. Interestingly, Metatron tells Ishmael that he is none other than Enoch. "Metatron," according to S. Lieberman, derived from an earlier word form, *synthronos.* The literal meaning of this Greek word is "a throne placed side by side with the throne of a king or a god." Metatron, therefore, is one who is seated on a throne next to God.[56]

Metatron in this book is the archangel who "acts as a vice-regent or divine plenipotentiary" (Gruenwald).[57] God bestows on him special knowledge regarding the secrets of heaven and earth and appoints him "as a prince and ruler over all the denizens of heights. . . . Any angel and any prince who has anything to say in my (God's) presence should go before him and speak to him" (10:3–4). He is placed on "a throne like the throne of Glory" (10:1).

Holding such a prominent office, Metatron is even called "the Lesser Yahweh." This name also appears, interestingly enough, in some Gnostic literature (*Pistis Sophia,* ch. 7) indicating a divine figure. This may be an instance of Gnostic influence on Jewish mysticism. In our text, however, the figure is not divine but the transformed Enoch. P. Alexander is of the opinion that Metatron in the Hekhalot literature stemmed from "circles acquainted with the Palestinian apocalyptic Enoch traditions."[58] The transformation of Enoch is not attested to in the apocalyptic writings; it is a speculative product of the mystics of the Hekhalot literature.

Another distinctive feature found in the Hekhalot literature (but absent in the Book of the Hekhalot) is the theurgic techniques. For example, some songs and magical seals are used for the purpose of incantation. The text called "Merkabah Rabbah" deals with the subject of the theurgic devices of angels for revealing the secrets of heaven and earth to humans. It teaches what kind of preparation the mystics should have—such as fasting, ritual baths, and incantation. Protective seals and special prayers of invocation for the angel's descent and ascent are in order as well. The text also includes further detailed instructions for the mystic's ritual, moral, and intellectual training. P. Alexander accurately points out that "these hymns, prayers, formulae, and invocations have one thing in common: they all involve the rhythmic repetition of certain words, sounds, or ideas." This device seems to correspond to Hindu and Buddhistic mantra— a sacred formula which one can use to seek enlightenment.

Shiur Komah

The image of God's chariot-throne also occurs in the unique literature of Jewish mysticism, which is commonly referred to as Shiur Kommah ("measurement of the body"). Rabbis Akiba, Ishmael, and Nathan (a student of Ishmael) are purportedly the recipients of the revelation concerning the exact measurements of the body of God sitting on the exalted chariot-throne. Metatron (who is called "the great prince of testimony") tells them about it, beginning from God's feet and tracing up to the head, giving the size and esoteric names of each of the parts of the body. The reported dimensions are indeed enormous; it is said in section B that the height, for example, is 2,300,000,000 parasangs, the length from the right arm to the left arm is 770,000,000 (according to section D, 120,000,000) parasangs, the distance between the eyeballs is 300,000,000 parasangs, and the size of the head is 3,000,003⅓ (according to section D, 10,000,033⅓) parasangs. We read in section E: "Every parasang is four miles, and every mil is ten thousand cubits, and each cubit is three *zeratot* (fingers). And His *zeret* (finger) fills the entire universe."[59] The secret designations of the limbs are combinations of unintelligible letters. The message of all these incredibly vast dimensions is obviously to suggest the immeasurability of God; God is simply beyond our comprehension.

Scholem points out that there is a scriptural basis for this mystical notion of the "measurements of the divine body." The Canticles, a collection of lyrics celebrating nuptial love, contains praise of the physical beauty of the lover (e.g., 5:10ff.). In the same vein, the mystics feel justified in praising God by describing him in physical terms, since the love which the Canticles extols is interpreted according to such an eminent rabbi as Akiba as the love relationship between God and Israel.

The text of the Shiur Komah came perhaps from the early medieval age, but such esoteric speculation already existed during the second century A.D. It is interesting to note that II Enoch (late first century A.D.) contains a passage which says: "I (Enoch) have seen the extent of the Lord, without measure and without analogy, who has no end" (39:6). Mystical speculation pertaining to a divine body appears to have begun in the very early century A.D. Scholem envisages the "possibility of a continuous flow of specific ideas from the Qumran sect to the Merkabah mystics and rabbinic circles in the case of the Shiur Komah as well as in other fields."[61] M. S. Cohen, however, presents a more cautious view in his recent study of the Shiur Komah, suggesting that the tradition of the Shiur Komah originated and developed in Palestine, but was given a literary framework by Jewish mystics in Babylonia in the early medieval period.[62]

Scholem also notes that the Jewish mystic notion of Shiur Komah influenced some Gnostics, for instance, Marcus (second century A.D.) who talked about the "body of truth."[63] The relationship between Jewish mysticism and Gnosticism has been suggested not only by Scholem but also by many other scholars. It is an exciting but also difficult subject to ascertain with exactness. Was there Jewish Gnosticism? Was ancient Jewish mysticism a fountainhead of Gnosticism? Was the Qumran sect a preGnostic (if not Gnostic) group, since it embraced esoteric teachings and organization? These are the questions which will be dealt with in the next section.

6. Jewish Mystic Tradition and Gnosticism

(1) What Is Gnosticism?

This is a notoriously difficult question. The word "Gnosticism" did not exist in ancient and medieval times. There has never been anything like a Gnostic canon, nor a universally accepted Gnostic doctrine. Yet the religio-philosophical trend which we call Gnosticism was a formidable reality from the first to the ninth century A.D. and spread from Iran in the east and to Gaul in the west. There were numerous different sects and groups as well, the better known of which include the Valentinians, Basilidians, Encratites, and Ophites.[64] The diversity of opinions that existed among them can be illustrated by the words of Irenaeus, the Bishop of Lyons, about 180 A.D.: "Let us look at the inconsistent opinions of those heretics (for there are two or three of them), how they do not agree in treating the same points but alike, in things and names, set force opinions mutually discordant."[65]

Literary Sources

In the face of enormous difficulty, how do we explore the teaching of the Gnostics? What ancient sources are available to us? Many references to them are found in the writings of the church fathers, including Justin Martyr (c. 100-c. 165), Irenaeus (c. 130-c. 202), Clement of Alexandria (c. 150-c. 215), Hippolytus (c. 170-c. 236), Tertullian (c. 160-c. 220), Origen (c. 185–c. 254), Eusebius of Caesaria (c. 260–c. 340), Epiphanius (c. 315-c. 402), Augustine (354-430), John of Damascus (c. 675-c. 749), and some others. They asserted that Gnostic teachings were false and misleading the people.

As ancient-Gnostic documents have been discovered, we have learned about Gnosticism from the proponents' side as well. Two manuscripts written in Coptic (a later form of the ancient Egyptian language written with the Greek alphabet) were acquired by two British collectors in the eighteenth century: one by Askew and the other by S. J. Bruce. They include *Pistis Sophia* and *The Two Books of Jeu,* both Gnostic Christian works from the third century A.D. Also, the same milieu produced *The Gospel of Mary, The Apocryphon (Secret Book) of John, The*

Sophia Christi, and *The Acts of Peter;* they became available to modern audiences toward the end of the last century.

Then in 1945, a fascinating discovery of Gnostic codices was made accidentally near a town called Nag Hammadi on the Nile River in Egypt. Reportedly, they were found in a large jar under a boulder at the foot of the cliffs near the river.[66] The discovered materials comprise thirteen leather-bound volumes containing fifty-two separate tractates written on more than eleven hundred pages. They were most likely copied in Coptic in the fourth century A.D., but scholarly consensus assumes that the original documents were written in Greek.

Nag Hammadi codex

The end of the *Second Treatise of the Great Seth* and the beginning of the *Apocalypse of Peter.*

All of these codices were collected by Gnostic Christians in the early centuries of the Christian era. A leading scholar of the Nag Hammadi texts, J. M. Robinson, in the English translation of the whole literature (of which he is the general editor) aptly draws an analogy between these Gnostic Christians and the Essenes. Prior to the discoveries of their writings, both of these groups were too little known to modern scholars to be treated with the seriousness they deserved. Coincidentally, their writings were discovered about the same time (1945–1947). The jars which housed those priceless ancient documents for centuries, when broken, brought to us a great variety of information of enormous value. "The history of Gnosticism, as documented in the Nag Hammadi library, takes up about where the history of the Essenes, as documented by the Dead Sea Scrolls, breaks off."[67] As well, both the Qumran Essenes and the Gnostic Christians were apparently oppressed by the main or orthodox streams of the respective religions.

The Nag Hammadi collection includes a diversity of literature. There are several works of Gnostic apocalypses, two books modeled on the New Testament Acts, letters addressed to readers, dialogues, "secret books" of revelation, wisdom and speculative treatises, and prayers. Interestingly, a copy of a portion of Plato's *Republic* is also found among the others.

Gnostic Teachings

What kind of teachings do these ancient writings contain? What was the basic doctrine of Gnosticism? It is beyond the scope of our present interest to elucidate the Gnostic system of thought, which, after all, never existed in any clear-cut form. But Gnostics, although demonstrating great diversity, shared a basic belief that one could attain spiritual liberation from the illusive world through knowledge *(gnosis)*—the knowledge which enabled one to discover the presence of a divine spirit hidden deep within oneself. They affirmed that the spirit, when ignited by a spark of gnosis, would enjoy a flight from the entrapment of the flesh to the divine world of light. A redeemer, the heavenly emissary, would release the divine component imprisoned in the ignorant self. Therefore, Gnostics were "those who know" the secrets of salvation.

Fundamental to this teaching is a dualistic view of reality: the corporeal world is false and transient, while the divine world is true and eternal. Gnostics maintained, consequently, that the world, dominated by darkness, was created by the Demiurge, a malevolent force, an assertion which diametrically opposed a belief in the monotheistic Creator God of Judaism and Christianity. The Gnostic god was utterly unfathomable, so transcendent from every form of existence that he was paradoxically called the "non-existent one." The transcendence of the biblical God, however, included his nearness. The world was, for Jews and Christians, in contrast to the Gnostics' negative view, essentially good and important, despite its sinful condition. The Gnostic belief in the innate divine nature of humans was also in dissonance with the Judaeo-Christian position which professed a qualitative disparity between God and persons. Gnosis, as the way of salvation, was, needless to say, not acceptable to the synagogues and church.

In essence, Gnosticism was hence radically different from either of these two religions, yet it borrowed extensively words, ideas, and images from both of them. Does this suggest that Gnosticism stemmed historically from Judaism and/or Christianity? Or did it derive from some other source, as from Greek philosophy or Iranian religion? Or was it a hybrid of all of these? For our inquiry, the question of a possible Jewish background for Gnosticism is of particular significance. And that is the next task in our discussion.

(2) Incipient Gnosticism

Our adumbration of Gnosticism in the previous section is, as we noted, based on many patristic writings and the Nag Hammadi literature from the early centuries of the Christian era. This is indicative of the fact that this Gnosticism must have been a rather popular religio-philosophical movement from the second to fourth centuries A.D. As Professor Frend, who has just recently published a voluminous work on early Christian history, puts it, "the middle years of the second century belong to the Gnostics."[68] Gnostic influence dominated Christian intellectual life all over the Mediterranean basin during that period. Valentinus and Basilides, above all others, were the better-known Gnostic teachers active in such cultural and political centers as Rome and Alexandria.

The trend was formidable and even threatening to "orthodox" Christianity, so much so that the church fathers had to vigorously resist condemning them as heretics. However, Christianity finally succeeded in becoming the officially accepted religion of the Roman empire after the conversion of the Emperor Constantine in the early fourth century A.D., and Gnosticism lost ground. The Gnostic Christians who left their writings in a jar near Nag Hammadi were seemingly among the persecuted victims eradicated at that time.

Gnostic Provenance

Where and when was Gnosticism born? There is no extant document which indubitably originated with the Gnostics from the first century A.D. It seems, however, likely that there were some antecedents of the Gnosticism which became full-blown in the second century. Interestingly, some ancient authors point to Samaria, where the "antecedents" might possibly have existed.

In Acts 8:9–25, there is a reference to a magus named Simon in Samaria who "amazed the nation," and people "gave heed to him, from the least to the greatest, saying, 'This man is *dynamis* (power) of God which is called Great'" (v. 10). Upon encountering the Christian evangelistic work of Philip, Simon was converted to Christianity and was baptized by the evangelist. (*Dynamis,* [*geburah* in Hebrew] is an appellative of God in the apocalyptics, the Gospels [Mt 26:64; Mk 14:62], and the Hekhalot literature.[69])

Justin Martyr (*The First Apology,* chap. 26) and Irenaeus (*Against Heresies,* I, 23, 1–4), Hippolytus (*Refutation of All Heresies,* VI, 9–15) and some others[70] also make mention of Simon's teachings and activities as a magician and the head of a heretical group in Samaria called Simonians. He was worshipped by his followers as the "first God," and his companion, a former prostitute named Helena, was said to be the "first thought" and the mother of all, as she descended to the lower regions and created the angels and powers. These angels and powers supposedly created the world without knowing at all the existence of the higher God. They also entrapped Helena in human flesh so as not to let her return to her heavenly origins. Simon, a heavenly redeemer, came to deliver her.

If the information of these patristic writings is accurate, Simon Magus and his followers apparently held gnostic ideas: belief in the unknown supreme God, a dualistic world view (the heavenly world of Light versus this corporeal world of Darkness), the assertion of the imprisonment of the divine spirit ("the first thought") in the flesh, the assumption of a heavenly redeemer (Simon), and other teachings. K. Rudolph, an eminent scholar on Gnosticism, therefore, concludes that "it must undoubtedly be assumed that he (Simon) founded a gnostic community in Samaria which was considered by expanding Christianity as serious competition, especially as the Simonians themselves annexed Christian doctrines and thus threatened to subvert the Christian community, as did most of the later gnostics."[71]

Hippolytus tells us that Simon came into conflict with St. Peter in Rome and perished there because his magical power failed him. (He instructed his disciples to bury him alive, but, contrary to his prediction, he never arose after three days. See in *op. cit.,* chap. 15.) He seems to have had disciples and friends who were said to be Gnostics. An apocryphal writing putatively called the Pseudo-Clementines (written perhaps in Syria during the first half of the third century A.D.) contains a brief reference to Dositheus. He is said to have been Simon's disciple and later superior. Both of them were among the thirty disciples of John the Baptizer (*Homilies,* II, 23–24). Dositheus must have had some connection with the Gnostics, for one of the Nag Hammadi documents, usually called *The Three Stele of Seth,* mentions "the revelation of Dositheus" (the name appears only here).[72] There was another disciple of Simon Magus whose name was Menander. He came from Samaria as well and became a target of the denunciation of the second century church fathers.

As for Dositheus, the Pseudo-Clementines also says that he was a Sadducee, which most likely means in the context (*Recognitions,* I, 54) a Zadokite, i.e., an Essene.[73] His possible relationship with the Essenes may have been alluded to by Origen, a well-known ecclesiastical scholar from Alexandria (c. 185-c. 254). He wrote that Dositheus insisted on a strict observance of the Sabbath, and he applied to himself the prophecy of Deuteronomy 18:18 ("I [God] shall raise a prophet to them from among their brothers, like you [Moses], and I will put my words in his mouth, and he shall speak to them all that I shall command him.")

The identical passage, expressing the sect's expectation of an eschatological prophet, is quoted in a document from Qumran Cave IV (4QTest). (The New Testament equates this "prophet like Moses" with John the Baptizer, though Acts 3:21ff. identifies him with Jesus.) If indeed Dositheus and Simon were disciples of John the Baptizer (as the Pseudo-Clementine Homilies suggests), who might have had some connection with the Qumran Essenes (as we have discussed in the previous chapter), it is then conceivable that Dositheus and Simon were at least influenced by Essenism.

Finally, Hegesippus, a converted Jew from Palestine, who in the second century wrote five books in opposition to the Gnostics (which survived only in fragments mostly in Eusebius' *Ecclesiastical History*), traced the Gnosticism of his time back to a Jewish ancestry of Jesus' time via certain groups of Jewish Christians (*Eccl. Hist.*, IV, 22, 4–7).

If these ancient sources reflect accurate historical facts, they intimate a very intersting link: the Essenes—Dositheus and Simon—the "heretics" in Samaria—the Gnostics. However, a lack of reliable evidence prevents us from drawing a clear picture of this whole development. It is not certain, for example, that the Simon of Acts was indeed the same Simon referred to by the church fathers.[74] It is difficult to prove conclusively that Dositheus and Simon were truly associated with the Essenes. Nonetheless, it remains a formidable historical possibility. This, of course, does not suggest that the Essenes were Gnostics. There is no evidence that Gnosticism existed before the time of Jesus. The Dead Sea Scrolls yield nothing to allude to that as fact.

New Testament References to Gnostic Trends

Although we have no Gnostic documents from the first century A.D., the Gnostic movement in its inchoate form was apparently alive at that time. Several passages in the New Testament, for example, appear to suggest that the Christian leaders were engaged in a dispute with the Gnostics. As contemporary New Testament scholars often acknowledge, St. Paul's letters to the Christians in Corinth seem to indicate the existence of a trend which later became Gnosticism in that town.[75] The heretical movement which Colossians criticizes may also be an early form of Gnosticism; the epistle warns against "philosophy and vain deceit according to the tradition of men, according to the elements of the world (i.e., the angels) and not according to Christ" (2:8).[76] When Ephesians encourages a combat against "the principalities, against the powers, against the rulers of this world of the darkness of this age, against the spiritual powers of evil in the heavenly regions" (6:12), we just may be detecting here a response to an incipient Gnostic movement in Ephesus.[77]

In 1 Timothy, there are counsels against "myths and endless genealogies" (1:4) and "deceiving spirits and teachings of demons" (4:1). This may well be referring to Gnostic speculations concerning the origin of the universe and the doctrine of the archons ("rulers").[78] The epistle also admonishes that one must "guard the deposit, avoiding the profane babblings and opposing theories of the falsely called gnosis" (6:20). The spiritualization of the resurrection referred to 2 Timothy 2:18 ("The resurrection has already taken place") may be an indication of characteristic Gnosis (cf. 1 Cor 15:12).

The Gospel of John has been regarded by some scholars as having Gnostic connections.[79] John uses a characteristically dualistic scheme, such as light vs. darkness, heaven vs. the world below, spirit vs. flesh, and so on. Jesus is described as the heavenly redeemer and as the pre-existent logos which descended to earth to be tabernacled in a human form, then to ascend again to the world above. Words and ideas which are found in Gnostic literature also occur in this Gospel, such as "knowledge (gnosis)," "paraclete," "good shepherd," and others. Yet John makes a polemical attempt to oppose the Gnostics by asserting that the logos became flesh (1:4). A well-known New Testament scholar, R. Bultmann, insists that there is a connection between John's Gospel and the Mandaean literature. Madaeism is a syncretic and gnostic religion which originated at least as early as the second century A.D. (Some scholars maintain its pre-Christian origin.) It claims John the Baptizer as its ancestor, and its literature, though much later, shows many parallels to the fourth Gospel. The alleged relationship between this Gospel and Gnosticism, however, remains ambiguous.

Nowhere in the New Testament is there a clear identification of Gnosticism, nor is any specific form thereof found. The New Testament portions referred to above, nonetheless, do suggest the fact that there was in the first century an incipient form of the second century Gnosticism. It may be, consequently, better to use the term proto- or pre-Gnosticism, or simply Gnosis.[80] Is it possible then for us to trace its provenance further back to the pre-Christian period? Does the existence of Simon Magus indicate that Gnosis has a Palestinian origin? Is a heterodox Judaism its cradle-place?

(3) Possible Sources of Early Gnostic Ideas

Scholars have suggested various possible sources for the Gnostic phenomena from the early centuries A.D. K. Rudolph, for example, assumes that the idea of the eschatological judgment, and the resurrection of the dead, the scheme of the ages, and dualism—all characteristically attested to in Gnosticism— were derived ultimately from Zoroastrianism of ancient Persia through the apocalyptic Jewish filter.[81] Not only these thematical ideas, he further notes, but also more specifically Iranian elements are found in Gnostic writings like *The Acts of Thomas* from the third century. They derived from ancient Iran, independent of the Jewish tradition. A Persian word for "attendants" is, in fact, used in the extant Syriac text.

Iranian Influence

Iranian influence on Manichaism has also been suggested by scholars. Manichaism is a Gnostic religion which thrived in the third and fourth centuries. The founder, Mani (c. 215–275), was said to have been born in Persia, grew up in a Gnostic (Mandaean?) environment, and taught a highly syncretic religion (e.g., Jesus, Buddah, the prophets, and other religious geniuses, including himself, were supposedly sent from heaven to release particles of Light captured in the human body). But the evidence shows that Mani came from a Jewish-Christian baptist sect called the Elchasaites of the third century.[82]

Available data do not seem to lend support to the alleged Iranian derivation of Gnostic ideas. First, we possess little documentation regarding very early Zoroastrianism. Second, the Zoroastrian view of the world is affirmative, unlike the total pessimism of Gnosticism. Therefore, the Zoroastrian influence on the inchoate Gnostic thought appears to have been minimal.

Greek Influence

The ancient Greek world has also been considered by scholars as a possible source of influence on Gnosticism. The Christian and non-Christian Gnostics of the second century often used words and ideas borrowed from Greek religion (e.g., the Greek theosophical school, Orphism) and from Greek philosophy (e.g., Platonism). The notion of the "unknown god," Demiurge, the descent and return of the soul, the origin of evil, and Platonic dualism, (spirit and matter, soul and body) appears to comport with Gnostic thought. Hippolytus, whom we have referred to earlier, traces all Gnostic teachings back to Greek philosophy, which is of course an inaccurate over-simplification. Platonic dualism, for example, never implies a total rejection of the world as does the Gnostic scheme of thought. Modern scholars, such as A. H. Armstrong, say that "any influence which may have been exerted by any kind of Greek philosophy on Gnosticism was not genuine but extraneous and, for the most part, superficial."[83]

A body of theosophical literature ascribed to Hermes (Greek name for Thot, the ancient Egyptian god of wisdom), from the early centuries of our era, also shows a mixture of Greek philosophy (Platonic dualism, Stoic pantheism, etc.) and Gnostic ideas. (Some Hermetic writings are found in Nag Hammadi.) The Hermetic teaching, however, is clearly different from Gnosticism; it does not preach, for example, a total rejection of the world as Gnosticism does. (G. Quispel calls it "vulgar Egyptian Gnosticism," however.[84])

Summing up, early Gnostic thought (not "Gnosticism") was possibly influenced by a variety of sources, including Iranian religion and the philosophy and mythology of the Hellenistic world. But these influences were superficial. Gnosticism did not have one specific root. It was certainly not just a product of Christian heresy, as scholars once assumed. The incipient Gnosis evidently antedated Christianity. If such is the case, Judaism, particularly the apocalyptic and mystical trends of Judaism, was possibly the most significant source for early Gnostic conceptions.

(4) Jewish Background of the Early Gnosis

K. Rudolph presents a most forceful argument for the Palestinian provenance of early Gnostic thought. For support, he cites the patristic references; they point again and again to Samaria, in particular, as the place of origin for the first Gnostics (as we have previously mentioned). These church fathers also indicate that the Gnostic teachings owe a debt to the Jewish biblical tradition. Rudolph states: "Particularly the Coptic texts from Nag Hammadi have lent support to the thesis that the majority of gnostic systems came into existence on the fringes of Judaism."[85]

It is true that there are numerous paraphrases of Old Testament passages found in the Gnostic writings. Old Testament personalities such as Adam, Seth, Cain, Shem, and Noah are claimed to be important ancestors by the Gnostics. The Law and the Prophets are attributed to Yaldabaoth, the Demiurge, who is identified with the Old Testament Creator God. Irenaeus tells us:

> They distribute the prophets in the following manner: Moses, and Joshua the son of Nun, and Amos, and Habakkuk, belong to Iadabaoth; Samuel, and Nathan, and Jonah, and Micah, to Iao; Elijah, Joel, and Zechariah, to Sabaoth; Isaiah, Ezekiel, Jeremiah, and Daniel, to Adonai; Tobias and Haggai to Eloi; Micaiah and Nahum to Oraus; Esdras and Zechariah to Astanphaeus.[86]

These cosmic rulers (called archons) are given Hebrew names. "Yaldabaoth" has been analyzed by some scholars to mean "son (yaldo) of chaos (baoth)," but G. Scholem tenders a convincing alternative, "the begetter of (S)abbaoth" (*oth* is a "magic suffix"). Scholem also suggests that Ariel was an older name of Yaldabaoth, as attested to by an amulet of the Orphic Gnostics. The amulet has the inscription of Yaldabaoth and Ariel in Greek letters with a lion-headed figure. Ariel is a Hebrew name meaning "the lion of God." The "lion" was derived from one of the four faces of the living creatures carrying the chariot-throne in Ezekiel chapter one.[87] So, then, it appears that the name of this important Demiurge of the Gnostics originally came from the Merkabah mysticism. Scholem suggests that this secret name was produced by "a Jew who had joined the Gnostic camp of the *minim* (heretics) consciously."[88]

As for the other archons' names, "Yao" is obviously Yahweh, the name of the biblical God. It occurs quite frequently both in the Hekhalot literature as well as the gnostic writings.

"Sabaoth" is a divine epithet used in the Old Testament usually translated "hosts," but its exact meaning is uncertain. Sabaoth is said to be the son of Yaldabaoth (his mother is "Matter"). He inherits his father's blasphemous nature but repents and condemns his parents, which accords him the merits of being enthroned in the seventh heaven. Interestingly, it is said that Sabaoth "made himself a huge four-faced chariot of cherubim, and infinitely many angels to act as ministers, and also harps and lyres" (*The Hypostasis of the Archons,* 95, 25–30). Another text from Nag Hammadi, usually called *On the Origin of the World,* also describes Sabaoth's "great throne on a four-faced chariot called cherubim" which has the form of a lion, bull, human, and eagle (105, 1–10). These forms agree exactly with the faces of Ezekiel's creatures.

What we have here is, of course, the familiar scene of Merkabah in Ezekiel, *The Songs of Sabbath Sacrifices* from Qumran, some apocalyptic literature, and the Hekhalot writings. We are compelled, therefore, to assume that the Gnostic reference to the chariot-throne was derived from an older source which must be, so far as evidence indicates, of the Jewish apocalyptic tradition.

Another intriguing feature of Sabaoth is, as F. Fallon indicates, that the figure resembles the archangel Michael in Jewish apocalyptic literature.[89] Just as Michael is said to be an opponent of Satan, a master over chaos, the leader of the angels and the prince of Light, so is Sabaoth. His position is lower than the high

God, yet he is enthroned, an opponent of Satan, a commander with authority over chaos, and the maker and leader of the angels. Furthermore, these two figures seem to correspond to Metatron in the Hekhalot literature. The apocalyptic image of the archangel, therefore, evidently has contributed to forming the Gnostic portrayal of Sabaoth.

In the above-quoted portion of *The Hypostasis of the Archons,* we also read that Pistis Sophia placed the angel of wrath on the left side of Sabaoth, representing "the unrighteousness of the realm of absolute power above." On his right is Life. Zoe ("life" in Greek) represents a feminine hypostasis of divine wisdom, which apparently came from the Old Testament wisdom literature in which Wisdom (*hochmah,* a Hebrew feminine noun) is described as a hypostatized figure assisting God in creation (Proverbs 8, Ecclesiasticus 24, Wisdom 6–10).[90] In First Enoch, wisdom is said to return to heaven after failing to find her abode among men, because of human iniquities (chap. 42).

The separation described here (righteousness on the right as against unrighteousness on the left) comes close to the division of good and evil portrayed in the Manual of Discipline 3:13ff. This Qumran text teaches that the "God of wisdom" has given people two spirits: righteous (the prince of Light) and unrighteous (the angel of Darkness). The dualistic ideas at Qumran, however, are eminently ethical, whereas the Gnostic dualism is essentially cosmological or ontological. The eradication of evil, according to the Qumran sectarians (and other apocalyptists), takes an historical process which culminates in the final victory of the good. The Gnostic scheme, by contrast, presents a vertical stratification (though the horizontal eschatological direction is not excluded). There is an ascent to the divine realm above and a fleeing from the dark world below.

The Gnostic view of this world is thus utterly negative. The one who is responsible for creating the world, therefore, is evil. The true God has nothing to do with the Demiurge; he is far beyond, unknowable, an existence beyond existence. It is paradoxical that the Gnostics, on the one hand, denounce the Old Testament Creator God, but, on the other hand, adopt the Jewish notion of the transcendent God. From the post-exilic period onward, the Jewish conception of God became increasingly transcendent, mainly because of the tragic historical conditions confronting the Jews; God was felt to be far removed from the tumultuous world. As a result, belief in intermediaries grew ever more important as a means to fill the gap—wisdom, a messiah, angels, etc. Such a spiritual and social situation seems to have provided the fertile seedbed where Gnostic ideas were nurtured. Gnosticism is, as K. W. Tröger puts it, a protest religion; it protests and revolts against the anti-divine nature of the whole cosmos.[91]

R. M. Grant has advanced the thesis that the trauma of the fall of Jerusalem in A.D. 70 precipitated a deep disillusionment toward the world on the part of the Jewish apocalyptists and drove them to Gnosticism.[92] His view has been criticized because the origin of Gnosticism cannot be explained simply in inner-Jewish terms.[93] Also, Gnostic trends in their incipient form seem to antedate A.D. 70. Nonetheless, Grant's insight seems to be on the right track in that he draws a correlation between the rueful historical experience and the Gnostic rejection of this world. B. A. Pearson states: "It is quite possible that an important factor in the development of this Gnostic attitude was a profound sense of the failure of history, such as appears to be reflected in the way in which the Gnostic sources depict the foibles and machinations of the Creator."[94]

There is no reason to deny that some apocalyptists were indeed drawn toward a gnostic type of speculation. There are, as we have observed thus far, so many points of contact between apocalypticism and Gnosticism that their historical connection cannot be simply dismissed. The massive use of Jewish tradition by the Gnostics is an implacable indication that the Jewish lineage constitutes a significant component in Gnosticism. The very fact that there is a vigorous Gnostic rejection of the Creator God of the Old Testament intimates a close relationship to Judaism. If Gnosticism had nothing to do with Judaism, why does it have to react so violently against the Jewish God? This Jewish God the Gnostics defy.

In N. Dahl's opinion, the real target of the Gnostic revolt is the Creator God rather than the world itself. "According to widespread gnostic opinion, the world is indeed better than its Creator. The Demiurge thought that he had created the world by his own power but, without knowing it, he had been inspired by his mother, Wisdom; he modeled his work after the pattern of higher realms."[95] Such a protest to this God can only be understandable as an endeavor within Judaism. Gruenwald draws an analogy: just as Christianity, while stemming from Judaism, yet rejected it, so, too, did Gnosticism.[96]

It is interesting to note, as Gruenwald points out,[97] the fact that the author of *The Apocryphon of John* repeatedly asserts that Moses did not transmit accurate information. In other words, the Gnostic writer attempts to correct the Old Testament accounts. Unless the Old Testament is an important source book for him, why does he have to do this?

Gruenwald also raises another important point which is related to what we have noted above: "Only Jews could see the full relevance of the Gnostic argument made through the Jewish scriptures."[98] That is, the Gnostic writings which contain the Jewish material were written by Jews (or, more likely, ex-Jews) and written for Jews (again, ex-Jews) who needed to be convinced of both the falsity of the Jewish interpretation of scripture and the truth of the Gnostic treatment of the Bible. It is, however, far from certain how many of these "Jewish Gnostics" actually existed. Yet it is very possible that there were a number of such Jews (ex-Jews).

It is of interest to recall at this juncture that Irenaeus said that the disciples of Basilides (the famous Gnostic leader of the second century A.D.) "declare that they are no longer Jews and not yet Christians" (*Against Heresies,* I, 24, 6). This statement is indicative of the Jewish origin of Basilides' disciples.

Another instance of "Jewish conversion" to Gnosticism is found in Rabbi Elisha ben Abuyah, who came to hold the view of Two Powers in heaven. (He is one of the four rabbis who are said to have ascended to heaven, as we have mentioned earlier.) Scholem, who has suggested that the name of the Gnostic Demiurge, Yaldabaoth, was created by a Gnostic Jew, says, "If I say a Jew, I have in mind Jews who went over to Gnostic heresies, such as the famous Tannaitic teacher Elisha ben Abuyah in the first half of the second century, who surely was not the first Gnostic sectarian (Hebrew: *min*), but only the most widely known."[99] This rabbi was called "Aḥer," which literally means "other" but seemingly connotes "apostate" or "unorthodox," as it does in the Tannaitic literature.

In conclusion, it is reasonable to assume from what we have discussed thus far that Gnosticism has its important roots in Judaism. The esotericism expressed in the Dead Sea Scrolls and some other apocalyptic literature (the Enochian tradition, in particular) seem to have provided fertile soil for the incipient Gnostic thought (not yet Gnosticism). The Gnostic texts from Nag Hammadi, as J. M. Robinson says, "may provide some of the documentation that bridges the gulf from Qumran to Christian Gnosticism, and thus contribute to our understanding of the context in which Christianity emerged."[100]

This, however, does not mean that Judaism is the only source for the Gnostic development. Mythological material from the eastern world (as from Iran) and Greek philosophical and religious ideas and images also influenced it to a degree. Conflicts with rabbis and Christian leaders perhaps radicalized it into a full-blown Gnosticism in the second century A.D.

Be that as it may, the discovery of the documents at Qumran has thus shed invaluable light on a significant Jewish trend in the pre-Christian period which seems to have been an influence in the birth of Gnosticism. It has also afforded important textual evidence of the earliest Merkabah mysticism within the Jewish tradition.

Conclusion

The contribution of recent archaeological finds in the wilderness of Judaea has proved to be invaluable, indeed. We have observed this in respect to our understanding of the Jewish history of the Second Temple period, Old Testament textual problems, Christian beginnings and the New Testament, and the development of mystic and Gnostic trends. The discovered materials have shed light on hitherto unknown or ambiguous areas of these subjects.

The information from the finds has focused our attention, in particular, on various events involving the so-called "fringe" segments of Judaism. The Essenes at Qumran is a case in point. Before the Dead Sea Scrolls became available, the Essenes were an almost totally unknown fringe group deemed more or less insignificant compared to the Pharisaic-rabbinic Judaism of the day, which was once customarily regarded as "normative" Judaism. Scholarly treatment of the Judaism of the Second Temple period was, therefore, inaccurate and lopsided; the historical reality has been found to be far more complex. The Qumran sect represented a legitimately significant aspect of the Jewish religious situation of its day. The biblical texts from the Qumran caves demonstrate to us that there existed an intriguing diversity in textual tradition at that time.

The finds from Judaea, other than those in Qumran, chiefly provide us with traces of information concerning the Jewish fighters who opposed Rome. Here again we detect the activities of some "fringe" groups—the Sicarii and the Zealots. We note the enormous involution of the social, political and religious movements in Palestine. Many sites in Judaea have also

201

revealed the intensity of Bar-Kosiba's war with the Romans. Another rueful remain found at Wadi ed-Daliyeh illustrates the cruelty of the human affair as well. All of these finds furnish us priceless evidence of history—the history of these "losers" in battles. History, as often popularly espoused, is written by victors, but the archaeological discoveries inform us about the other side of history—the losers' stories. And they oftentimes echo more honest voices.

Christianity was born in a "losers'" milieu. The Dead Sea Scrolls attest to the fact that those who possessed (and originated) the scrolls were akin to the early Christians in many respects—closer than any other of the known Jewish groups at that time. Essene conversions to Christianity may indeed have occurred. ("Conversion" is not really a proper word, for those "converts" must have believed that the Christian movement was a genuine form of their own religious heritage, rather than some new and different religion.) Many literary expressions and theological ideas contained in the scrolls illuminate those used in the New Testament. Tantalizing, however, is the paucity of evidence which prevents us from drawing any direct line between Qumran and Christianity.

The mystic trend has been considered simply a peripheral phenomenon in antiquity. But mysticism has always been an integral part of any religion (so long as it is authentic). But because of its very nature, mysticism has not been discussed often enough. In the Judaeo-Christian tradition as well, mysticism had been a neglected topic until recently. But we now know that it was alive as a vital religious movement at Qumran. G. Scholem and others have contributed to investigating its heritage preserved in Judaism, thereby generating interest in this significant subject. Gnosticism, in spite of its negative attitude toward Judaism, intimates that its strongest possible progenitor is the Jewish tradition. All of these questions must and should be explored further.

Any believers belonging to a specific religion tend to search for and adopt historical and archaeological data for the sake of fortifying their own religious commitment. Believers of the Bible are also tempted to do so; they attempt to "prove" biblical stories. That is understandable, but may result in a biased use of supposedly objective scientific research. Such a misuse and abuse should, needless to say, be noted and restricted. This does not mean that the use of the data is to be monopolized by a handful of specialists. Religious phenomena are not found simply floating in the air, nor was the Bible born in a vacuum. Given material such as the Bible and the Dead Sea Scrolls should be studied by all and with any available means, including the study of history, archaeology, paleography, theology, and other disciplines. Those who are seriously interested in a religion, whether specialist or lay person, share both a privilege and a responsibility to pursue a more accurate and exact understanding of what they believe in. The academic height achieved by specialists should be supported by wider circles of non-specialists. Our small endeavor in this book intends to intensify support for the further investigation of the Bible and its background.

Notes

Introduction

1. For the story of the discovery, see G. L. Harding, *DJD* I, pp. 1–7; W. H. Brownlee, "Muhammed ed-Deeb's Own Story of His Scroll Discovery," *INES* 16 (1957) pp. 236–39. A. Y. Samuel, *Treasure of Qumran: My Story of the Dead Sea Scrolls* (Westminster, 1966); J. C. Trever, *The Dead Sea Scrolls: A Personal Account* (Eerdmans, 1978).

2. Cf. P. J. King, "The Contribution of Archaeology to Biblical Studies," *CBQ* 45 (1983) pp. 1–16.

1. Finds in the Judaean Wilderness

1. For a complete list of publications of the discovered manuscripts, see *The Dead Sea Scrolls Major Publications and Tools for Study* (Society of Biblical Literature and Scholars Press, 1977) by J. A. Fitzmyer.

2. Translation by E. Isaac in *The Old Testament Pseudepigrapha,* vol. 1, ed. by J. H. Charlesworth (Doubleday, 1983) p. 86.

3. See, e.g., M. Black, *The Scrolls and Christian Origin: Studies in the Jewish Background of the New Testament* (Scribners, 1961) p. 193.

4. See, e.g., G. Vermes, *Scripture and Tradition in Judaism: Haggadic Studies* (Leiden: Brill, 1961) p. 124.

5. J. A. Fitzmyer, *The Genesis Apocryphon of Qumran Cave 1: A Commentary* (Rome: Pontifical Biblical Institute, 1966) p. 9. After a thorough comparison of 1QapGen with the Targums of Neofiti 1, Pseudo-Onkelos, and Onkelos, he makes

the observation that 1QapGen is "more frequently a paraphrase of the biblical text. The phrases which are literarily translated are incorporated into its own account. And therefore it cannot be regarded simply as a targum." He also concludes that "it is prior to the Targums" (p. 32).

6. For the meaning of *serek,* see Y. Yadin, *The Scroll of the War of the Sons of Light against the Sons of Darkness,* tr. by Batya and Chaim Rabin (London: Oxford University Press, 1962) pp. 148–150.

7. Cf. F. M. Cross, "The Development of the Jewish Scripts," in *The Bible and Ancient Near East,* ed. by G. Wright (Anchor Books, 1965) p. 258, n. 116.

8. See his "La genèse litéraire de la Règle de la Communauté," *RB* 76 (1969) pp. 528–549. He postulates four stages of the process: (1) 1QS 8:1–16a and 9:3–10:8a—the nucleus of the literature written in a pre-sectarian period, (2) 8:16b–19 and 8:20–9:20—the earliest penal legislation composed shortly after the birth of the sect, (3) 5:1–13a and 5:15b–7:25—the portion which reflects the heyday of the sect, and (4) additions and reductions were made.

9. See his *1QM, The War Scroll from Qumran: Its Structure and History* (Rome: Biblical Institute Press, 1977).

10. *Ibid.,* p. 123.

11. Y. Yadin presented the view of a single authorship of the scroll in his commentary on the War Scroll *(op. cit.).* But J. van der Ploeg disagreed with him by postulating an original version preserved in cols. 1, 10–12, and 15–19. See his *Le rouleau de la Guerre: Traduit et annoté avec une introduction* (Leiden: Brill, 1959). In J. Becker's opinion, (similar to that of Davies), there are two recensions: (1) cols. 1, 7–8, 15–19; (2) 2, 3–7, 10–14. See his *Das Heil Gottes: Heils- und Sündenbegriffe in den Qumrantexten und im Neuen Testament* (Göttingen: Vandenhoeck & Reprecht, 1964). P. van der Osten-Sacken, *Gott und Belial* (Göttingen: Vandenhoeck & Ruprecht, 1969) even identifies the prince of evil power, Belial, with Antiocus IV, the archfoe of the Maccabeans.

12. See also G. R. Driver, *The Judaean Scrolls. The Problem and a Solution* (Oxford: Blackwell, 1965) pp. 180ff.

13. This expression is used by C.-H. Hunzinger in his "Fragmente einer älteren Fassung der Buches Milhamā aus Höhle 4 von Qumrān," *ZAW* 69 (1957) pp. 131–151. He thinks that a fragment of the War Scroll from Cav IV (4QMa) suggests some pre-Qumran reading of the text.

14. "*bnê ḥesed*" in Hebrew. J. T. Milik suggests that it may be an allusion to the *Ḥassîdîm*, the pious fighters of the Maccabean war against the Greeks. See his *Ten Years of Discovery in the Wilderness of Judaea*, tr. by J. Strugnell (London: SCM Press, 1959) p. 77, n. 1.

15. Cf. D. P. Hopkins, "The Qumran Community and IQ Hodayot: A Reassessment," *RQ* 10 (1979–81) pp. 331–336.

16. Th. Gaster, *The Dead Sea Scriptures* (Anchor Books, 1964) p. 124.

17. C. F. Kraft, "Poetic Structure in the Qumran Thanksgiving Psalms," *Biblical Research* 2 (1957) p. 17.

18. H. Ringgren, *The Faith of Qumran: Theology of the Dead Sea Scrolls* (Fortress, 1963) p. 14.

19. D. P. Hopkins says that any further attempt to identify the poetic form of the Hymn should be abandoned. See *op. cit.,* p. 331. But other researchers insist that it is wrong to interpret the Hymns rigidly according to biblical category and that the Hymns should be treated on their own merit. See B. P. Kittel, *The Hymns of Qumran* (Scholars Press, 1981).

20. Cf. J. A. Fitzmyer, *The Gospel According to Luke I–IX* (Doubleday, 1981) pp. 358f., 376–378, 420.

21. G. Vermes, *The Dead Sea Scrolls: Qumran in Perspective* (Collins & World Publishing Company, 1978) p. 57.

22. H. Bardtke, "Considérations sur les cantiques de Qumrân," *RB* 63 (1956) pp. 220–233, esp. pp. 229–231.

23. J. M. Allegro, *The Treasure of the Copper Scroll* (Doubleday, 1960). See also K. G. Kuhn, "Les rouleaux de cuivre de Qumrân," *RB* 61 (1954) pp. 193–205.

24. E.-M. Laperrousaz, *Qoumrân: L'establissement essénien des bords de la Mer Morte. Historie et archéologie du site* (Paris: Picard, 1976) pp. 131–147.

25. F. M. Cross, *The Ancient Library of Qumran and Modern Biblical Studies,* rev. ed. (Baker Book House, 1980) pp. 20–25. (This book will be henceforth referred to as *Library.*) J. T.

Milik, the editor of the scroll, also points out its fictitious nature. In his view, it did not belong to the sect. See his "Le rouleau de cuivre provenant de la grotte 3Q (3Q15)," *DJD* III, pp. 199–302.

26. *Op. cit.,* p. 29.

27. See R. Levy's readable article about the discovery of the Cairo geniza documents with several photographs of the synagogue, "First 'Dead Sea Scrolls' Found in Egypt Fifty Years Before Qumran Discoveries," *BAR* 8 (1982) pp. 38–53.

28. S. Schechter, *Documents of Jewish Sectaries* (Cambridge: Cambridge University Press, 1910).

29. Cf. J. M. Allegro, *Qumran Cave 4,* I (*DJD* V) 1968; J. T. Milik, *Qumran Grotte 4,* II (*DJD* VI) 1977; M. Baillet, *Qumran Grotte 4,* III (*DJD* VII) 1982.

30. Some scholars suspect that the Qumran sect may not be in all aspects identical with the sect of the Damascus Document. The latter presupposes registered members of women and children, as well as private property, which the former seemingly does not. See P. R. Davies, *The Damascus Document* (Shefield: Journal for the Study of the Old Testament Press, 1982) p. 18.

31. F. M. Cross (*Library,* pp. 81f.) and many other scholars. Vermes explains that the symbolic use of "Damascus" in the Damascus Document is a good example of Jewish exegetical tradition which associates the eschatological temple with Damascus. See his *Scripture and Tradition in Judaism,* pp. 43–49.

32. Cf. J. T. Milik, *Ten Years of Discovery in the Wilderness of Judaea,* pp. 87–93.

33. See I. Rabinowitz, "A Reconsideration of 'Damascus' and '390 years' in the 'Damascus' (Zadokite) Fragments," *JBL* 73 (1954) pp. 11–35; J. Murphy-O'Connor, "The Essenes and Their History," *RB* 81 (1974) p. 221.

34. Cross, *Library,* p. 82.

35. Y. Yadin, *Megillat Hammiqdāsh,* 3 vols. (Jerusalem: Israel Exploration Society, 1977); the English translation by the same publisher in 1983.

36. Cf. also J. Milgrom, "'Sabbath' and 'Temple City' in the Temple Scroll," *BASOR* 232 (1978) pp. 25–27, and J. Kampen, "The Temple Scroll, the Torah of Qumran?" in *Proceedings, Eastern Great Lakes Biblical Society* 1 (1981) ed. by P. Siegal, pp. 37–54.

37. Yadin identified some unpublished fragments from Qumran Cave IV in the Rockefeller Museum in Jerusalem as part of this literature and published them in the Supplement to the third volume. There is, however, doubt about some of them. See, e.g., B. A. Levine, "The Temple Scroll: Aspects of its Historical Provenance and Literary Character," *BASOR* 232 (1978) p. 6.

38. *Op. cit.*

39. See L. H. Schiffman, *Sectarian Law in the Dead Sea Scrolls: Courts, Testimony and the Penal Code* (Scholars Press, 1983) p. 14. Cf. also his "The Temple Scroll in Literary and Philological Perspective," in *Approaches to Ancient Judaism* 2, ed. by W. S. Green (Scholars Press, 1980) pp. 143–158.

40. This scroll refers to *kohen gadol* (high priest). This expression never occurs in the rest of the Qumran literature. In its place, *kohen rôsh* (chief priest) is used. Another peculiar fact is that the festival of oil is mentioned in the document, but according to Josephus (*War* 2:123), the Essenes strictly avoided any contact with oil. Finally, it is not so clear, as Yadin claims, whether the scroll's calendar is indeed the same as the one the sectarians espoused (cf. B. A. Levine, *op. cit.,* pp. 231ff.).

41. P. Benoit, J. T. Milik, and R. de Vaux, *Les grottes de Muraba'ât, DJD* 2 (Oxford: Clarendon, 1961).

42. "Palimpsest" means a parchment which has been written on more than once, the previous writing having been imperfectly erased.

43. For an archaeological report, see G. R. H. Wright, "The Archaeological Remains at El Mird in the Wilderness of Judaea," *Biblica* 42 (1961) pp. 1–21, and an appendix by J. T. Milik, "The Monastery of Kostellion," pp. 21–27.

44. For a list of the published documents from Mird, see J. A. Fitzmyer, *The Dead Sea Scrolls, Major Publications and Tools for Study,* p. 52.

45. Preliminary reports were published in *IEJ* 11 (1961) and 12 (1962).

46. Y. Aharoni, "The Caves of Naḥal Ḥever," *'Atiqot* III (1961) pp. 146–162; *idem., IEJ* 12 (1962) p. 186–199.

47. Cf. M. R. Lehmann, "Studies in the Muraba'at and Nahal Hever Documents," *RQ* 13 (1963) pp. 51–81.

48. Cf. Y. Yadin, *Bar-Kokhba* (Random House, 1971) pp. 222–253.

49. Y. Yadin, *IEJ* 11 (1961) pp. 36–52; *idem, The Finds from the Bar Kokhba Period in the Cave of Letters* (Jerusalem: The Israel Exploration Society, 1963).

50. F. M. Cross, "The Discovery of the Samaritan Papyri," *BA* 26 (1963) pp. 110–121; Paul and Nancy Lapp, "Discoveries in the Wadi ed-Daliyeh," *The Annual of the American School of Oriental Research* XLI (1974).

51. Cross states that in addition to hundreds of small fragments, "perhaps twenty pieces are worthy of being numbered as 'papyri,'" and "the original deposit may have been in excess of a hundred documents." See his "The Papyri and Their Historical Implications," *ibid.,* p. 19.

52. *Ibid.*

53. Lapp., *op. cit.,* p. 8. G. E. Wright's excavation at Schechem also seem to confirm this historical reconstruction. Cf. his *Schechem: The Biography of a Biblical City* (McGraw-Hill, 199) pp. 170–184. Several Hellenistic coins of the fourth century B.C. found in the caves also reinforce the case. Cf. F. M. Cross, "Papyri of the Fourth Century B.C. from Daliyeh: A Preliminary Report on Their Discovery and Significance," in *New Direction in Biblical Archaeology,* ed. by D. N. Freedman and J. C. Greenfield (Doubleday, 1971) pp. 48–51.

54. M. Avi-Yona, N. Avigad, Y. Aharoni, I. Dunayevsky, and S. Gutman, "The Archaeological Survey of Masada 1955–1956," *IEJ* 7 (1957) pp. 1–60.

55. Y. Yadin, "The Excavation of Masada 1963/64: Preliminary Report," *IEJ* 15 (1965) pp. 1–120; *idem., Masada: Herod's Fortress and the Zealots' Last Stand,* tr. by H. Pearlman (Random House, 1966).

56. Cf. Yadin, *Masada,* pp. 181–189; G. Foerster, "The Synagogues at Masada and Herodium," *JJA* 3–4 (1977) pp. 6–11; M. J. S. Chiat, *Handbook of Synagogue Architecture* (Scholars Press, 1982) pp. 248–251.

57. Cf. Foerster, *op. cit.;* H. Shanks, *Judaism in Stones: The Archaeology of Ancient Synagogues* (Harper & Row, 1979) pp. 28–30; D. Chen, "The Design of the Ancient Synagogues in Judaea: Masada and Herodium," *BASOR* 239 (1980) pp. 37–40.

58. Cf. Chiat, *op. cit.*, pp. 201f.

59. Cf. Y. Yadin, *The Ben Sira Scroll from Masada* (Jerusalem: Israel Exploration Society and the Shrine of the Books, 1965).

60. J. Strugnell, "The Angelic Liturgy at Qumran—4Q Serek Šîrôt 'Olat Haššabbāt," *VT, Suppl.* VII (1960) pp. 318–345.

61. Cf. A. Kloner, "The Subterranean Hideaways of the Judaean Foothills and the Bar-Kokhba Revolt," in *The Jerusalem Cathedra* 3, ed. by L. I. Levine (Jerusalem: Yad Izhak Ben-Zvi Institute—Wayne State University Press, 1983) pp. 114–135. An abbreviated version of this article was published in *BA* 46 (1983) pp. 210–221.

62. Kloner cites the references to Jewish rebels' intense efforts of making such underground installations in Josephus' *War* 4:512, Dio's *Roman History* 69, 12, Eikha Rabba 1, and the Babylonian Talmud Shabbat 60a (*The Jerusalem Cathedra* 3, pp. 130–132).

2. Judaean Finds and Ancient Jewish History

1. M. Gaster, *The Samaritans: Their History, Doctrine, and Literature* (London: The British Academy, 1925).

2. J. MacDonald, *The Theology of Samaritans* (London: SCM Press, 1964).

3. *Ibid.*, p. 29.

4. J. A. Montgomery, *The Samaritans: The Earliest Jewish Sect* (J. C. Winston, 1907); G. Fohrer, *Geschichte des israelitischen Religion* (Berlin: W. de Gruyter, 1969) pp. 379f.; A. H. J. Gunneweg, *Geschichte Israels bis Bar Kockba* (Stuttgart: W. Kohlhammer, 1972) p. 142.

5. H. H. Rowley points out "anti-Samaritan bias" of the Chronicler. See his "The Samaritan Schism in Legend and History," in *Israel's Prophetic Heritage*, ed. by B. W. Anderson & W. Harrelson (London: Preacher's Library, 1962) p. 219.

6. For this question, see R. J. Coggins, *Samaritans and the Jews: The Origins of Samaritanism Reconsidered* (John Knox Press, 1975) pp. 93–99.

7. F. M. Cross, "Discoveries in the Wadi ed-Daliyeh," p. 21f.; *idem,* "A Reconstruction of the Judaean Restoration," *JBL* 94 (1975) pp. 1–18.

8. See G. E. Wright, *Shechem: The Bibliography of a Biblical City* (McGraw-Hill, 1965) pp. 170ff.

9. The papponymy was widely practiced by Phoenicians, Egyptians, and Greeks as well as Jews. For example, the Tobias family recorded nine generations of papponymy. Cf. B. Mazar, "The Tobiads," *IEJ* 7 (1957) p. 235.

10. Cf. R. Pummer, "The Present State of Samaritan Studies: I," *JSS* 21 (1976) p. 51f.

11. M. Smith, *Palestinian Parties and Politic That Shaped the Old Testament* (Columbia University Press, 1971) p. 185.

12. *Op. cit.; idem,* "The Samaritan Problem: A Case Study in Jewish Sectarianism in the Roman Era," in *Traditions in Transformation: Turning Points in Biblical Faith,* ed. by B. Halperin and J. D. Levenson (Eisenbrauns, 1981) pp. 323–350, esp. pp. 334–337.

13. Pummer, *op. cit.,* p. 51. R. J. Coggins thinks that "the decisive formative period for Samaritanism was the epoch from the third century B.C. to the beginning of the Christian era" (*op. cit.,* p. 164).

14. For the Dositheans, cf. H. G. Kippenberg, *Gerizim und Synagoge: Traditionsgeschichtliche Untersuchung zur samaritanischen Religion der aramaischen Periode* (Berlin: W de Gruyter, 1971); S. J. Isser, *The Dositheans: A Samaritan Sect in Late Antiquity* (Leidon: Brill, 1976).

15. For scholarly research into these questions, see Pummer, *JSS* 22 (1977) pp. 27–44.

16. Josephus in *Antiquities* 18:23 counts the militant nationalistic group led by Judas the Galilean as the fourth school. We will discuss this movement in the next section.

17. J. Neusner, "Pharisaic-Rabbinic Judaism: A Clarification," *History of Religions* 12 (1972–73) p. 251. See his detailed study, *The Rabbinic Traditions about the Pharisees before 70,* 3 vols. (Leiden: Brill, 1971).

18. *Ibid.*

19. Josephus, *War* 2:119–161; *Ant.* 18:18–22; Philo, *Quod omnis probus liber sit* 75–91; *Apologia pro Judaeis* preserved in

Eusebius' *Praeparatio evangelica* viii, 11, 1–8. Their information basically coincides except for a few instances: Philo says in one place (*Quod . . . ,* 75) that they fled from ungodly cities and lived in villages, while in another place (*Apologia,* 1) he writes that they lived in a number of towns in Judaea. According to Josephus, they settled "in large numbers in every town" (*War* 2:124). Another disagreement is found in their report about the Essene view of marriage. Philo (*Apologia* 14) and Josephus (*War* 2:121) tell us of the Essene abstinence from marriage due to the fact that they despised women, whereas the latter mentions also "another order of Essenes, which, while at one with the rest in its mode of life, customs, and regulations, differs from them in its views on marriage," and goes on saying that women, like men after a three years' probation, can marry (*War* 2:160–161).

20. Some modern scholars suspect that the term "Essenes" in Philo and Josephus is a generalization including many smaller sects. See L. H. Schiffman, *The Halakha at Qumran* (Leiden: Brill, 1975) p. 136.

21. Recently, R. Eisenman has asserted anew the sect's identity with the Sadducees, a group older than the one portrayed by Josephus and the New Testament writers. He says, "Qumran can almost be considered a training center for the Jerusalem priesthood" (p. 25), and it "is fed by waves of refugees from the corrupt Pharisaic/Sadducean regime of the procurators" (p. 26). See his *Maccabees, Zadokites, Christians and Qumran* (Leiden: Brill, 1983). The Sadduceism he talks about, however, lacks historical evidence.

22. Cf. S. Lieberman, "Light on the Cave Scrolls from Rabbinic Sources," *Proceedings of the American Academy for Jewish Research* 1951, pp. 395–404.

23. Chaim Rabin, *Qumran Studies* (Schocken Books, 1975) p. 69. He does not, however, seem to have succeeded in proving that the sect was not the Essenes.

24. See R. de Vaux, *Archaeology and the Dead Sea Scrolls* (Oxford: Oxford University Press, 1973) pp. 133–137.

25. This testimony of Dio is preserved by Sybesius of Cyrene (A.D. 370–413) in his *Dio Chrysostom,* vol. 5 of the Loeb Classical Library, tr. by H. L. Crosby, p. 379.

26. Cf. G. Vermes, *The Dead Sea Scrolls: Qumran in Perspective* (Collins & World Publishing Co., 1978) p. 128.

27. L. H. Schiffman insists that the sect still cannot be identified with any previously known group, despite its affinities with the Pharisaic and Essene traditions. See *op. cit.*, p. 136. But he does not really deny that the sect was the Essenes.

28. G. R. Driver, *The Judaean Scrolls: The Problem and a Solution* (Oxford: Blackwell, 1965). C. Roth, *The Historical Background of the Dead Sea Scrolls: A New Historical Approach* (Norton, 1965).

29. These fragments were published by J. Strugnell, "The Angelic Liturgy at Qumran—4Q Serek Šîrôt 'Ôlat Haššabāt," *VT, Suppl.* (Leiden: Brill, 1960) pp. 318–45.

30. Cf. Y. Yadin, *Masada*, p. 174.

31. Cf. J. C. Trever, "1QDanᵃ, the Latest of the Qumran Manuscripts," *RQ* 7 (1970) pp. 277–286.

32. See S. Zeitlin, *The Dead Sea Scrolls and Modern Scholarship* (Dropsie College, 1956). He and S. B. Hoenig have published a series of articles in *Jewish Quarterly Review* since 1949 insisting vehemently on the medieval Karaits theory. For a strong refutation of this theory, see N. Wieder, *The Judaean Scrolls and Karasim* (London: Horovitz Publishing Co., 1962). Wieder acknowledges that there exists "a close kinship" between these two groups (*ibid.*, p. v).

33. J. L. Teicher represents this view. See his articles which appeared in *JSS* 2–5 (1950–54). Cf. also Y. Baer, "Serekh ha-Yahad—The Manual of Discipline. A Jewish-Christian Document from the Beginning of the Second Century CE," *Zion* 29 (1960) pp. 1–60 (Hebrew).

34. See R. de Vaux, *Archaeology and the Dead Sea Scrolls.* Despite some attempts at reassessment (see E. M. Laperrousaz, *Qoumrân: L'éstablissement essénien des bords de la mer Morte* [Paris: Picard, 1976]. See also reviews of this book by J. Vanderkam in *JBL* 97 (1978) pp. 310f. and by J. A. Sanders in *BASOR* 231 (1978) pp. 79f.; the great majority of contemporary scholars still follow de Vaux's archaeological analysis. Cf. also a recent and readable book on Qumran by P. R. Davies, *Qumran* (Eerdmans, 1982).

35. Some scholars believe that Jehoshaphat, king of Judah (870–848 B.C.) had earlier built a town there (cf. 2 Chr 17:12). But no archaeological evidence indicates an occupation prior to the eighth century B.C.

36. Some suggest the possibility of an attack by the Parthians who invaded Syria, Phoenicia, and Palestine in 40 B.C. See J. H. Charlesworth, "The Origin and Subsequent History of the Authors of the Dead Sea Scrolls: Four Transitional Phases Among the Qumran Essenes," *RQ* 38 (1980) pp. 225f.

37. See J. Murphy-O'Connor, "The Essenes and Their History," *RB* 81 (1974) pp. 215–244; *idem,* "The Essenes in Palestine," *BA* 40 (1977) pp. 94–124.

38. Murphy-O'Connor, *RB* 81 (1974) p. 226.

39. Murphy-O'Connor, *BA* 40 (1977) pp. 114f. He is called *ha-kohen* (the priest) in 1QpHab 2:8; 4QPsa 2:19; 3:15.

40. Some scholars, however, take Murphy-O'Connor's theory seriously. See, e.g., P. R. Davies, *The Damascus Document;* J. A. Fitzmyer, "The Dead Sea Scrolls and the New Testament after Thirty Years," *Theology Digest* 29 (1981) pp. 357f. Davies denies the existence of the Hasidim as a party. See his "Hasidim in the Maccabean Period," *JJS* 28 (1977) pp. 127–140.

41. Among many scholarly works, the following two are particularly important: J. Jeremias, *Der Lehrer der Gerechtigkeit* (Göttingen: Vandenhoeck & Ruprecht, 1963) esp. pp. 36–78, and H. Stegemann, *Die Entstehung der Qumrangemeinde* (Bonn: privately published, 1971) esp. pp. 205–246. The eminent French scholars, M. Delcor ("Où en est le problème du Midrash d'Habacuc?" *Revue d'histoire des religions* 142 [1952] pp. 129–146) regards Alexander Jannaeus (103–76 B.C.), and A. Dupont-Sommer (*The Essene Writings from Qumran,* tr. by G. Vermes [World Publishing Co., 1962] *loc. cit.*) regards Hyrcanus II (67, 63–40 B.C.) as the Wicked Priest.

42. Cross, *Library,* pp. 127–160.

43. *Ibid.,* p. 140.

44. See, e.g., Stegemann, *op. cit.,* pp. 111–114. He takes it as a reference to Jonathan's capture and execution by the Greek general Tryphon (cf. 1 Macc 13). Incidentally, among the Hasmonean rulers, Aristobulus I (104–103 B.C.) and Alexander Jan-

naeus (103–76 B.C.) are known to have suffered from severe diseases. Some scholars thus name Alexander Jannaeus to be the Wicked Priest. See, e.g., J. Carmignac, *Les Textes de Qumran* (Paris: Editions Letouzey et Ané, 1963) p. 108.

45. Cross relates it to Simon who was assassinated while drunk (*op. cit.,* pp. 143–146). But the text says: "He walked in the way of drunkenness" (i.e., a habit of heavy drinking).

46. Stegemann interprets the phrase to mean "in a foreign land" (*op. cit.,* pp. 114–115), but this passage is definitely eschatological.

47. W. H. Brownlee, "The Wicked Priest, the Man of Lies, and the Righteous Teacher—The Problem of Identity," *JQR* 83 (1982) p. 4.

48. For the question of the sectarian calendar, cf. A. Jaubert, "Le Calendrier des Jubilés et de la Secte de Qumrân: Ses origines bibliques," *VT* 3 (1955) pp. 250–264. This calendar, according to Jaubert, is also used by the Priestly author of the Tetrateuch, the writers of the late books of the Old Testament (Ezekiel, Haggai, Zechariah, Ezra, Nehemiah, and the Chronicler), and those of the pseudepigraphical books such as Jubilees and I Enoch 72–82. Thus this calendrial system was in use from the exilic time to the Christian era. Cf. J. C. VanderKam, "The Origin, Character, and Early History of the 364-Day Calendar: A Reassessment of Jaubert's Hypothesis," *CBQ* 41 (1979) pp. 390–411. VanderKam suggests that the lunar calendar began to be used in the temple because it was forced upon them as the official cultic calendar by Antiochus IV, a fierce Greek aggressor in 167 B.C. The Hasidim who fought against the Greek king with the Maccabean family held fast to the traditional Zadokite priestly solar calendar. The Qumran Essenes inherited this calendrial tradition. See his "2 Maccabees 6, 7a and Calendrical change in Jerusalem," *Journal for Study of Judaism* 12 (1981) pp. 52–74. Disagreeing with VanderKam, P. R. Davies thinks that the solar calendar had already been abandoned by Judaism soon after the exile, but exilic communities like the Essenes preserved it. See his "Calendrical Change and Qumran Origin: An Assessment of VanderKam's Theory," *CBQ* 45 (1983) pp. 80–89.

49. Cf. S. Talmon, "The Calendar Reckoning of the Sect from the Judaean Desert," *Scripta Hierosolymitana* IV (Jerusalem: Magness Press, 1965) p. 167.

50. Cf. L. Schiffman, *The Halakha at Qumran, and Sectarian Law in the Dead Sea Scrolls: Courts, Testimony and the Penal Codes* (Scholars Press, 1983).

51. See a report of this conference in *The Biblical Archaeology Review* 10 (July/August, 1984) pp. 17f. Unfortunately, a complete publication of this important letter will not be made soon.

52. A. S. van der Woude, "Wicked Priest or Wicked Priests? Reflections on the identification of the Wicked Priest in the Habakkuk Commentary," *JJS* 33 (1982) pp. 349–359.

53. W. H. Brownlee, *op. cit.*

54. A. S. van der Woude, *op. cit.,* pp. 357f. He thinks that the Teacher died from this persecution and that it fits in the historical context in terms of his age (presumably seventy years old). But the text is not necessarily interpreted to mean his death. Cf. G. Vermes' rendering in *The Dead Sea Scrolls in English* (Penguin Books, 1962) pp. 241f.

55. Josephus, *Ant.* 13:288–298. For this identification, see J. Murphy-O'Connor, *RB* 81 (1974) pp. 239–242, and J. H. Charlesworth, *RQ* 10 (1980) pp. 223f.

56. S. Freyne, *Galilee from Alexander the Great to Hadrian: 323 B.C.E. to 135 C.E. A Study of Second Temple Judaism* (M. Glazier and the University of Notre Dame Press, 1980) pp. 241f.

57. S. Zeitlin, "A Survey of Jewish Historiography: From the Biblical Books to the *Sefer ha-Kabbalah* with Special Emphasis on Josephus," *JQR* 60 (1969) p. 67.

58. *Ibid.,* p. 48.

59. For criticism of Josephus' inaccuracy, see S. J. D. Cohen, *Josephus in Galilee and Rome, His Vita and Development as a Historian* (Leiden: Brill, 1979).

60. Cf. M. Broshi, "The Credibility of Josephus," *JJS* 33 (1982) pp. 379f.

61. *Ibid.,* p. 382.

62. See, e.g., M. Smith, "Zealots and Sicarii, Their Origins and Relation," *HTR* 64 (1971) pp. 1–19; D. M. Rhoads, *Israel*

in Revolution 6–74 C.E.: A Political History Based on the Writings of Josephus (Fortress, 1976); R. A. Horsley, "Josephus and the Bandits," *JSJ* 10 (1979) pp. 37–63. Horsley indicates that a popular messianic movement was operative particularly among the Jewish masses. See his "Popular Messianic Movements around the time of Jesus." *CBQ* 46 (1984) pp. 471–495.

63. David took a census of his people, an act which was punished by God (2 Sam 24:1–17; 1 Chr 21).

64. M. Hengel, *Die Zeloten* (Leiden: Brill, 1976, 2nd ed.) p. 337.

65. W. Farmer attempts to trace the direct ideological continuity from the Maccabeans to the Zealots. See his *Maccabees, Zealots, and Josephus* (Columbia University Press, 1956). See also Hengel, *op. cit.*, p. 89, etc.; S. Applebaum, "The Zealots: The Case for Reevaluation," *Journal of Roman Studies* 61–62 (1971–72) pp. 159ff.; D. M. Rhoads, *op. cit.*, pp. 54ff.

66. Cf. Applebaum, *op. cit.*, p. 159; M. Stern, "Society and Religion in the Second Temple Period," in *The World History of the Jewish People*, ed. by Avi-Yona & Z. Bares (Jerusalem: Masad Publication Ltd., 1977) p. 280; S. Spero, "In Defence of the Defenders of Masada," *Tradition* 11 (1970) pp. 31–43.

67. E. Schürer, *Geschichte des jüdischen Volkes im Zeitalter Jesu Christi* (Leipzig, 1886–1890).

68. Y. Yadin, *Masada, Herod's Fortress and the Zealots' Last Stand* (Random House, 1966).

69. M. Hengel, "Zeloten und Sikarier," in *Josephus-Studien, Otto Michel zum 70 Geburstag gewidmet*, ed. by O. Betz, *et. al.* (Göttingen: Vandenhoeck & Ruprecht, 1974) pp. 189f. See also his *Zeloten*, pp. 47–54.

70. Cf. Y. Meshorer, *Jewish Coins of the Second Temple Period*, tr. by I. H. Levine (Tel Aviv: Am Hassefer, 1967) pp. 88–91, 154–158.

71. Hengel, *Zeloten*, p. 66.

72. Smith, *op. cit.*, pp. 10f. See also Hengel's rebuttal in "Zeloten und Sikarier," pp. 184f.

73. *Op. cit.*, pp. 11, 16. Therefore, "Simon surnamed the Zealot" in Luke 6:15 and Acts 1:13 should mean "zealous one" not "Zealot."

74. Another area of disagreement between Hengel and Smith pertains to the basic nature of the Zealots. Hengel believes that the core of the party was made up of the lower priestly group, while Smith insists that it derived from the peasantry of Judaea. Both views, however, seem to lack hard evidence.

75. Sulpicius Severus (c. 363-c. 420) wrote in his *Chronica* 2, 30, perhaps following a lost writing of Tacitus (c. 56-c. 120), that Titus ordered the temple to be burned.

76. Cf. B. Mazar, *The Mountain of the Lord: Excavation in Jerusalem, loc. cit.*

77. See N. Avigad, "The Burnt House Captures a Moment in Time," *BAR* 9 (1983) pp. 66–72.

78. See Mazar *op. cit.,* pp. 232f.

79. See M. R. Scherer, *Marvels of Ancient Rome* (New York & London: Phaidon Press, 1955) pp. 75f., plates 119–123.

80. See Mazar, *op. cit.,* p. 94.

81. Cf. Cohen, *op. cit.,* pp. 394ff.

82. See, e.g., T. Weiss-Rosmarin, "Masada Revisited," *Jewish Spectator* 34 (1969) pp. 29–32.

83. Yadin, *op. cit.,* p. 13.

84. See R. Alter, "The Masada Complex," *Commentary* 56 (1973) pp. 19–24.

85. *Ibid.,* p. 21.

86. S. Zeitlin does not regard the Sicarii at Masada as heroes because "they had no interest in the freedom of their country" (*op. cit.,* p. 61). They, he says, did not attempt to fight in defense of Jerusalem and Masada. "Masada did not fall to the Romans. . . . They simply delivered Masada to the Romans" ("The Sicarii and Masada," *JQR* 57 (1966) p. 262).

87. A recent thorough study of sources concerning the Second Revolt by P. Schäfer evaluates as reliable Eusebius, Dio, some inscription (legio XXII Deiotariana), the Muraba'at documents, and Jewish coins from this period. See his *Der Bar Kokhba-Aufstand: Studien zum zweiten jüdischen Krieg gegen Rom* (Tübingen: J. C. B. Mohr, 1981).

88. Shimon Applebaum, *Prolegomena to the Study of the Second Jewish Revolt (A.D. 132–135)* (Oxford, 1976) p. 8. His reasons for this judgment include the fact that Dio lived closer

to the event, and also that Eusebius had a bias against the Jews for he considered the Jewish misfortune to be a punishment for their sins.

89. E. M. Smallwood, *The Jews Under Roman Rule from Pompey to Diocletian* (Leiden: Brill, 1976) p. 433.

90. Y. Meshorer, *Jewish Coins of the Second Temple Period,* tr. by I. H. Levine (Tel Aviv: Am Hassefer, 1967) p. 93.

91. As for Dio's report of the construction of Jupiter's temple on the site of the Jerusalem temple, J. Wilkinson, G. W. Bowersock and others question its meaning. As they point out, ancient eyewitnesses (e.g., Origen, Jerome, and others) made mention of only two statues there. The temple of Jupiter was built farther west. Dio perhaps meant simply that the Roman temple replaced the Jewish one. Even so, however, it was offensive to the Jews. See J. Wilkinson, *Jerusalem As Jesus Knew It* (London: Thames and Hudson, 1978) pp. 178f., and G. W. Bowersock, "A Roman Perspective on the Bar Kochba War," in *Approaches to Ancient Judaism,* vol. II, ed. by W. S. Green (Scholars Press, 1980) p. 137.

92. *Op. cit.,* pp. 429 and 431.

93. Smallwood cites as the main support for her view the Roman policy of guaranteeing Jewish religious liberty (p. 431). H. Mantel, however, contends that Hadrian's policy was not really at the root of the problem for he, on the contrary, "pursued peace at all cost." See his "The Causes of the Bar Kokhba Revolt," *JQR* 58 (1968) pp. 224–242; 274–296. Denying the accuracy of the ancient information mentioned above, Mantel opts to rely on the church historian Eusebius, who cited the desire of the Jews for freedom and salvation as the reason for the war. The Bishop of Caesarea also referred to the belief in Bar Kokhba as the messiah as the second motive for the rebellion. Mantel's view, however, has failed to convince other scholars. The Romans do not seem to have been that mild or "democratic." They were often rather insensitive. Mishnah, Aboth 3:12 says that Rabbi Elazar who lived at the time of the revolt made the accusation that a man who "makes void of the covenant of Abraham" (i.e., circumcision) had no share in the world to come. Applebaum quotes Rabbi Ishmael (dead before the revolt) who commented on the ban (*op. cit.,* p. 7). He also uses

the Epistle of Barnabas 9:4 as a reference to it (*ibid.*, p. 8). It was written toward the end of the first century A.D. This reference, however, is uncertain.

94. *Op. cit.*, p. 4.

95. See also Lamentation Rabba 2, 4. These are the only references in the rabbinic literature to any direct contact between Akiba and Bar Kosiba.

96. In lieu of "and a staff shall rise from Israel" in the Hebrew text, the Septuagint has "a man shall spring out of Israel." Targum Onkelos: "when a king shall arise from Jacob, and the Messiah be anointed from Israel"; Targum Pseudo-Jonathan: "when a mighty king of Jacob's house shall reign, and the Messiah and a powerful scepter be anointed from Israel"; Fragmentary Targum and Codex Neofiti: "a king is to arise from the house of Jacob, and a redeemer and ruler from the house of Israel." CD 7:18f.: "The star is the interpreter of the Law who shall come to Damascus, as it is written 'a star shall come forth from Jacob, and a scepter shall rise from Israel." See Hengel, *Die Zeloten,* pp. 243ff.

97. For this question, see P. Schäfer, "Rabbi Aqiva and Bar Kokhba," in *Approaches to Ancient Judaism,* vol. II, ed. W. S. Green (Scholars Press, 1980) p. 118.

98. See Mur. 24, B, C, E, G; 5/6 ḤevEp 1, 4, 8, 11, 12, 14; 5/6 ḤevEp gr.

99. See Meshorer, *op. cit.,* pp. 94f., 159ff.

100. Cf. G. G. Porton, "The Grape-cluster in Jewish Literature and Art of Late Antiquity," *JJS* 27 (1976) pp. 159–76.

101. *Op. cit.,* pp. 93f.

102. *Op. cit.,* p. 58.

103. Cf. B. Lifshitz, "The Greek Documents from Nahal Seelim and Naḥal Mishmar," *IEJ* 11 (1961) pp. 60ff.

104. See Y. Yadin, *Bar-Kokhba* (Random House, 1971) pp. 130ff.

105. *Ibid.,* pp. 125f.

106. For a detailed explanation of Mur 24, see J. A. Fitzmyer, *Essays,* pp. 324–330, and M. R. Lehman, "Studies in the Muraba'at and Nahal Ḥever Documents," *RQ* 4 (1963/64) pp. 56, 72–78. The date suggested by J. T. Milik, A.D. 131 (*DJD* II, p. 67), has been rejected by other scholars in favor of 132.

107. M. Avi-Yona thinks that the rebels were rather well prepared. See his *The Jews of Palestine* (Schoken Books, 1976) pp. 12f.

108. Cf. G. W. Bowersock, *op. cit.,* p. 133.

109. Mur 43 refers to "Galileans" in Bar Kosiba's troops. But they were not the people from Galilee but from Galil from Judaea. See P. Schäfer, *Der Bar Kokhba-Aufstand,* p. 118. There is no evidence of Galilean involvement (see S. Freyne, *Galilee from Alexander the Great to Hadrian,* p. 245). Applebaum states that no single find of Bar Kosiba coins could be authenticated in the north of the country (*op. cit.,* p. 23).

110. Cf. L. Mildenberg, "Bar Kokhba Coins and Documents," *Harvard Studies in Classical Philology* 84 (1980) p. 325.

111. B. Mazar who excavated the southwestern side of the wall of Jerusalem reports that only two of Bar Kosiba's coins were discovered. He admits that it is "guesswork" but assumes Bar Kosiba's successful capture of the city. See his *The Mountain of the Lord,* p. 20. See also Applebaum, *op. cit.,* n. 241. N. Avigad, who excavated the Jewish quarter near the Temple mount, found no coins of Bar Kosiba there. See his "Archaeological Discoveries in the Jewish Quarter of Jerusalem," *Israel Museum* (1976) pp. 24f.

112. *Op. cit.,* p. 444. See also Schürer, *op. cit.,* p. 550. Eusebius also refers to Hadrian's siege of Jerusalem (*Eccl. Hist.* 4, 5, 2).

113. B. Kanael contends, on the basis of the discovered coins, that "the insurgents would have held Jerusalem for the spring (or summer) of 132 till the spring (or the summer) of 134. In the spring (or the summer) of 135 the Romans retook Jerusalem and Bar Kokhba retreated to Bether." See his "Notes on the Dates Used During the Bar Kokhba Revolt," *IEJ* 21 (1971) p. 45. But this reconstruction is highly speculative.

114. *IEJ* 12 (1962) p. 199.

3. The Significance of the Judaean Finds for Old Testament Studies

1. The Masoretic text most widely used today, *Biblia Hebraica Stuttgartensia,* ed. by K. Elliger and W. Rudolph

(Stuttgart: Deutsche Bibelgesellschaft, 1983) goes back to the edition of Aaron ben Moses ben Asher dated A.D. 1008 which was discovered by P. Kahle in the public library in Leningrad in 1926 (its siglum: B19a or L).

2. This papyrus fragment contains the Ten Commandments and Deut 6:4–5. It was acquired in Egypt in 1902 by W. L. Nash.

3. Paul de Lagarde, *Anmerkungen zur griechischen Übersetzung der Proverbien* (Leipzig: Brockhaus, 1863) p. 2.

4. Paul Kahle, "Untersuchungen zur Geschichte des Pentateuchtextes," *Theologische Studien und Kritiken* 88 (1915) pp. 299–439. Kahle also insists that there was no one original Septuagint text, but instead Greek translations of the Old Testament were made in random places and in diversified ways without textual affinity. However D. Barthélemy has proved the opposite by publishing a Greek translation of the fragments of the Minor Prophets from Naḥal Ḥever in his *Les Devanciers d'Aquila* (Leiden: Brill, 1963). This material is a revision of the Septuagint from the first century A.D.

5. See four of his articles reprinted (originally published in various journals) in *Qumran and the History of the Biblical Text,* ed. by F. M. Cross & S. Talmon (Harvard University Press, 1975).

6. *Ibid.,* p. 283.

7. *Ibid.,* p. 187.

8. *Ibid.,* p. 184.

9. S. Talmon, "The Old Testament Text," *ibid.,* pp. 36f. (This article was previously published in *The Cambridge History of the Bible,* vol. 1, ed. by P. R. Ackroyd & C. F. Evans (Cambridge: Cambridge University Press, 1970) pp. 159–199.)

10. "History of Hebrew Text," in *IDB, Suppl.* Barthélemy agrees with Cross on the identity of the Proto-Masoretic with the Babylonian text.

11. See H. J. Venetz, *Die Quinta des Psalteriums, Ein Beitrag zur Septuaginta und Hexaplaforschung* (Heidelscheim, 1974) pp. 80ff., and also D. Barthélemy, *ibid.,* and A. van der Kooij, "On the Place of Origin of the Old Greek of Psalms," *VT* 33 (1983) pp. 67–74.

12. E. Tov, *The Text-Critical Use of the Septuagint in Biblical Research* (Jerusalem: Simor Ltd., 1981) p. 260. After all, the Letter of Aristeas (written in the last third of the second century B.C. in Alexandria) tells of the Jerusalem provenance of the Greek translation of the Hebrew Torah. B. Z. Wacholder states: "A reasonable solution may be that the Septuagint represented a work of collaboration between the two main centers of third century Judaism" (*Eupolemus: A Study of Judaeo-Greek Literature* [Hebrew Union College, 1974] p. 276).

13. G. Howard, "Frank Cross and Recensional Criticism," *VT* 21 (1971) p. 442.

14. E. Tov, "A Modern Textual Outlook Based on the Qumran Scrolls," *HUCA* 53 (1982) p. 26.

15. *Qumran and the History of the Biblical Text,* pp. 325f.

16. *Ibid.,* pp. 378f.

17. P. W. Skehan, "Exodus in the Samaritan Recension from Qumran," *JBL* 74 (1955) pp. 182–187. The untimely death of the Monsignor prevented a full publication of the material from Cave IV for which he had been responsible. It will be completed and published by E. Ulrich.

18. *Ibid.,* p. 182.

19. F. M. Cross, *Library,* p. 184.

20. *Ibid.,* pp. 185f.

21. D. N. Freedman, "The Leviticus Scroll from Qumran Cave 11," *CBQ* 36 (1974) pp. 525–534.

22. *Ibid.,* p. 533.

23. *Ibid.*

24. F. M. Cross, *Library,* p. 43.

25. P. W. Skehan, "A Fragment of the 'Song of Moses' (Deut. 32) from Qumran," *BASOR* 136 (1954) pp. 12–15. Cf. also Cross, *Library,* pp. 182f.

26. F. M. Cross, "A New Qumran Fragment Related to the Original Hebrew Underlying the Septuagint," *BASOR* 132 (1953) pp. 15–26; *idem,* "The Oldest Manuscripts from Qumran," *JBL* 74 (1955) pp. 165–172.

27. E. C. Ulrich, "4QSam^c: A Fragmentary Manuscript of 2 Samuel 14–15 from the Scribe of the Serek Hay-yahad (1QS)," *BASOR* 235 (1979) pp. 1–25.

28. F. M. Cross, *BASOR* 132 (1953) p. 18.

29. The Codex Vaticanus of the Septuagint lacks "of it." See the text of 4QSam[b] published by F. M. Cross in *JBL* 74 (1955) p. 167.

30. E. C. Ulrich, *op. cit.*

31. D. Barthélemy, *Les Devanciers d'Aquila* (Leiden: Brill, 1963).

32. E. C. Ulrich, *op. cit.*

33. Cf. *ibid.,* p. 14. This type of scribal mistake is usually called "homoioteleuton."

34. E. C. Ulrich, *The Qumran Text of Samuel and Josephus* (Scholars Press, 1987).

35. In addition to Ulrich's study, cf. also the textual notes in the *Anchor Bible, I Samuel* (Doubleday, 1980) by P. K. MacCarter, Jr.

36. Cf. E. Tov, "Lucian and Proto-Lucian—Toward a New Solution of the Problem," *RB* 79 (1972) pp. 101–113. Cf. also T. Muraoka, "The Greek Texts of Samuel–Kings: Incomplete Translations or Recensional Activity?" *Abr-Nahrain* 21 (1982–83) pp. 28–49.

37. E. Tov, "The Textual Affiliations of 4QSam[a]," *JSOT* 14 (1979) pp. 37–53.

38. They were published by J. G. Janzen, *Studies in the Text of Jeremiah* (Harvard University Press, 1973) pp. 174–184.

39. Janzen provides a summary explanation of various scholarly views on this question; see *ibid.* pp. 1–9.

40. F. M. Cross, *Library,* p. 187.

41. For these textual features as well, cf. Janzen's book.

42. E. Tov, *Text-Critical Use of the Septuagint in Biblical Research,* p. 276.

43. B. J. Roberts, "The Second Isaiah Scroll from Qumran," *BJRL* 42 (1959–60) p. 143.

44. E. Y. Kutscher, *The Language and Linguistic Background of the Isaiah Scroll (1QIs[a])* (Leiden: Brill, 1979) p. 77.

45. J. Hoegenhaven, "The First Isaiah Scroll from Qumran (1QIs[a]) and the Masoretic Text. Some Reflections with Special Regard to Isaiah 1–12," *JSOT* 28 (1984) p. 25.

46. *The Dead Sea Scrolls of St. Mark's Monastery,* vol. 1 *(The Isaiah Manuscript and the Habakkuk Commentary)* ed. by M. Burrows (The American Oriental Research, 1950).

47. H. Wildberger, *Jesaja, Biblischer Kommentar Altes Testament* (Neukirchen: Neukirchener Verlag, 1966) p. 136. Other translations (KJV, NEB, JB), however, emend the word *ki* in this verse to *kᵉwîyyā* (burn or scar).

48. Cf. H. Bauer-P. Leander, *Historische Grammatik der hebräischen Sprach* (Hildescheim: Georg Olms Verlagsbuchhandlung, 1965), reprint of the 1922 edition, Section 54r.

49. W. H. Brownlee, *The Meaning of the Qumran Scrolls for the Bible with Special Attention to the Book of Isaiah* (Oxford University Press, 1964) p. 185.

50. K. Stendahl thinks that Matthew's reading stems from an intentional change. The parents did not name him, but they (impersonally) will call him Immanuel. See his *The School of Matthew and Its Use of the Old Testament* (Fortress Press, 1968) p. 98.

51. H. M. Orlinsky, "Studies in the St. Mark's Isaiah Scroll, IV," *JQR* 43 (1952–53) pp. 336f. Orlinsky published six of his articles in this series involving his study of 1QIsᵃ in various journals. He consistently attempts to defend the superiority of the Masoretic text. In fact, he concluded that the Qumran Isaiah manuscript is a vulgar text, largely if not wholly orally contrived and worthless in any study of the Masoretic text (*ibid.,* p. 339). This is, however, too tendentious a verdict to accept. J. R. Rosenbloom in *The Dead Sea Isaiah Scroll: A Literary Analysis* (Eerdmans Publishing Company, 1970) follows the same line of approach.

52. But in Habakkuk 2:15 where the same exchange is found, the Masoretic text is better.

53. Cf. K. Elliger, *Deuterojesaja, Biblischer Kommentar* XI/1 (Neukirchen: Neukirchener Verlag, 1978) pp. 21f., etc.; J. Muilenburg, *The Interpreter's Bible* 5 (Abingdon, 1956) p. 429.

54. D. Barthélemy, "Le grand rouleau d'Isaïe trouvé près de la Mer Morte," *RB* 57 (1950) p. 548.

55. W. H. Brownlee, *op. cit.,* p. 198. Cf. also J. V. Chamberlain, "The Function of God as Messianic Titles in the Complete Qumran Isaiah Scroll," *VT* 5 (1955) pp. 366f. Chamberlain tries to find messianic implication in other passages in 1QIsᵃ as well. But he seems to force the issue too far in his attempt.

56. *Ibid.,* p. 201.

57. S. Mowinckel, *He That Cometh,* tr. by G. W. Anderson (Oxford: Clarendon Press, 1959) pp. 234ff., 249.

58. C. R. North, *The Second Isaiah* (Oxford: Clarendon Press, 1964) pp. 242–246.

59. C. Westermann, *Isaiah 40–66, A Commentary* (Westminster Press, 1969) p. 207.

60. J. Lindblom, "Die Ebed Jahwe Orakel in der neuentdeckten Jesajahandschrift (DSIsa)," *ZAW* 63 (1951) pp. 246f.

61. H. M. Orlinsky, "The So-Called 'Servant of the Lord' and 'Suffering Servant' in Second Isaiah," *VT Suppl.* 14 (Leiden: Brill, 1977) p. 61.

62. Allegro, *DJD* V, pp. 31–34. Cf. L. A. Sinclair, "A Qumran Biblical Fragment: Hosea 4Q XXII[d]," *BASOR* 239 (1980) pp. 61–65.

63. See Milik, *DJD* I, pp. 77–80, and Allegro, DJD V, p. 36. Cf. L. A. Sinclair, "Hebrew Text of the Qumran Micah Pesher and Textual Traditions of the Minor Prophets," *RQ* 11 (1983) pp. 253–263.

64. See Allegro, *DJD* V, p. 64.

65. See *ibid.,* pp. 37–42.

66. See Milik, *DJD* I, p. 80, and Allegro, *DJD* V, p. 42.

67. Cf. W. H. Brownlee, *The Text of Habakkuk in the Ancient Commentary from Qumran* (Society of Biblical Literature and Exegesis, 1959) pp. 77f. This book gives a comprehensive list of textual variants of the scroll. Cf. also J. B. Harris, *The Qumran Commentary on Habakkuk* (London: A. R. Mowbray, 1966) pp. 28–35.

68. For 11QPs[a], see J. A. Sanders, *DJD* IV, and *The Dead Sea Psalms Scroll* (Cornell University Press, 1967). The fragment E of this scroll was first published by Y. Yadin in "Another Fragment (E) of the Psalm Scroll from Qumran Cave 11 (11QPs[a])," in *Textus* V, ed. by S. Talmon (Jerusalem: Magness Press, 1966) pp. 1–10 with five plates. For 11QPs[b], see J. van der Ploeg, "Fragments d'un manuscrit de Psalmes de Qumran (11QPs[b])," *RB* 74 (1967) pp. 408–412.

69. See their articles in *Textus* V.

70. Talmon, *ibid.,* p. 13.

71. Cf. *op. cit.,* and "The Qumran Psalms Scroll (11QPs[a]) Reviewed," in *On Language, Culture, and Religion: In Honor*

of Eugen A. Nida, ed. by M. Black and W. A. Smalley (The Hague: Mouton, 1974) pp. 79–99, esp. pp. 95–99. According to Sanders, S. Talmon changed his view and holds the same position as Sanders. But Talmon says that "Sanders has overstrained my own willingness to consider his point of view—willingness not to be construed as full assent" (S. Talmon, "The Emergence of Institutionalized Prayer," in *Qumrân: sa piété, sa théologie et son milieu,* ed. by M. Delcor (Louvain: Louvain University Press, 1978) p. 275, n. 24).

72. P. W. Skehan, "Qumran and Old Testament Criticism," *ibid.,* p. 164.

73. P. W. Skehan, "A Liturgical Complex in 11QPs^a," *CBQ* 35 (1973) p. 204.

74. *Op. cit.,* pp. 163–172.

75. F. M. Cross, "The History of the Biblical Text in the Light of Discoveries in the Judaean Desert," in *Qumran and the History of the Biblical Text,* p. 182.

76. P. W. Skehan, "Jubilees and the Qumran Psalter," *CBQ* 37 (1975) pp. 343–347.

77. J. A. Sanders, *DJD* IV, p. 75.

78. While Sanders follows (*DJD* IV, p. 75) M. Noth who concludes the Syriac version's dependency on the Greek ("Die fünf syrisch überlieferten apokryphen Psalmen," *ZAW* 48 (1930) pp. 12f.), Goshen-Gottstein insists that the Syriac was translated directly from the Hebrew original as the Greek Ps 151 was (*op. cit.,* p. 32, n. 45). Cf. also J. Strugnell, "Notes on the Text and Transmission of the Apocryphal Psalms 151, 154 (= Syr. II) and 155(= Syr. III)," *HTR* 59 (1966) pp. 257–281.

79. M. Dahood, *The Anchor Bible, Psalms* III (Doubleday, 1970) p. 231.

80. Hans-Joachim Kraus, *Psalmen* 2 *(Biblischer Kommentar Altes Testament)* (Neukirchen: Neukirchener Verlag, 1961) p. 895.

81. *Op. cit.,* pp. 262f.

82. Cf. P. W. Skehan, "Qumran and Old Testament Criticism," p. 171.

83. J. M. P. van der Ploeg & A. S. van der Woude, *Le Targum de Job de la Grotte XI de Qumran* (Leiden: Brill, 1971).

84. M. Sokoloff, *The Targum to Job from Qumran Cave XI* (Ramat-Gan: Bar-Illan University, 1974) p. 6; R. Weiss, "Recensional Variations between the Aramaic Translation to Job from Qumran Cave 11 and the Masoretic Text," *Shnaton* 1 (1975) pp. 123–127. Some others think that the Hebrew original of this Targum was different from the Masoretic text. See, e.g., J. Jongeling, C. L. Labuschagne, & A. S. van der Woude, *Aramaic Texts from Qumran* (Leiden: Brill, 1976) p. 7.

85. *Library,* p. 34, n. 48. Cf. also M. McNamara, *Targum and the New Testament* (Eerdmans, 1972) pp. 63–65.

86. Other ancient versions agree with the Masoretic text. This passage is cited in B. Jongeling, "The Job Targum from Cave 11 (11QtgJob)," *Folia Orientalia* 15 (1974) pp. 191f.

87. Rabbinic views of Job recorded in the Babylonian and Jerusalem Talmuds vary considerably, ranging from praise for him as a "righteous proselyte" to condemnation as a Gentile whom God would banish from the next world. Cf. "Job, in the Aggadah," in *Encyclopedia Judaica* (Jerusalem: Keter Publishing Company, 1971).

88. Van der Ploeg and van der Woude, *op. cit.,* pp. 2–4.

89. J. A. Fitzmyer, "Some Observations on the Targum of Job from Qumran Cave 11," *CBQ* 36 (1974) p. 510.

90. Muraoka agrees with the editors on (1), but differs on (3). See his "The Aramaic of the Old Targum of Job from Qumran Cave XI," *JJS* 25 (1974) pp. 425–443. As for the language of the Genesis Apocryphon, E. Kutscher (with whom Muraoka concurs) contends that it was the western Aramaic of the first century A.D. See his "The Language of Genesis Apocryphon: A Preliminary Study," in *Scripta Hierosolymitana* IV, *Aspects of the Dead Sea Scrolls,* ed. by C. Rabin and Y. Yadin (Jerusalem: Magnes Press, 1965) p. 22.

91. J. A. Fitzmyer, *op. cit.,* pp. 512, 517.

92. C. Rabin, "Hebrew and Aramaic in the First Century C.E.," in *The Jewish People in the First Century,* vol. II ed. by S. Safrai & M. Stein (Assen/Amsterdam: Van Gorcum, 1976) p. 1031.

93. Cf. J. A. Fitzmyer, *A Wandering Aramean: Collected Aramaic Essays* (Scholars Press, 1979) p. 6.

94. For discussion concerning these words of the New Testament, see J. A. Emerton, "MARANATHA and EPHATHA," *JTS* 18 (1967) pp. 427–431; *idem,* "The Problem of Vernacular Hebrew in the First Century A.D. and the Language of Jesus," *JTS* 74 (1972) pp. 18–21.

95. K. Beyer, *Semitische Syntax im Neuen Testament,* Bd. I (Göttingen: Vanderhoeck & Ruprecht, 1968). But some scholars doubt that there was such influence (e.g., Fitzmyer, *ibid.,* pp. 12–14).

96. M. H. Segal, *A Grammar of Mishnaic Hebrew* (Oxford: Clarendon Press, 1927) pp. 1–20.

97. H. Birkeland, *The Language of Jesus* (Oslo: Jakob Dywad, 1954) pp. 25f.

98. This description is used in J. Barr, "Which Language Did Jesus Speak?—Some Remarks of a Semitist," *BJRL* 53 (1970–71) pp. 9–29.

99. E. Y. Kutscher, "Aramaic," in *Encyclopedia Judaica,* p. 1028. See also his "The Language of the 'Genesis Apocryphon,'" in *Scripta Hierosolymitana* IV, pp. 1–35, and J. A. Fitzmyer, *The Genesis Apocryphon of Qumran Cave 1: A Commentary* (Rome: Pontifical Biblical Institute, 1966) pp. 17–25.

100. A bibliographical reference for this matter is found in E. Schürer, *The History of the Jewish People in the Age of Jesus Christ,* vol. II, rev. ed., p. 24, n. 90; p. 25, n. 92–95. Cf. also E. M. Meyers & J. F. Strange, *Archaeology, the Rabbis and Early Christianity* (Abingdon, 1981) pp. 74–78.

101. These Aramaic texts are collected and translated by J. A. Fitzmyer and D. J. Harrington in their *A Manual of Palestinian Aramaic Texts: Second Century B.C.–Second Century A.D.* (Rome: Biblical Institute, 1978). Cf. Fitzmyer's evaluation of scholarly research regarding this question in "Methodology in the Study of the Aramaic Substratum of Jesus' Sayings in the New Testament," in *Jésus aux origines de la christologie,* ed. by J. Dupont (Louven: Louven University Press, 1975) pp. 73–102.

102. M. Black, *An Aramaic Approach to the Gospels and Acts* (Oxford: Clarendon Press, 1967, 3rd. ed.) pp. 73–102.

103. *JNES* 31 (1972) p. 60. Likewise J. A. Fitzmyer says: "So in the long run the bulk of Aramaic texts from Qumran remains the best available material for the study of the Aramaic

substratum of the sayings of Jesus in the Greek New Testament" ("Methodology in the Study of the Aramaic Substratum of Jesus' Sayings in the New Testament," p. 86).

104. Fitzmyer, *ibid.,* pp. 92f.

105. *Ibid.,* pp. 94f.

106. Fitzmyer, "The Contribution of Qumran Aramaic to the Study of the New Testament," *NTS* 20 (1974) pp. 386–391.

107. E.g., R. Bultmann, *Theology of the New Testament* (Scribners, 1951) vol. 1, p. 51.

108. *Op. cit.,* pp. 391–394.

109. "'Peace upon Earth Among Men of His Good Will' (Lk 2:14)," in *Essays on the Semitic Background of the New Testament,* pp. 101–104.

110. R. Brown, *The Birth of Messiah,* p. 246.

111. For this question, see *ibid.,* pp. 244–250. Fitzmyer points out literary parallels between the birth story of Noah in the Genesis Apocryphon and the stories of child Jesus in the Gospels. See *NTS* 20 (1974) pp. 388f.

112. David Flusser, "Healing Through the Laying-On of Hands in a Dead Sea Scroll," *IEJ* 7 (1957) pp. 107–108. A. Dupont-Sommer speculates that the Qumran sect inherited this practice from Babylonian exorcism ("Exorcismes et guérisons dans des écrits de Qumran," *VT Suppl.* 7 [1960] pp. 246–261).

113. Fitzmyer furthermore gives a list of literary parallels between the New Testament and the Aramaic documents from Qumran. See *NTS* 20 (1974) pp. 400f. Cf. also his commentary on Luke in the *Anchor Bible* series (Doubleday, 1981) p. 117.

114. *CBQ* 32 (1970) p. 529. This does not mean that the sectarians were not familiar with Mishnaic Hebrew; some Mishnaic influences are detectable in the style and vocabulary of their language.

115. C. Rabin, "Hebrew and Aramaic in the First Century," in *The Jewish People in the First Century,* vol. II, p. 1018. His contention that "the Pharisees abandoned the use of biblical Hebrew in order to distinguish their own teaching clearly from that of the sectarians" (*ibid.,* p. 1015) stems from his view that the sect branched off from the Pharisees and, therefore, was not the Essenes. As considered in the previous chapter, this view has

not gained wide acceptance. Cf. also his *Qumran Studies* (Oxford: Oxford University Press, 1957) pp. 67–69.

116. "Hebrew and Aramaic in the First Century," p. 1036. M. Greenfield describes it: "Hebrew was used in the village of Galilee during this period, Aramaic was used in the Jewish urban areas and in the Galilee, while Greek was used in the Hellenistic cities throughout the land and along the coast" in his "The Language of Palestine, 200 BCE–200 CE," in *Jewish Languages: Themes and Varieties,* ed. H. Paper, p. 149.

117. For a meager amount of Latin inscriptions from Palestine of this period, cf. E. M. Meyers and J. F. Strange, *op. cit.,* pp. 88–90. For example, at the well-known Jewish catacombs in Beth Shearim, the great majority of the inscriptions are Greek and only about ten percent are Hebrew or Palmyrene (cf. J. Kaplan, "'I, Justus, Lie Here': The Discovery of Beth Shearim," *BA* 40 [1977] p. 170).

118. Cf. V. Tcherikover, *Hellenistic Civilization and the Jews,* tr. by S. Applebaum (The Jewish Publication Society of America, 1959) pp. 40f.

119. For a discussion of this passage, see J. N. Svenster, *Do You Know Greek? How Much Greek Could the First Jewish Christians Have Known?* (Leiden: Brill, 1968) pp. 65–71.

120. T. Rajak, *Josephus: the Historian and His Society* (Fortress Press, 1983) p. 63. Cf. also pp. 46–64.

121. See S. Liebermann, *Greek in Jewish Palestine in the II–IV Centuries CE* (Jewish Theological Seminary of America, 1942) p. 30.

122. *Op. cit.,* p. 188.

123. *Ibid.,* p. 189. He goes as far as to say that "the obvious assumption is that they (the Jewish Christians) often had a better knowledge of Greek than their Jewish compatriots on the whole, since they belonged to a Christian congregation" *(ibid.).*

124. *Op. cit.* p. 1007.

125. Cf. Fitzmyer, *op. cit.,* pp. 507, 516.

126. M. Hengel, *Acts and the History of Earliest Christianity* (Fortress Press, 1980) p. 71.

127. Cf. C. F. D. Moule, "Once More, Who Were the Hellenists?" *Expository Times* 70 (1958–59) pp. 100–102; J. A. Fitzmyer, "Jewish Christianity in Acts in the Light of the Qumran

Scrolls," in *Essays in the Semitic Background of the New Testament,* pp. 277–278; E. Haenchen, *The Acts of the Apostles: A Commentary* (Westminster Press, 1971) p. 260.

128. O. Cullmann, "The Significance of the Qumran Texts for Research into the Beginning of Christianity," in *The Scrolls and the New Testament,* ed. by K. Stendahl (Harper and Brothers Publishers, 1957) pp. 26–30. C. S. Mann also insists that the "hellenistai were hellenized Jews" in J. Munck, *The Acts of the Apostles, The Anchor Bible* Series 31 (Doubleday, 1967) pp. 301–304.

4. The Significance of the Judaean Finds for New Testament Studies

1. *The Mishnah,* tr. by H. Danby (Oxford: Oxford University Press, 1933) p. 148. The same sentence appears also in Eduyoth 5,2.

2. The Sibylline Oracles 4:165 also mentions: "and wash your whole bodies in ever-running rivers." This passage is dated to the second half of the first century A.D. (cf. H. C. O. Lanchester, "The Sibylline Oracles," in *Apocrypha and Pseudepigrapha of the Old Testament,* ed. by R. H. Charles [Oxford: Oxford University Press, 1913] p. 373).

3. W. H. Brownlee, "John the Baptist in the New Light of Ancient Scrolls," in *The Scrolls and the New Testament,* ed. by K. Stendahl (Harper & Brothers, 1957) pp. 33–53: J. Jeremias, "Der Ursrung der Johannestaube," *ZNW* 28 (1929) pp. 312–320; *idem,* "Proselytentaube und Neues Testament," *TZ* 5 (1949) pp. 418–428.

4. C. H. H. Scobie, "John the Baptist," in *The Scrolls and Christianity,* ed. by M. Black (S.P.C.K., 1969) pp. 58–69. The proselyte baptism, however, antedates Christian baptism. H. H. Rowley states: "It is unlikely that Judaism first established this rite during the early days of the church, and borrowed it from a body to which it was so strongly opposed." See his "The Baptism of John and the Qumran Sect," in *New Testament Studies in Memory of T. W. Manson,* ed. by A. J. B. Higgins (Manchester: Manchester University Press, 1959) p. 225. H. Koester also

denies the relationship because there was no eschatological component in the proselyte baptism. See his *History and Literature of Early Christianity,* vol. 2 (Fortress Press, 1982) p. 72.

5. R. Schütz, *Johannes der Täufer* (Zürich/Stuttgart: Zwingli Verlag, 1967) p. 43.

6. Cf. W. H. Brownlee, *op. cit.,* pp. 38f. B. Pixner contends that there was a quarter in Jerusalem (the southwestern hill of the city) inhabited by the Essenes in ancient time. Some evidence of Essene *mikveh,* according to him, is still detectable there. See his *An Essene Quarter in Mount Zion?* (Franciscan Printing House, 1976) pp. 272ff.

7. G. Vermes takes this word to signify the sacred meal of the sect. See his *The Dead Sea Scrolls in English* (Penguin Books, 1975, 2nd ed.) p. 27. But the passages cited in the following clearly indicate the lustral rite using water.

8. B. E. Thiering, "Inner and Outer Cleansing at Qumran as a Background to New Testament Baptism," *NTS* 26 (1980) pp. 266–277.

9. Mt 3:1 ("in the wilderness of Judaea"). But his activity was perhaps not confined to Judaea. Luke separates Jordan from the Judaean wilderness (3:2–3), perhaps because, as scholars note, he was not familiar with the geography of Judaea. Jn 1:28 locates the cite of his baptismal ministry in "Bethany across the Jordan." But such a town beyond the Jordan River has not been located. Therefore, Origen, who lived in Palestine in the third century A.D., identified it as Bethabara (his Commentary on John 1:28). This town is mentioned in the Babylonian Talmud Pesahim 53a. Furthermore, Jn 3:23 says that he was baptizing people "at Aenon near Salim, because there was much water there." The location of Aenon is also vague; one tradition places it in Perea beyond the Jordan, another tradition fixes it eight miles south of Scythopolis (Beth-shan) in the Jordan valley west of the ruin, an area abundant in water. The name "Aenon" is from the Aramaic word for "spring." The third possibility is modern 'Ainun, four miles southwest of Shechem, in Samaria. For this question, see R. E. Brown, *The Gospel According to John I-XII, The Anchor Bible* (Doubleday, 1966) p. 151.

10. A number of scholars have suggested that Luke 1–2 perhaps originated with the followers of John the Baptizer. Cf.

W. Wink, *John the Baptist in the Gospel Tradition* (Cambridge University Press, 1968) pp. 60–79. Cf. also R. E. Brown, *The Birth of Messiah*, pp. 265–279.

11. Cf. 1QS 6:4–5. A pejorative use of *yayin* is found in CD 8:9–11 (= 19:22–23). According to St. Jerome (*Adv. Jovinianum* II, 14), the Essenes drank grape juice (*tîrōsh* in Hebrew), but not wine. A rabbinic source (Jerusalem Talmud Nedarim 40b) also distinguishes *tirōsh* from *yayin* as unfermented grape juice. J. M. Baumgarten comments: "The production of ritually pure fermented wine was, as indicated in Mishnah Tohoroth, as difficult a process as that of oil since it, too, is a liquid and constantly exposed to contamination. TYRWŠ, on the other hand, aside from its benefits with regard to sobriety, for which the Essenes were noted (*War* II, viii, 5, 133), has the considerable advantage of assured purity if the grapes are squeezed shortly before the priest pronounces the blessing" (*Studies in Qumran Law*, p. 96, n. 42). J. T. Milik, however, insists that it must have been lightly fermented sweet wine (*Ten Years of Discovery in the Wilderness of Judaea*, p. 105).

12. J. A. Fitzmyer, *Luke I-IX, The Anchor Bible*, p. 389.

13. The teaching of eschatological judgment by fire is said to have been of Iranian origin. Many scholars have indicated the probable influence of Zoroastrianism on Qumran theology; see, e.g., D. Winston, "The Iranian Component in the Bible, Apocrypha, and Qumran: A Review of the Evidence," *History of Religions* 5 (1966) pp. 183–216; J. Neusner, "Jews and Judaism under Iranian Rule: Bibliographical Reflections," *History of Religions* 8 (1968) pp. 159–177; J. C. Greenfield and S. Shaked, "Three Iranian Words in the Targum of Job from Qumran," *ZDMG* 122 (1972) pp. 37–45; S. Shaked, "Qumran and Iran: Further Consideration," *Israel Oriental Studies* 2 (1972) pp. 433–446.

14. Concerning this difference between Matthew and Luke, Fitzmyer says, "Given the form of address, 'Brood of vipers,' it is easier to see the Matthean audience as the more original" (*Luke I-IX, The Anchor Bible*, p. 467). But a pairing of these mutually unfriendly parties by Matthew (also in 16:6, 11, 12) has prompted some scholars to deny its historicity (see, e.g., J. P. Meier, "John the Baptist in Matthew's Gospel," *JBL* 99 [1980]

p. 389). Nonetheless, C. H. Krealing appears correct when he indicates that this accusation sounds a bit too bitter and specific to have been addressed to the people in general but rather to the priestly aristocracy. See his *John the Baptist* (Scribners, 1951) p. 51. Matthew uses this curse also in Jesus' denunciation of the Pharisees (12:34) and the scribes and Pharisees (23:33). In Luke it occurs only in this passage.

15. R. H. Gundry, *Matthew: A Commentary on His Literary and Theological Art* (Eerdmans, 1982) p. 46.

16. "The venom of serpents" also occurs in CD 8:9 where "serpents" are said to be "the kings of the nations." The identity of this reference is uncertain, however.

17. Mark makes no mention of baptism by fire. Does Mark include fire with the spirit as they are sometimes combined? Does he consider the judgment with fire not to be associated with Jesus' ministry? Or perhaps he did not receive the tradition concerning it, unlike the Q source.

18. For this question, see F. Lang, "Erwägungen zur eschatologischen Verkündigung Johannes des Täufers," *Jesus Christus in Historie und Theologie: Festschrift für H. Conzelmann zum 60 Geburstag,* ed. by G. Strecker (Tübingen: J. C. B. Mohr, 1975) pp. 466–473.

19. W. H. Brownlee, for example, stated: "It was John the Essene who proclaimed the coming Messianic Age in the wilderness" (*op. cit., p. 52).

20. Joseph Thomas, *Le Mouvement Batiste en Palestine et Syrie (150 av. J.-C.—300 ap. J.-C.)* (Gembloux: J. Duculot, 1935), presents a comprehensive study of this subject. Cf. also J. Daniélou, *The Theology of Jewish Christianity,* tr. by J. A. Baker (London: Darton, Longman & Todd, 1964); H.-J. Schoeps, *Theologie und Geschichte des Judentums* (Tübingen: J. C. B. Mohr, 1949) and also his shorter book, *Jewish Christianity: Factional Dispute in the Early Church,* tr. by D. R. A. Hare (Fortress Press, 1969); M. Simon, *Jewish Sects at the Time of Jesus,* tr. by J. H. Farley (Fortress Press, 1967) pp. 85–107.

21. Various parallels between the Qumran sect and the Ebionites have drawn modern scholarly attention. As we have noted in chapter 2, Teicher, for example, equated these two groups; his view, however, has not gained many supporters. But

Schoeps and others have recognized that the Ebionites were successors of "Essenism" (*Urgemiende Judenchristentum, Gnosis* [Tübingen: J. C. B. Mohr, 1956] pp. 77–86), and although this does not necessarily mean that the Qumran sectarians became the Ebionites, one cannot escape noticing the strong influence of the former on the latter.

22. *Op. cit.*, p. 110.

23. Cf., e.g., O. Cullmann, "The Significance of the Qumran Texts for Research into the Beginnings of Christianity," in *The Scrolls and the New Testament,* ed. by K. Stendahl, pp. 27–31.

24. See Acts 19:1–7. This passage reveals Luke's theological emphasis on the Holy Spirit and the ideal unity of Christianity. For this question, see E. Käsemann, "The Disciples of John the Baptist in Ephesus," in *Essays on New Testament Themes* (Fortress Press, 1982) pp. 136–148.

25. I. Rabinowitz translates *pesher* "presage" so as to underscore its prognostic sense. See his "'Pēsher/pittārōn': Its Biblical Meaning and Its Signficance in the Qumran Literature," *RQ* 8 (1973) pp. 219–32. See also critical comments on Rabinowitz's view by W. H. Brownlee in *The Midrash Pesher of Habakkuk* (Scholars Press, 1979) pp. 26–28.

26. "Le document de Qumrân sur Melkisédeq," *RQ* 7 (1969–71) pp. 360f.

27. The Hebrew word *pesher* occurs only once (Eccl. 8:1) in the Old Testament. In the Hebrew portion of Daniel, several words (e.g., *byn, yd', śkl, ngd*) are used to convey the same notion as *pesher*.

28. Cf. K. Elliger, *Studien zum Habakkuk-Kommentar vom Toten Meer* (Tübingen: Mohr-Siebeck, 1953) pp. 118–164.

29. W. H. Brownlee raises the following six points as the purposes of pesher: (1) to vindicate the Teacher of Righteousness against his enemies, (2) to vindicate the followers of the Teacher against their opponents, (3) to strengthen the faith and endurance of the Teacher's adherents, (4) to warn the wavering of the dangers of apostasy, (5) to prepare the way of Yahweh in the Judaean wilderness through study and obedience, and (6) to instruct the Community regarding the future (*op. cit.*, pp. 35f.).

30. This does not mean that the Qumran writers never cited the Old Testament in the same sense as in the original book. J. A. Fitzmyer (*Essays,* pp. 18–20) lists the following passages which contain this type of quotation: CD 7:8–9 (Num 30:17), CD 9:2 (Lev 19:18), CD 9:5 (Nahum 1:2), CD 9:7–8 (Lev 19:17), CD 10:16f. (Dt 5:12), CD 16:6f. (Dt 23:24), CD 3:7 (Dt 9:23).

31. See M. P. Horgan, *Pesharim: Qumran Interpretations on Biblical Books* (Catholic Biblical Association, 1979) p. 31.

32. D. Patte, *Early Jewish Hermeneutic in Palestine* (Scholars Press, 1975) p. 307.

33. A. Wright, *The Literary Genre Midrash* (Alba House, 1967) p. 74.

34. R. Bloch, *Dictionaire de la Bible, Supplément,* ed. by L. Pirot, *et al.* (Paris: Letouzey et Ané, 1957) cols. 1263–81; ET by M. H. Callaway in *Approaches to Ancient Judaism Theory and Practice,* ed. by W. S. Green (Scholars Press, 1978) pp. 29–50.

35. In his opinion, the contemporarization of the text is exactly that which marks the difference between midrash and pesher. See his "Unriddling the Riddle: A Study in the Structure and Language of the Habakkuk Pesher (1QpHab)," *RQ* 3 (1961) pp. 323–64.

36. *Ibid.* He indicates that in the rabbinic midrash, the Aramaic word *petirah* stands in place of the Hebrew *pesher* and that some midrash even contains as well the interpretation of dreams.

37. *Op. cit.,* and his other books and articles.

38. *Op. cit.,* p. 85. He also points out the differences as well. Pesher (1) is apocalyptic, (2) does not list other biblical books or the opinions of teachers, (3) does not derive essentially from the text itself, (4) is less detailed than midrash, (5) does not elucidate the biblical text as does midrash, but instead determines the application of certain biblical prophecies to current events (*ibid.,* pp. 81f.).

39. L. H. Schiffman, *The Halakha at Qumran* (Leiden: Brill, 1975) p. 60.

40. J. Neusner, *The Rabbinic Traditions about the Pharisees Before 70,* Part III (Leiden: Brill, 1971) pp. 76f.

41. *Op. cit.,* p. 309.

42. Modern scholars fail to reach a consensus in this regard. See G. Brooke, "Qumran Pesher: Towards the Redefinition of a Genre," *RQ* 40 (1981) pp. 483–503.

43. The authoritative source of the Qumran-style scriptural interpretation is undoubtedly the Teacher of Righeousness. There is also a counsel consisting of twelve men and three priests who are "perfect in all which is revealed from the entire Torah" (1QS 8:1–2). They are called *maskîl* (wise teacher). The rest of members of the sect are instructed by them regarding the truths (which are purportedly revealed only to them). For this question, see L. H. Schiffman, *op. cit.,* pp. 22–32. We read in 1QS 6:6–8: "And in a place where the ten are, let there not lack one who studies the Law day and night continuously, according to the arrangement, one after another. And let the many watch together the third part of every night of the year, reciting from the book, studying commandment and bless together." W. H. Brownlee comments: "If they did this in shifts, the whole of every night as well as every day would be filled with interpretation" (*op. cit.,* p. 188).

44. J. de Waard's *A Comparative Study of the Old Testament Text in the Dead Sea Scrolls and in the New Testament* (Leiden: Brill, 1965) suggests that some quotations of the Old Testament found in the New Testament (e.g., Acts 13:17–41; 15:16; etc.) seem to indicate the fact that the Hebrew text used by the author might be the same as the one which the sectarians possessed. This is a good possibility, but is not a firmly established fact.

45. *Introduction to the Old Testament* (Harper, 1941) p. 511.

46. *Paul's Use of the Old Testament* (London: Oliver & Boyd, 1957) p. 12.

47. *Ibid.,* p. 15.

48. See his "The Use of Explicit Old Testament Quotations in the Qumran Literature and in the New Testament," in *Essays,* pp. 3–16. See also C. F. D. Moule, "Fulfillment-Words in the New Testament: Use and Abuse," *NTS* 14 (1968) pp. 293–320. For a comparison of quotation formulae between the Mishnah and the New Testament, see B. M. Metzger, "The Formulas

Introducing Quotations of Scripture in the New Testament and the Mishnah," *JBL* 70 (1951) pp. 297–307. Fitzmyer says, "The Hebrew equivalents of the New Testament introductory formulae are far more numerous in the Qumran literature than in the Mishnah. Consequently, the comparative study of the Qumran and the New Testament introductory formulae would tend to indicate a closer connection of the New Testament writings with the contemporary Qumran material than with the later Mishnah" (*op cit.*, pp. 15f.).

49. *Ibid.*, p. 13.

50. B. Lindars, *New Testament Apologetic* (London: SCM Press, 1961) p. 192.

51. Matthew's "the land of Judah" is a contemporization of the old name, "Ephratha."

52. See, e.g., B. Gärtner, "The Habakkuk Commentary (DSH) and the Gospel of Matthew," *Studia Theologica* 8 (1955) pp. 1–24; R. H. Gundry, *The Use of the Old Testament in St. Matthew's Gospel with Special Reference to the Messianic Hope* (Leiden: Brill, 1967) pp. 155–159. Stendahl compares Matthew with the Habakkuk Commentary, but the Damascus Document seems to provide closer parallels. This fact is also clearly seen in the quotation formulae which we have noted above.

53. Mishnah Sanhedrin 2,4 permits the king to have eighteen wives. It is not expressly stated how many wives an ordinary man could have, but there are references to four wives (e.g., Ketuboth 10, 5) and five wives (Kerithoth 3, 7).

54. This law refers specifically to the king, but it can also be taken to mean the commoners as well (cf. J. R. Mueller, "The Temple Scroll and the Gospel Divorce Texts," *RQ* 10 [1980] p. 251).

55. Cf. Chaim Rabin, *The Zadokite Fragments*, p. 17.

56. Cf. J. R. Mueller, *op. cit.*, pp. 255f.

57. F. W. Beare, *The Gospel according to Matthew*, pp. 389f.

58. Cf. Babylonian Talmud, Shabbat 128b. For this question, see L. H. Schiffman, *The Halakha at Qumran*, p. 122.

59. Paul's quotation agrees with the Septuagint as against the Masoretic text which has "by God" but lacks "on a tree."

60. For a detailed exegesis of Gal 3:6–14, see H. D. Betz, *Galatians, Hermeneia* series (Fortress Press, 1979) pp. 137–153. Some scholars attempt to draw a parallel between Paul's theology of "justification by faith" and Qumran soteriology (see, e.g., W. Grundmann, "The Teacher of Righetousness of Qumran and the Question of Justification by Faith in the Theology of the Apostle Paul," in *Paul and Qumran: Studies in New Testament Exegesis,* ed. by J. Murphy-O'Connor [Priority Press, 1968] pp. 85–114). True, divine grace bestowed on powerless humans is repeatedly mentioned particularly in the Hymn Scroll, but the sectarians never accepted a teaching like "justice outside the Law" which Paul emphatically advocates (Rom 1:17; 3:21).

61. In E. E. Ellis' opinion, the pesher method is not used extensively in Paul's quotation from the Old Testament, and where it occurs, it often appears to go beyond the Greek to reflect an interpretation of the Hebrew original text. He also asserts that some of the most significant instances (e.g. Rom 12:19; 1 Cor 14:21, 15:45; 2 Cor 6:16ff.) appear to point back to pre-Pauline usage in the early church. See his *Paul's Use of the Old Testament,* p. 146.

62. Josephus reports this incident in *Ant* 13:379–383.

63. "Pesher Nahum (4QpNahum) Reconsidered," *IEJ* 21 (1971) pp. 1–12 (+pl. 1). J. A. Fitzmyer follows Yadin. See his "Crucifixion in Ancient Palestine, Qumran Literature, and the New Testament," in *To Advance the Gospel: New Testament Studies* (Crossroad, 1981) p. 132. J. M. Baumgarten disagrees with Yadin and insists that Jews never crucified but, instead, hanged offenders. See his "Does TLH in the Temple Scroll Refer to Crucifixion?" *JBL* 91 (1972) pp. 472–81. Baumgarten's assertion, however, is refuted convincingly by D. J. Halperin in "Crucifixion, the Nahum Pesher, and the Penalty of Strangulation," *JJS* 32 (1981) pp. 32–46. One may recall in this connection that the bones of a crucified Jewish man (dated the first century A.D.) were discovered in a tomb in the vicinity of Jerusalem. An iron nail was found still piercing the bones of the heel. Albeit many literary references to crucifixion, this is the only available archaeological evidence. See V. Tzaferis, "Jewish Tombs at and near Giv'at ha-Mivtar, Jerusalem," *IEJ* 20 (1970) pp. 18–32; N. Haas, "Anthropological Observations on the Skeletal Remains

from Giv'at ha-Mivtar," *ibid.,* pp. 38–59; Y. Yadin, "Epigraphy and Crucifixion," *IEJ* 23 (1973) pp. 18–22.

64. Cf. M. Wilcox, "'Upon the Tree'—Deut 21:22–23 in the New Testament," *JBL* 96 (1977) pp. 85–99.

65. Scholars have thought for many years that the author of Hebrews used the Septuagint alone, and, therefore, that the Epistle could not have been written in Palestine and for the Palestinian Jewish Christians. Recent studies, however, have shown that the question is quite complicated. See, for example, G. Howard, "Hebrews and the Old Testament Quotations," *Novum Testamentum* 10 (1968) pp. 208–216. G. W. Buchanon insists that Hebrews was written in Jerusalem before its destruction. See his *To the Hebrews, The Anchor Bible* (Doubleday, 1972) p. 263.

66. Cf. O. Cullmann, *The Christology of the New Testament,* tr. by S. C. Guthrie and C. A. M. Hall (Westminster, 1959) p. 188; G. W. Buchanon, *op. cit.,* pp. 27, 39ff.

67. The eschatological and christological reinterpretation of Ps 8:7b is also found in 1 Cor 15:27 and Eph 1:22.

68. See other examples in Hebrews 3:7ff., 10:5ff., 12:5ff.

69. See, e.g., F. Schröger, *Der Verfasser des Hebräerbriefes als Schriftausleger* (Regensburg, 1968) pp. 301–307.

70. Cf. S. G. Sowers, *The Hermeneutics of Philo and Hebrews* (Zürich: EVZ-Verlag, 1965) pp. 91f.; C. K. Barrett, "The Eschatology of the Epistle to the Hebrews," in *The Background of the New Testament and Its Eschatology: Studies in Honor of C. H. Dodd,* ed. by W. D. Davies and D. Daube (Cambridge: Cambridge University Press, 1954) pp. 363–393; R. Williamson, *Philo and the Epistle to the Hebrews* (Leiden: Brill, 1970) pp. 493–538.

71. See his "The Dead Sea Scrolls and the Epistle to the Hebrews," in *Scripta Hierosolymitana,* pp. 36–55. This theory is also held by J. Daniélou in *The Dead Sea Scrolls and Primitive Christianity,* p. 111–114, and C. Spicq, "L'Épître aux Hébreux, Apollos, Jean-Batiste, les Hellénistes et Qumrân," *RQ* 1 (1959) pp. 365–390. Spicq thinks that the author was Apollos who only knew of the baptism of John (cf. Acts 18:24f.).

72. For references to "messiah(s)," see also CD 12:23–13:1; 14:19; 20:1. These three passages of the Damascus Docu-

ment have "messiah (singular) of Aaron and Israel." Many scholars think either that the phrase means "the messiah from Aaron and (the messiah) from Israel" (e.g., Barthelemy & Milik, *DJD* I, p. 129) or that the singular form originated from the medieval copyists (e.g., K. G. Kuhn, "The Two Messiahs of Aaron and Israel," in *The Scrolls and the New Testament*, p. 59). Others disagree: G. J. Brooke, for example, proposes a view that the belief in one messiah was held by a minority of the sectarians, while the majority opinion included two messiahs. See his "The Amos-Numbers Midrash (CD 7:13b–8:1a) and Messianic Expectation," *ZAW* 92 (1980) pp. 397–404.

73. For a different and unlikely rendering of this passage, see M. Dahood, *Psalms* III, *The Anchor Bible* (Doubleday, 1970) pp. 117f.

74. This prince of Darkness is also called 'Melchiresha (king of evil)" in 4QAmram[b] and 4Q280 2, the direct opposite of Melchizedek (king of righteousness). The texts of these documents are found in P. J. Kobelski, *Melchizedek and Melchiresa'* (The Catholic Biblical Association of America, 1981).

75. This is the consensus of modern scholars. See A. S. van der Woude, "Melchisedek als himmlische Erlösergestalt in den neugefundenen eschatologischen Midraschim aus Qumran Höhle XI," *Oudtestamentische Studien* XIV (1965) pp. 354–373; J. A. Fitzmyer, "Further Light on Melchizedek from Qumran Cave 11," in *Essays*, pp. 245–267; D. Flusser, "Melchizedek and the Son of Man," *Christian News from Israel*, April, 1966, pp. 23–29; P. J. Kobelski, *op. cit.* J. Carmignac questions this view and considers Melchizedek to be a terrestrial being who was expected to reproduce the figure of the biblical Melchizedek. See his "Le document de Qumrân sur Melchisédeq," *RQ* 27 (1970) pp. 343–378. M. Delcor refutes this view, however. See his "Melchizedek from Genesis to the Qumran Texts and the Epistle to the Hebrews," *JSJ* 2 (1971) pp. 133f. In 4QAmram, Melchizedek is identified with the archangel Michael, who appears as the leader of the heavenly forces of good as in Daniel, Jude, Revelation, Jubilees, I Enoch, The Testament of Levi, and other pseudepigrapha.

76. For a detailed discussion of this point, see Kobelski, *op. cit.*, pp. 54, 59f., 62–64.

77. The "Similitudes of Enoch" (I Enoch 37–71) contains references to the son of man. No text of this portion of I Enoch has been discovered at the Qumran caves. The most recent scholarly opinion is that it is a Jewish product of the first century A.D. Cf. J. H. Charlesworth, "The SNTS pseudepigraphic Seminars at Tübingen and Paris on the Books of Enoch," *NTS* 25 (1978–79) pp. 315–23; M. A. Knibb, "The Date of the Parables of Enoch: A Critical Review," *ibid.,* pp. 345–59; C. L. Mearus, "Dating the Similitudes of Enoch," *ibid.,* pp. 360–69.

78. See W. O. Walker, "The Son of Man: Some Recent Developments," *CBQ* 45 (1983) pp. 584–607. He insists that the Son of Man Christology was born in the exegetical exercise of the early Greek-speaking Christian community. He suggests that Psalm 8 was used as a connecting link between Ps 110:1 and Dan 7:13 in this exegetical process. O. J. F. Seitz, on the other hand, thinks that Ps 80:17 served as the link. See his "The Future Coming of the Son of Man: Three Midrashic Formulations in the Gospel of Mark," *SE* VI (1973) pp. 478–94.

79. Cf. J. J. Collins, *The Apocalyptic Vision of the Book of Daniel* (Scholars Press, 1977) pp. 144ff.

80. These instances are cited in Kobelski, *op cit.,* p. 136.

81. Cf. its preliminary publication by J. A. Fitzmyer, "The Contribution of Qumran Aramaic to the Study of the New Testament," *NTS* 20 (1974) pp. 391–94, also by D. Flusser, "The Hubris of the Antichrist in a Fragment from Qumran," *Immanuel* 10 (1980) pp. 31–37.

82. P. Wernberg-Møller attempts to interpret the spirits of good and evil psychologically, not cosmologically; "Spirit" indicates a disposition or temperament resembling the rabbinic idea of good and evil *yezer* (inclination). He, therefore, discounts the alleged Zoroastrian influence. See his "A Reconsideration of the Two Spirits in the Rule of the Community (1QSerek III, 13–IV, 26)," *RQ* 3 (1961–62) pp. 413–441. True, the "psychological" implication is an important dimension of the Qumran dualism, but the cosmic dimension based on God's creation is fundamental as well.

83. D. D. Hopkins contends that Qumran dualism should be understood not simply as "black and white," for the two sides

are "neither mutually exclusive nor congruent, but rather inter-secting" (*op. cit.*, pp. 354f.).

84. E. H. Merill, *Qumran and Predestination: A Theological Study of the Thanksgiving Hymns* (Leiden: Brill, 1975) p. 58.

85. There are many scholarly works on the dualism of Zoroastrianism, Jewish apocalypticism, John, Hellenism, and Gnosticism. See, for example, O. Böcher, *Der johanneische Dualismus im Zusammenhang des nachbiblischen Judentums* (Gütersloh: Verlagshaus G. Mohn, 1965); J. H. Charlesworth, "A Critical Comparison of the Dualism in 1QS 3:13–4:26 and the 'Dualism' Contained in the Gospel of John," in *John and Qumran,* ed. by J. H. Charlesworth (London: Geoffrey Chapman, 1972) pp. 76–106.

86. Cf. R. E. Brown, "The Paraclete in the Fourth Gospel," *NTS* 13 (1966–67) pp. 113–32; Kobelski, *op. cit.,* pp. 99–114. The "spirit of Truth" is mentioned, besides the Qumran Scrolls, only in the Testament of Judah 20:1–5 in the pre-Christian Jewish literature.

87. To express this idea, scholars have often used the phrase, a "spiritualization of temple," or a "spiritual temple." See, e.g., H. Wenschkewitz, *Die Spiritualisierung der Kultusbegriffe Tempel, Priester, und Opfer im Neuen Testament, Angelos,* Beiheft 4 (Leipzig: Pfeiffer, 1932); Yves M.-J. Congar, *The Mystery of the Temple or the Manner of God's Presence to His Creatures from Genesis to the Apolcalypse,* tr. by R. E. Trevett (Newman, 1962); B. Gärtner, *The Temple and the Community in Qumran and the New Testament* (Cambridge: Cambridge University Press, 1965). R. J. McKelvey in *The New Temple: The Church in the New Testament* (Oxford: Oxford University Press, 1969) cautiously uses the term because the dichotomy between the material and the spiritual is not quite applicable to the biblical and ancient tradition. E. S. Fiorenza points out an anti-cultic meaning in the use of this word, and prefers expressions like "transference" or "reinterpretation." See her "Cultic Language in Qumran and in the New Testament," *CBQ* 38 (1976) pp. 159–77.

88. See also CD 3:18–4:10. G. Vermes and others have suggested that the council of the community which is identified with "Lebanon" in 1QpHab 12:3f. also indicates a temple. See

his *Scripture and Tradition in Judaism,* pp. 26–39. In 4QFlorilegium 1:6 the expression "sanctuary of man *(miqdāsh 'ādām)*" occurs. Some scholars have interpreted it to mean a temple-community (cf. B. Gärtner, *op. cit.,* pp. 30–42; J. M. Baumgarten, *Studies in Qumran Law,* pp. 82–83). Many other scholars translate it: "a sanctuary among men," thereby denying any symbolic implication of the temple, for the passage in question refers rather to a future temple. See, e.g., Y. Yadin, "A Midrash on 2 Sam. 7 and Ps. 1–11 (4QFlorilegium)," *IEJ* 9 (1959) pp. 95–98; R. J. McKelvey, *op. cit.,* pp. 50f. Furthermore, Yadin maintains that the Temple Scroll 29:8–10 (this section contains a statement of God's act of creating his temple) confirms this translation. See his *Megîllat Hammiqdāsh,* vol. 1, pp. 143f.; D. R. Schwartz, "The Three Temples of 4QFlorilegium," *RQ* 10 (1979) pp. 83–91.

89. Some remains of animal bones buried in the community center most likely do not indicate a practice of offering burnt sacrifices. No sacrificial altar has been discovered at Qumran. Cf. R. de Vaux, *Archaeology and the Dead Sea Scrolls,* pp. 14f.; J. M. Baumgarten, *Studies in Qumran Law,* pp. 59–61. 11QTemple 52:13–16 prohibits killing animals qualified for sacrifice outside the temple within a radius of a three days' journey, which includes Qumran. Those bones, therefore, must have come from animals unfit for sacrifices. According to CD 11:19f., sending sacrifices to the Jerusalem temple seems to have been prohibited by the sect. Josephus reports that the Essenes were barred from the precincts of the temple where sacrifices were offered because they "employed a different ritual of purification" *(Ant* 18:19). The meaning of this "different ritual" is not clear. Baumgarten's suggestion that the Essenes had "some form of segregation within the precincts of the temple" seems too vague to be convincing *(op. cit.,* p. 67). See also J. Nolland, "A Misleading Statement of the Essene Attitude to the Temple," *RQ* 9 (1978) pp. 555–562. Furthermore, Philo states that the Essenes "have shown themselves especially devout in the service of God not by offering sacrifices of animals but by resolving to sanctify their minds" *(Quod omnis probus liber sit* 75).

90. J. A. Fitzmyer, "Qumran and the Interpolated Paragraph in 2 Cor 6:14–7:1, in *Essays,* p. 217. Cf. also J. Gnilka, "2

Cor 6:14–7:1 in the Light of the Qumran Texts and the Testament of the Twelve Patriarchs," in *Paul and Qumran,* pp. 48–68. H. D. Betz argues that the addressees of this paragraph must have been Jewish Christians for whom the Law was still of central importance, and that the tenet of this passage was, therefore, "anti-Pauline." See his "2 Cor 6:14–7:1: An Anti-Pauline Fragment?" *JBL* 92 (1973) pp. 88–108. For an unknown reason, Betz says, the redaction of the Pauline corpus has transmitted this document. Incidentally, it is found in every important ancient manuscript.

91. Cf. R. J. McKelvey, *op. cit.,* pp. 126–130. Rom 12:1 also urges: "Present your bodies as a living sacrifice, holy and acceptable to God, which is your spiritual worship."

92. For this restored part, see M. P. Horgan, *Pesharim: Qumran Interpretation of Biblical Books,* p. 129.

93. The text is not clear as to whether there should be twelve men in addition to the three priests or whether the three priests were to be included in the twelve. As for "three," it is interesting to note that Peter, James, and John seem to form the inner circle among the disciples of Jesus. Paul mentions the three pillars of the Jerusalem church (Gal 2:9).

94. D. Flusser, "Qumran und die Zwölf," in *Initiation,* ed. by C. J. Bleeker (Leiden: Brill, 1965) pp. 134–146. J. M. Baumgarten elaborates further the close connection between 4QpIs[d] and Revelation 21 by pointing out that just as the former mentions the twelve priests and the twelve heads of the tribes, the latter refers to the twelve disciples and the twelve angels of the tribes (21:12). See his "The Duodecimal Courts of Qumran, Revelation, and the Sanhedrin," *JBL* 95 (1976) pp. 59–78.

95. The reasons for this view are: (1) the references to the twelve disciples in Mark (the oldest Gospel) belong to a more recent tradition, and (2) when Paul used an early tradition concerning Jesus' resurrection, the risen Lord is said to have appeared to the twelve (1 Cor 15:5). This leads Schmithals to insist that Judas' betrayal occurred after Easter. (Matthius' selection as one of the twelve apostles takes place after Jesus' ascension. See Acts 1:26.) (3) There is no evidence that the twelve disciples as a unit played an important role in the early Christian history. Paul, for instance, does not seem to have been aware of

the twelve apostles. See his *The Office of the Apostles in the Early Church,* tr. by J. E. Steely (Abingdon, 1969). Cf. also K. H. Rengstorf, "dôdeka," in *TNDT* II, p. 326.

96. B. Gärtner, *op. cit.,* p. 100.

97. G. Klinzing, *Die Umdeutung des Kultes in der Qumrangemeinde und im Neuen Testament* (Göttingen: Vandenhoeck & Ruprecht, 1971) p. 210.

98. *Op. cit.,* p. 139.

99. Some small Aramaic fragments (1Q32, 2Q24, 5Q15, 11QJN ar) also describe the new Jerusalem. Because the city plan described is too large to be realistic, scholars consider it as an "ideal" temple. The very fragmentary state in which the manuscripts were discovered prevents us from correlating them with the Temple Scroll. See J. Licht, "An Ideal Town Plan from Qumran—The Description of the New Jerusalem," *IEJ* 29 (1979) pp. 44–59.

100. *Op. cit.,* p. 217.

101. *Ibid.,* p. 225.

102. Cf. L. H. Schiffman, *Sectarian Law in the Dead Sea Scrolls,* p. 14.

103. In B. Z. Wacholder's opinion, the scroll's temple is meant to be the final and eternal one which God creates (cf. *op. cit.,* esp. pp. 21–24). If so, however, why is it necessary to give so many detailed plans for its construction? He provides no answer to this question (see p. 27).

104. Consequently, it is beyond our reach to reconstruct a comprehensive system of the Qumran temple theology. The notion of the symbolic temple is mentioned in 1QS, CD, and 1QpHab, but not in other writings, while in 1QM, 1QpPs37, 4QF1, and 11QTemple, expectations of a future and final temple are referred to. The Temple Scroll presents an actual and desirable, but not final, temple. The first three contain no anticipation of a future temple, and the second group (four documents) tender no symbolic ideas concerning the temple. The references to these three temples are scattered in these writings.

This diversity might suggest a theological evolvement in Qumran history, but it is too speculative to trace its process on the basis of the available texts. However, one fact should be stressed and that is that these references, instead of conflicting with each other, rather complement one another. The Essenes had their own theological understanding of the temple, cult, and laws, which is reflected in the writings such as CD and 11QTemple. Their criticisms of the Jerusalem officials prompted them to embrace the symbolic notion of the temple and also to stress ever strongly the temple-structure and the purity laws as seen in 11QTemple. Yet they expected that the final temple would be built by God himself.

105. Notice the ambiguity of these passages. Mark reports that the witnesses did not agree (14:56, 59). Matthew has Jesus saying: "I am able to destroy . . ." (26:61) instead of Mark's: "I will destroy . . ." (14:58). According to John 2:19, Jesus says to the Jews, "Destroy the temple, and in three days I will raise it up."

106. It, therefore, does not refer to the heavenly temple as Haenchen assumes (cf. his commentary on Acts, p. 272, n. 1). For this question, see D. Juel, *Messiah and Temple* (Scholars Press, 1977).

107. The same expression is used also in Heb 9:11 and 24.

108. *Op. cit.,* p. 85.

109. Stephen was "falsely" accused of attacking "the temple and the law" (6:13) and was quoted as saying that Jesus would destroy the temple. It is striking that this was, according to Mark and Matthew, the exact charge brought up against Jesus by false witnesses. Luke, who does not mention this indictment against Jesus in his Gospel, seems to draw a parallel between Jesus and Stephen by citing the same allegation.

110. Philo also reports the Essene communal meal (*Quod omnis liber sit* 86).

111. Cf. K. G. Kuhn, "The Lord's Supper and the Communal Meal at Qumran," in *The Scrolls and the New Testament,* pp. 67–72.

112. *Op. cit.,* pp. 10–13.

113. See his *Sectarian Law in the Dead Sea Scrolls,* pp. 191–210.

114. J. Neusner, *The Rabbinic Traditions about the Pharisees before 70,* Part III, p. 88.

115. *Ibid.,* p. 89.

116. J. Jeremias attempts to recover Jesus' words at the Last Supper. See his *The Eucharistic Words of Jesus,* tr. by N. Perrin (Fortress Press, 1966). Cf. also another excellent but shorter study by W. Marxen, *The Lord's Supper as a Christological Problem* (Facet Books, 1970) which is a more tradition-historical approach. Many scholars view the Markan passage as representing the Eucharistic liturgical formula of the Palestinian communities, while the Pauline portion, that of the Hellenistic churches. Matthew depends on Mark, and Luke seems to rely on both. Their accounts, therefore, "are concerned first and foremost, not with providing a historical report of what occurred at the last supper, but with setting out the celebration of the eucharist on the basis of Christian actions" (A. Stöger, "Eucharist," in *Sacramentum Verbi,* vol. 1 [Herder & Herder, 1970] p. 228).

117. R. Bultmann, *The Gospel of John: A Commentary,* tr. by G. R. Beasley-Murray, *et al.* (Westminster, 1971) p. 465. Even so, John clearly knew about the Lord's Supper as shown in Jesus' feeding of the multitude and also in the statement of Jesus as the bread of life (both in ch. 6).

118. J. Jeremias strongly defends the accuracy of the Synoptic Gospels' report *(op. cit.),* while others opt for John (e.g., R. E. Brown, who suggests that "for unknown reasons," before the official Passover, Jesus ate "a meal that had Passover characteristics," as John tells us. The Synoptic writers made "too quick an assumption" that it was actually Passover because of these characteristics. See his *Anchor Bible* commentary on John, p. 556). But these explanations are no more convincing than Jaubert's theory which we refer to next.

119. A. Jaubert, *The Date of the Last Supper,* tr. by I. Rafferty (Alba House, 1965).

120. For critical comments on this theory, see, e.g., R. E. Brown, *New Testament Essays* (Image Books, 1968) pp. 214–217. M. Black sees the possibility that Jesus and his disciples celebrated an "illegal Passover." Mk 14:12ff. emphasizes the secret nature of the preparation for it. See his *Scrolls and Christian Origin,* p. 201. This suggestion, however, is purely speculative.

121. See, e.g., H. Koester, *Introduction to the New Testament,* vol. II, p. 84.

122. Cf. D. E. Aune, *The Cultic Setting of Realized Eschatology in Early Church* (Leiden: Brill, 1972) pp. 37–42.

123. Cf. H. -W. Kuhn, *Enderwartung und gegenwärtiges Heil: Untersuchungen zu den Gemeindeliedern von Qumran* (Göttingen: Vandenhoeck & Ruprecht, 1966) p. 179. Cf. also R. E. Brown's commentary on John in the *Anchor Bible* series, p. cxix. Kuhn contends that this convergence of the future and the present stems from the sectarians' symbolic understanding of the temple, i.e., the community as a symbolic temple where the heavenly and earthly dwelling place of God merges (p. 185).

124. *Op. cit.*, p. 66. The Ebionites, a Jewish Christian group, practiced an annual re-enactment of the Last Supper at Passover time.

125. Cf. *ibid.*, pp. 117–122. The word Eucharist (*eucharistia*, "thanksgiving") first appears in the Didache. Jeremias, who discounts a connection between the Essene meal and the meal of the Didache, points out the difference in the ordering of the elements between the two: the former bread and *tirōsh* (grape juice): the latter, wine and bread (*op. cit.*, p. 32).

126. R. Schnackenburg, *The Gospel According to St. John*, vol. 3 (Crossroad Publishing Co., 1982) p. 45.

127. G. Vermes, "The Impact of the Dead Sea Scrolls on the Study of the New Testament," *JJS* 27 (1976) pp. 107f.

128. S. R. Isenberg, "Power through Temple and Torah in Greco-Roman Palestine," in *Christianity, Judaism and Other Greco-Roman Cults: Studies for Morton Smith at Sixty*, part II (Leiden: Brill, 1975) p. 36.

129. G. Theissen, *Sociology of Early Palestinian Christianity*, tr. by J. Bowden (Fortress Press, 1978), and *The First Followers of Jesus: A Sociological Analysis of the Earliest Christianity* (SCM Press, 1978). She is of the opinion that Jesus' movement had its root in the hinterland of Judea. Cf. also W. A. Meeks, "The Social Context of Pauline Theology," *Interpretation* 36 (1982) pp. 266–277.

130. Paul mentions "the church in . . .'s house" (Rom 16:5; 1 Cor 16:19; Philemon 2; Col 4:15) as well as "the whole church" (Rom 16:23; 1 Cor 14:23) which also assembled on occasion. But the former was, as W. Meeks states, the "basic cells" of the Christian movement. See his *The First Urban Christians: The*

Social World of the Apostle Paul (Yale University Press, 1983) p. 75.

131. *Op. cit.*, p. 42.

5. Mysticism at Qumran and in Rabbinic, Christian, and Gnostic Literature

1. Besides *rāz*, a Hebrew synonym *sôd* is also used for mystery in the Dead Sea Scrolls.

2. See R. E. Brown, "The Pre-Christian Semitic Conception of 'Mystery,'" *CBQ* 20 (1958) pp. 417–43.

3. *Ibid.*, p. 443.

4. See, e.g., *TDNT* vol. 4, p. 824.

5. J. Strugnell, "The Angelic Liturgy at Qumran—4Q Serek Šîrôt 'ôlat Haššabbat," *VT, Suppl.*, pp. 318–45.

6. The present author would like to express deep gratitude for her generosity in sharing parts of her unpublished manuscripts.

7. See A. S. van der Woude, "Fragmente einer Rolle der Leider für das Sabbatopfer aus Höhle XI von Qumran (11QSirSabb)," in *Von Kanaan bis Kerala: Festschirift für Prof. Mag. Dr. J. P. M. van der Ploeg, O.P. zur Vollendung des siebzigsten Lebensjahres am 4, Juli 1979,* ed. by W. C. Delsmann *et al.* (Kevelaer: Butzon & Bercker: Neukirchen-Vluyn: Neukirchener Verlag, 1982) pp. 311–37.

8. C. Newsom and Y. Y. Yadin, "The Masada Fragment of the Qumran Songs of the Sabbath Sacrifice," IEJ 34 (1984) pp. 77–88.

9. *Op. cit.*, p. 318.

10. *Op. cit.*, p. 320.

11. L. H. Schiffman, "Merkavah Speculation at Qumran: The 4Q Serek Shirot 'Olat ha-Shabbat," in *Mystics, Philosophers, and Politicians: Essays in Jewish Intellectual History in Honor of Alexander Altman,* ed. by J. Reinharz and D. Swetschinski (Duke University Press, 1982) p. 19.

12. W. Zimmerli says it is whitegold. See his *Ezechiel, Biblischer Kommentar* (Neukirchen-VLuyn: Neukirchener Verlag, 1959) p. 1. G. R. Driver: brass. See his "Ezekiel's Inaugural Vision," *VT* 1 (1951) pp. 60–62. G. G. Cameron: inlay. See his

Persepolis Treasury Tablets (University of Chicago Press, 1948) pp. 129–130.

13. *Op. cit.,* p. 340.

14. H. Ringgren, *The Faith of Qumran: Theology of the Dead Sea Scrolls* (Fortress Press, 1963) p. 82.

15. Schiffman notes that the multiplicity of the chariot-throne is a familiar concept in Jewish mystical literature (see his *op. cit.,* p. 42).

16. Cf. *ibid.,* p. 37.

17. The words which are used to signify "knowledge" in the Qumran Scrolls are *da'at, bīnāh, śekel, ḥokmāh, 'ormah, tūshiyyah.*

18. *Op. cit.,* pp. 115f.

19. I. Gruenwald, "Knowledge and Vision—Towards a Clarification of Two Gnostic Concepts in the Light of Their Alleged Origin," *Israel Oriental Studies* III (1973) p. 76.

20. G. Scholem, *Major Trends in Jewish Mysticism* (Schoken Books, 1961) p. 41.

21. *Ibid.,* p. 42.

22. Cf. J. T. Milik and M. Black, *The Books of Enoch* (Oxford: Clarendon Press, 1976).

23. Translation by E. Isaac in *The Old Testament Pseude-pigrapha,* vol. 1, p. 21.

24. I. Gruenwald, *Apocalyptic and Merkavah Mysticism* (Leiden/Koln: Brill, 1980) p. 36.

25. *Op. cit.,* p. 45.

26. J. T. Milik, "Turfen et Qumran, Livre du Géants juif et manichéen," in *Tradition und Glaube: Des frühe Christentum in seiner Umwelt* (K. G. Kuhn Festschrift) ed. by G. Jeremias, *et al.* (Göttingen, 1971) pp. 117–27.

27. Cf. *The Old Testament Pseudepigrapha,* p. 7.

28. *Ibid.,* p. 698.

29. *Apocalyptic and Merkavah Mysticism,* pp. 55f.

30. A. Feuillet, *Johannine Studies,* tr. by T. E. Crane (Alba House, 1965) pp. 183–214.

31. *Apocalyptic and Merkavah Mysticism,* p. 65.

32. J. M. Ford, *Revelation, The Anchor Bible* (Doubleday, 1975) p. 79.

33. *Ibid.*

34. J. W. Bowker, "'Merkabah' Vision and the Vision of Paul," *JSS* 16 (1971) pp. 157–173.

35. E. Heinnecke, *New Testament Apocrypha,* vol. 2, ed. by W. Schneemelcher and R. Mcl. Wilson (Westminster Press, 1965) p. 767.

36. *Ibid.,* p. 777.

37. *Op. cit.,* p. 79.

38. Eusebius, *Preparation for the Gospel,* IX, 28f.; Clement of Alexandria, *Stromateis,* I, 23, 155ff. For the fragments of his work, see A.-M. Denis, *Fragmenta Pseudepigraphorum quae Supersunt Graeca* (Leiden: Brill, 1970) pp. 210–216.

39. W. A. Meeks, "Moses as God and King," in *Religions in Antiquity. Essays in Memory of R. E. Goodenough,* ed. by J. Neusner (Leiden: Brill, 1968) pp. 354–371.

40. A. F. Segal, *Two Powers in Heaven* (Leiden: Brill, 1977).

41. Translation by I. Epstein in *The Babylonian Talmud* (London: Soncino Press, 1938) p. 93.

42. P. W. van der Horst, "Moses' Throne Vision in Ezekiel the Dramatist," *JJS* 34 (1983) p. 28.

43. Cited in *op. cit.,* pp. 83f.

44. For a recent analysis of this question, see C. Rowland, *The Open Heaven: A Study of Apocalyptic in Judaism and Early Christianity* (Crossroad, 1982) chap. 11.

45. *Op. cit.,* p. 85.

46. *Major Trends in Jewish Mysticism,* p. 47.

47. *Ibid.*

48. *Ibid.,* p. 359, n. 24.

49. Cf. I. Gruenwald, *Apocalyptic and Merkavah Mysticism,* pp. 93–97.

50. I. Chernus, *Mysticism in Rabbinic Judaism* (Berlin/New York: Water de Gruyter, 1982). For examples from the Tannaic midrash, see chapter 1.

51. D. J. Halperin, *The Merkabah in Rabbinic Literature* (American Oriental Society, 1980).

52. *Ibid.,* pp. 183f.

53. Cf. G. Scholem, *Jewish Gnosticism, Merkavah Mysticism, and Talmudic Tradition* (The Jewish Theological Seminary of America, 1965, 2nd ed.) pp. 5–7, and also *The Old Tes-*

tament Pseudepigrapha, vol. 1, pp. 250f. According to Scholem, a work called *the Vision of Ezekiel* is the earliest (*op cit.,* p. 5). It is not really Hekhalot literature; the word *hekhal* does not occur in the extant text. It is a midrash on Ezekiel chapter one. Many of these texts have not been published yet. For detailed explanations of the content of these writings, see *Apocalyptic and Merkavah Mysticism,* pp. 134–234.

54. *Major Trends in Jewish Mysticism,* p. 45.

55. *Op. cit.,* p. 153.

56. *Apocalyptic and Merkavah Mysticism,* pp. 235–241.

57. *Ibid.,* p. 196. He fully accepts S. Lieberman's explanation of Metatron.

58. *Ibid.,* p. 244. These quotations from III Enoch are from P. A. Alexander's translations found in *the Old Testament Pseudepigrapha,* vol. 1, p. 264.

59. This quotation is from M. S. Cohen's translation in his *The Shiur Oomah: Liturgy and Theurgy in Pre-Kabbalistic Jewish Mysticism* (The University Press of America, 1983).

60. *Jewish Gnosticism, Merkabah Mysticism, and Talmudic Tradition,* p. 37.

61. G. Scholem, *Kabbalah* (New American Library, 1978) p. 16.

62. *Op. cit.,* p. 66.

63. *Ibid.,* p. 17. For other possible Gnostic connections, see G. Quispel, "Ezekiel 1:26 in Jewish Mysticism and Gnosis," *Vigilae Christianae* 34 (1980) pp. 1–13.

64. Epiphanius, Bishop of Constantia in Cyprus about 375 A.D., mentioned more than sixty Gnostic teachers.

65. Irenaeus, *Against Heresies,* I,11,1 in *the Anti-Nicene Fathers,* ed. by A. Roberts and J. Donaldson, vol. 1 (Christian Literature Publishing Co., 1887) p. 332.

66. For a report of the discovery and acquisition of the manuscripts, see J. M. Robinson, "The Discovery of the Nag Hammadi Codices," *BA* 42 (1979) pp. 206–224.

67. Ed. by J. M. Robinson, *The Nag Hammadi Library in English* (Harper & Row, 1981) p. 7.

68. W. H. C. Frend, *The Rise of Christianity* (Fortress Press, 1984) p. 195.

69. Cf. G. Scholem, *Jewish Gnosticism, Merkabah Mysticism, and Talmudic Tradition,* p. 67f.

70. For a concise summary of these sources, see K. Rudolph, *Gnosis: The Nature and History of Gnosticism,* tr. by R. Mcl. Wilson (Harper & Row, 1983) pp. 294–298.

71. *Ibid.,* p. 297.

72. *The Nag Hammadi Library,* p. 363.

73. Cf. R. Mcl. Wilson, "Simon Dositheus and the Dead Sea Scrolls," *Zeitschrift für Religions-und Geistesgeschichte* 9 (1957) pp. 21–30.

74. Cf. R. M. Grant, *Gnosticism and Early Christianity* (Columbia University Press, 1966, 2nd ed.) chap. 3.

75. W. G. Kümmel says of 1 Corinthians: "The whole letter manifests a front against a Gnostic perversion of the Christian message which attributes to the pneumatics, as those liberated from the *sarks* (flesh), a perfect redemptive state and an unconditional moral freedom." See his *Introduction to the New Testament,* tr. by H. C. Kee (Abingdon Press, 1975) p. 274. For an excellent analysis of the Gnostic presence in Corinth, see W. Schmithals, *Gnosticism in Corinth: An Investigation of the Letters to the Corinthians,* tr. by J. E. Steely (Abingdon Press, 1971).

76. Cf. E. Lohse, *Colossians and Philemon* (Fortress Press, 1971) p. 129; E. Schweitzer, *The Letter to the Colossians: A Commentary,* tr. by A. Chester (Augusburg Publishing House, 1982) pp. 125–34; W. Schmithals, "The *Corpus Pantinum* and Gnosis," in *The New Testament and Gnosis: Essays in Honor of Robert Mcl. Wilson,* ed. by A. H. B. Logan & A. J. M. Wedderburn (Edinburgh: T. & T. Clark, 1983) pp. 117–121.

77. Cf. K. G. Kuhn, "Der Epheserbrief im Lichte der Qumran Texte," *NTS* 7 (1960–61) pp. 334–46.

78. Cf. M. Debelius and H. Conzelmann, *The Pastoral Epistles* (Fortress Press, 1972) pp. 17, 65–57.

79. Cf., e.g., R. Bultmann, *The Gospel of John: A Commentary,* pp. 7–9.

80. R. Mcl. Wilson, for instance, insists that the incipient gnostic trends in the first century should be called Gnosis distinct from the Gnosticism of the second century. See his "Nag Hammadi and the New Testament," *NTS* 28 (1982) pp. 289–302. For definitions of Gnosticism and Gnosis, see also K.

Rudolph, "'Gnosis' and 'Gnosticism'—The Problems of Their Definition and Their Relation to the Writings of the New Testament," in *The New Testament and Gnosis: Essays in Honor of Robert Mcl. Wilson,* pp. 21–37.

81. K. Rudolph, *Gnosis,* pp. 282f.

82. Cf. E. M. Yamauchi, *Pre-Christian Gnosticism: A Survey of the Proposed Evidences* (Baker Book House, 1983, 2nd. ed.) pp. 207–210.

83. A. H. Armstrong, "Gnosis and Greek Philosophy," in *Gnosis, Festschrift für Hans Jonas,* ed. by U. Bianchi, *et al.* (Göttingen: Vandenhoeck & Ruprecht, 1978) p. 101.

84. G. Quispel, *Gnosis als Weltreligion* (Zürich: Origo Verlag, 1951) pp. 9f.

85. K. Rudolph, *Gnosis,* p. 277.

86. *Against Heresies,* I,30,11.

87. G. Scholem, *Jewish Gnosticism, Merkabah Mysticism, and Talmudic Tradition,* p. 72. See also his "Jaldabaoth Reconsidered," in *Mélanges d'Histoire des Religions offerts à H.-C. Puech* (Paris: Presse Universitaires de France, 1974) pp. 405–421.

88. *Ibid.,* p. 421.

89. F. Fallon, *The Enthronement of Sabaoth: Jewish Elements in Gnostic Creation Myths* (Leiden: Brill, 1978) p. 34.

90. For Sophia, see G. M. MacRae, "The Jewish Background of the Gnostic Sophia Myth," *Novum Testamentum* 12 (1970) pp. 86–101.

91. K. W. Tröger, "The Attitude of the Gnostic Religion towards Judaism as Viewed in a Variety of Perspectives," in *Bibliothéque Copte de Nag Hammadi Section ≪Etudes≫ -1- Colloque International sur les Textes de Nag Hammadi,* ed. by B. Barc (Quebec: Les Presse de L'université Laval; Louvain: Éditions Peaters, 1981) p. 88.

92. R. M. Grant, *Gnosticism and Early Christianity,* pp. 34f.

93. Cf. Yamauchi, *op. cit.,* p. 157. According to Yamauchi, Grant later abandoned his theory.

94. B. A. Pearson also says, "Hence it seems most plausible to conclude that the earliest Gnostics were Jewish intellectuals eager to redefine their own religious self-understanding,

and convinced of the bankruptcy of the traditional verities." See his "Jewish Elements in Gnosticism and the Development of Gnostic Self-Definition," in *Jewish and Christian Self-Definition,* vol. 1, ed. by E. P. Sanders (Fortress Press, 1980) p. 159.

95. N. Dahl, "The Arrogant Archon and Lewd Sophia: Jewish Traditions in Gnostic Revolt," in *The Rediscovery of Gnosticism,* vol. 2, ed. by B. Layton (Leiden: Brill, 1981) p. 689.

96. I. Gruenwald, "Aspects of the Jewish-Gnostic Controversy," in *The Rediscovery of Gnosticism,* vol. 2, ed. by B. Layton, p. 715.

97. *Ibid.,* p. 717. In Gruenwald's opinion, the Gnostic appraoch may have stemmed from an imitation of the Christian practice. But the Christian interpreters did not deny what the Old Testament said; their method of interpretation of the Old Testament, though decidedly Christological, was similar to that of the Jewish writers. No Christian writer of the early centuries ventured to insist: "Do not think it was as Moses said" and statements to that effect.

98. *Ibid.*

99. G. Scholem, "Jaldabaoth Reconsidered," pp. 418f.

100. J. M. Robinson, "The Coptic Gnostic Library Today," *NTS* 14 (1968) p. 380.

Bibliography

Sources

The Ante-Nicene Fathers, tr. by A. Roberts and J. Donaldson, 10 vols., American ed., Eerdmans, 1951.

The Apocrypha and Pseudepigrapha of the Old Testament, 2 vols., ed. by R. H. Charles, Oxford: Clarendon Press, 1913.

The Apostolic Fathers, tr. by K. Lake (Loeb Classical Library) 2 vols., London: Heinemann, 1919.

Babylonian Talmud, Engl. tr., ed. by I. Epstein, 18 vols., London: Soncino Press, 1961.

Biblia Hebraica Stuttgartensia, ed. by K. Elliger & W. Rudolph, Stuttgart: Deutsche Bibelgesellschaft, 1967/77, 1983.

Dio Cassius, *Roman History,* tr. by E. Cary (Loeb Classical Library) Harvard University Press/London: Heinemann, 1924.

Strolls from Qumran Cave I, photo. by J. C. Trever, Jerusalem: The Albright Institute of Archaeological Research and the Shrine of the Book, 1972.

Discoveries in the Judaean Desert, Oxford: Clarendon Press,
vol. I, *Qumran Cave I,* ed. by D. Barthélemy & J. T. Milik, 1955.
II, *Les Grottes de Muraba'at,* by P. Benoit, J. T. Milik, & R. de Vaux, 1960–1.

258

III, *Les 'Petites Grottes' de Qumran,* M. Baillet, J. T. Milik, & R. de Vaux, 1962.

IV, *The Psalms Scroll of Qumran Cave 11,* J. A. Sanders, 1965.

V, *Qumran Cave 4,* J. M. Allegro, 1968.

VI, *Qumran Grotte 4,* II, R. de Vaux & J. T. Milik, 1977.

VII, *Qumran Grotte 4,* III, M. Baillet, 1982.

English tr.—A. Dupont-Sommer, *The Essene Writings from Qumran,* tr. by G. Vermes, World Publishing Co., 1962; Th. Gaster, *The Dead Sea Scriptures,* Anchor Books, 1964; G. Vermes, *The Dead Sea Scrolls in English,* Penguin Books, 1962.

Eusebius, *The Ecclesiastical History,* tr. by K. Lake (Loeb Classical Library) Harvard University Press/London: Heinemann, 1926–32.

Josephus, F., *Jewish Antiquities, Jewish War, The Life* and *Contra Apionem,* tr. by H. St. J. Thackeray, R. Marcus, and L. H. Feldman (Loeb Classical Library) London: Heinemann, 1925–65.

Midrash Rabbah, tr. by H. Freedman and M. Simon, 10 vols. London: Soncino Press, 1951.

Mishnah, tr. by H. Danby, Oxford: Oxford University Press, 1972.

Nag Hammadi Library in English, ed. by J. M. Robinson, Harper & Row, 1981.

New Testament Apocrypha, 2 vols., E. Heinnecke, tr. by W. Scheemelcher & R. Mcl. Wilson, Westminster Press, 1965.

The Old Testament Pseudepigrapha, vol. 1, ed. by J. H. Charlesworth, Doubleday, 1983.

Philo, tr. by F. H. Colson, *et al.* (Loeb Classicial Library) 10 vols., London: Heinemann, 1929–61.

Septuaginta, 2 vols., ed. by A. Rahlfs, 7th ed., Stuttgart: Privileg. Wurtt. Bibelaustalt, 1962.

Yadin, Y., *Megillat Hammiqdash,* 3 vols. Jerusalem: Israel Exploration Society, 1977 (English tr. in 1983).

Encyclopedias and Dictionaries
Encyclopedia Judaica, 10 vols., Jerusalem: Keter Publishing Co., 1971.

Interpreter's Dictionary of the Bible, ed. by G. Buttrick, 4 vols., Abingdon, 1962; supplementary vol. ed. by K. Crim, 1976.

Jewish Encyclopedia, 12 vols., ed. by I. Singer, New York-London, 1901–7.

Theological Dictionary of the New Testament, 10 vols., ed. by G. Kittel and G. Friedrich, tr. by G. W. Bromiley, Eerdmans, 1968–.

Books and Articles
Agus, A., "Some Early Rabbinic Thinking on Gnosticism," *JQR* 71 (1980) 18–30.

Aharoni, Y., *et al.,* "The Expedition to the Judaean Desert, 1960–1961," *IEJ* 11–12 (1961–62).

———, "The Cave of Naḥal Ḥever," *'Atiqot* III (1961) 146–62.

Alexander, P. S., "Comparing Merkavah Mysticism and Gnosticism: An Essay in Method," *JJS* 35 (1984) 1–17.

Allegro, J. M., *The Treasure of the Copper Scroll,* Doubleday, 1960.

Applebaum, S., "The Zealots: The Case for Reevaluation," *Journal of Roman Studies* 61–62 (1971–72) 155–170.

————, *Prolegomena to the Study of the Second Jewish Revolt,* Oxford, 1976.

Armstrong, A. H., "Gnosis and Greek Philosophy," in *Gnosis, Festschrift für Hans Jonas,* ed., by U. Bianchi, *et al.,* Göttingen: Vandenhoeck & Ruprecht, 1978, 87–124.

Avigad, N., *Discovering Jerusalem,* T. Nelson, 1983.

Avi-Yona, M., *The Jews in Palestine,* Schoken Books, 1976.

————, Avigad, N., Aharoni, Y., Dunayevsky, I., & Gutman, S., "The Archaeological Survey of Masada 1955–1956," *IEJ* 7 (1957) 1–60.

Barr, J., "Which Language Did Jesus Speak?—Some Remarks of a Semitist," *BJRL* 53 (1970–71) 9–29.

Barthélemy, D., *Les devanciers d'Aquila,* Leiden: Brill, 1963.

Baumgarten, J. M., "Does TLH in the Temple Scroll Refer to Crucifixion?" *JBL* 91 (1972) 472–81.

————, "The Duodecimal Courts of Qumran, Revelation, and the Sanhedrin," *JBL* 95 (1976) 59–78.

————, *Studies in Qumran Law,* Leiden: Brill, 1977.

Becker, J., *Das Heil Gottes: Heiles- und Sündenbegriffe in den Qumran Texten und im Neuen Testament,* Göttingen: Vandenhoeck & Ruprecht, 1964.

Betz, H. D., "2 Cor 6:14–7:1: An Anti-Pauline Fragment?" *JBL* 92 (1973) 88–108.

Birkeland, H., *The Language of Jesus,* Oslo: Jakob Dywad, 1954.

Black, M., *The Scrolls and Christian Origin: Studies in the Jewish Background of the New Testament,* Scribners, 1961.

————, *An Aramaic Approach to the Gospels and Acts,* Oxford, Clarendon Press, 1967 (3rd ed.).

————, (ed.) *The Scrolls and Christianity,* SPCK, 1969.

Bloch, R., "Midrash," *Dictionaire de la Bible,* Supplément 5, ed. by L. Pirot, *et al.,* Paris: Letouzey et Ané, 1957, cols. 1263–81 (Engl. tr. in *Approaches to Ancient Judaism* 2, ed. by W. S. Green, Scholars Press, 1978, 29–50).

Böcher, O., *Das johaneische Dualismus im Zusammenhang des nachbiblischen Judentums,* Göttingen: Verlaghaus G. Mohn, 1965.

Böhlig, A., *Mysterion und Wahrheit,* Leiden: Brill, 1968.

Bowersock, G. W., "A Roman Perspective on the Bar Kokhba War," in *Approaches to Ancient Judaism* 2, ed. by W. S. Green, Scholars Press, 1980, 131–142.

Bowker J. W., "'Merkabah' Vision and the Vision of Paul," *JSS* 16 (1971) 157–73.

Brock, R. van den, "The Present State of Gnostic Studies," *Vigilae Christianae* 37 (1983) 4–71.

Brooke, G. J., "The Amos-Numbers Midrash (CD 7:13b–8:1a) and Messianic Expectation," *ZAW* 92 (1980) 397–404.

————, "Qumran Pesher: Towards the Redefinition of a Genre," *RQ* 40 (1981) 483–503.

Broshi, M., "The Credibility of Josephus," *JJS* 33 (1982) 379–84.

Brown, R. E., "The Pre-Christian Semitic Conception of 'Mystery,'" *CBQ* 20 (1958) 417–43.

————, "The Paraclete in the Fourth Gospel," *NTS* 13 (1966–67) 113–32.

————, *The Gospel according to John, The Anchor Bible,* Doubleday, vol. 1 (1966), vol. 2 (1970).

————, *The Birth of Messiah,* Doubleday, 1977.

Brownlee, W. H., *The Meaning of the Qumran Scrolls for the Bible with Special Attention to the Book of Isaiah,* Oxford: Oxford University Press, 1964.

————, *The Midrash Pesher of Habakkuk,* Scholars Press, 1979.

————, "The Wicked Priest, the Man of Lies, and the Righteous Teacher—The Problem of Identity," *JQR* 83 (1982) 1–37.

Burgmann, H., "Wer war der 'Lehrer der Gerechtigkeit?" *RQ* 40 (1981) 553–77.

Carmignac, J., *Les Textes de Qumran,* Paris: Editions Letouzey et Ané, 1963.

————, "Le document de Qumrân sur Melkisédeq," *RQ* 7 (1969–71) 343–78.

Charlesworth, J. H. (ed.) *John and Qumran,* London: G. Chapman, 1972.

————, "The SNTS Pseudepigraphic Seminars at Tübingen and Paris on the Books of Enoch," *NTS* 25 (1978–79) 315–23.

————, "The Origin and Subsequent History of the Authors of the Dead Sea Scrolls: Four Transitional Phases Among the Qumran Essenes," *RQ* 38 (1980) 213–233.

Chernus, I., *Mysticism in Rabbinic Judaism,* Berlin/New York: Walter deGruyter, 1982.

Chiat, M. J. S., *Handbook of Synagogue Architecture,* Scholars Press, 1982.

Coggins, R. J., *Samaritans and Jews: The Origins of Samaritanism Reconsidered,* John Knox Press, 1975.

Cohen, M. S., *The Shiur Qomah: Liturgy and Theurgy in Pre-Kabbalistic Jewish Mysticism,* The University Press of America, 1983.

Cohen, S. J. D., *Josephus in Galilee and Rome, His Vita and Development as a Historian,* Leiden: Brill, 1979.

Cross, F. M., "A New Qumran Fragment Related to the Original Hebrew Underlying the Septuagint," *BASOR* 132 (1953) 15–26.

————, "The Discovery of the Samaritan Papyri," *BA* 26 (1963) 110–21.

————, "The Development of the Jewish Scripts," in *The Bible and Ancient Near East,* ed. by G. Wright, Anchor Books, 1965, 170–264.

————, "Aspects of Samaritan and Jewish History in Late Persian and Hellenistic Times," *HTR* 59 (1966) 201–11.

————, "Papyri of the Fourth Century B.C. from Daliyeh: A Preliminary Report on Their Discovery and Significance," in *New Direction in Biblical Archaeology,* ed. D. N. Freedman & J. C. Greefield, Doubleday, 1971, 48–51.

————, "A Reconstruction of the Judaean Restoration," *JBL* 94 (1975) 1–18.

————, *The Ancient Library of Qumran and Modern Biblical Studies,* (rev. ed.) Baker Book House, 1980.

———— and Talmon, S. (ed.), *Qumran and the History of the Biblical Text,* Harvard Unviersity Press, 1975.

Dahl, N., "The Arrogant Archon and Lewd Sophia: Jewish Traditions in Gnostic Revolt" in *The Rediscovery of Gnosticism,* vol. 2, ed. by B. Layton, Leiden: Brill, 1981, 689–712.

Daniélou, J., *The Theology of Jewish Christianity,* tr. by J. A. Baker, London: Darton, Longman & Todd, 1964.

Davies, P. R., *1QM, The War Scroll from Qumran: Its Structure and History,* Rome: Biblical Institute Press, 1977.

————, *The Damascus Document,* Shefield: Journal for the Study of the Old Testament Press, 1982.

————, "Calendrical Change and Qumran Origin: An Assessment of VanderKam's Theory," *CBQ* 45 (1983) 80–89.

Delcor, M., "Melchizedek from Genesis to the Qumran Texts and the Epistle to the Hebrews," *JSJ* 2 (1971) 115–35.

———— (ed.), *Qumrân: sa piété, sa théologie et son milieu,* Louvain: Louvain University Press, 1978.

Driver, G., *The Judaean Scrolls, The Problem and a Solution,* Oxford: Blackwell, 1965.

Eisenman, R., *Maccabees, Zadokites, Christians, and Qumran,* Leiden: Brill, 1983.

Elliger, K., *Studien zum Habakkuk-Kommentar vom Toten Meer,* Tübingen: Mohr-Siebeck, 1953.

Ellis, E. E., *Paul's Use of the Old Testament,* London: Oliver & Boyd, 1957.

Emerton, J. A., "MARANATHA and EPHATHA," *JTS* 18 (1967) 427–31.

————, "The Problem of Vernacular Hebrew in the First Century A.D. and the Language of Jesus," *JTS* 74 (1972) 18–21.

Fallon, F., *The Enthronement of Sabaoth: Jewish Elements in Gnostic Creation Myths,* Leiden: Brill, 1978.

Farmer, W., *Maccabees, Zealots, and Josephus,* Columbia University Press, 1956.

Fiorenza, E. S., "Apocalyptic and Gnosis in the Book of Revelation and Paul," *JBL* 92 (1973) 565–81.

————, "Cultic Language in Qumran and in the New Testament," *CBQ* 38 (1976) 159–77.

Fitzmyer, J. A., *The Genesis Apocryphon of Qumran Cave 1: A Commentary,* Rome: Pontifical Biblical Institute, 1966.

————, *Essays on the Semitic Background of the New Testament,* Scholars Press, 1974.

————, "Some Observations on the Targum of Job from Qumran Cave 11," *CBQ* 36 (1974) 503–24.

————, *The Dead Sea Scrolls, Major Publications and Tools for Study,* Society of Biblical Literature and Scholars Press, 1977.

————, *A Wondering Aramean: Collected Aramaic Essays,* Scholars Press 1979.

————, "The Dead Sea Scrolls and the New Testament after Thirty Years," *Theology Today* 29 (1981) 351–68.

————, *To Advance the Gospel: New Testament Studies,* Crossroad, 1981.

————, *The Gospel according to Luke I-IX,* Doubleday, 1981.

———— and Harrington, D. J., *A Manual of Palestinian Aramaic Texts: Second Century B.C.—Second Century A.D.,* Rome: Biblical Institute, 1978.

Flusser, D., "Qumran und Die Zwölf," in *Initiation*, ed. C. J. Becker, Leiden: Brill 1965, 134–46.

————, "The Dead Sea Scrolls and the Epistle to the Hebrews," *Scripta Hierosolymitana* IV (1965) 36–55.

————, "Melchizedek and the Son of Man," *Christian News from Israel* April 1966, 23–29.

Foerster, W., "Die 'Ersten Gnostiker' Simon und Menander," in *The Origin of Gnosticism*, ed. by U. Bianchi, Lieden: Brill, 1970, 190–196.

Ford, J. M., *Revelation, The Anchor Bible*, Doubleday, 1975.

Freedman, D. N., "Variant Readings in the Leviticus Scroll from Qumran Cave 11," *CBQ* 36 (1974) 525–34.

Frend, W. H. C., *The Rise of Christianity*, Fortress, 1984.

Freyne, S., *Galilee from Alexander the Great to Hadrian: 323 B.C.E. to 135 C.E. A Study of Second Temple Judaism*, M. Glazier and the University of Notre Dame Press, 1980.

Gärtner, B., "The Habakkuk Commentary (DSH) and the Gospel of Matthew," *Studia Theologica* 8 (1955) 1–24.

————, *The Temple and the Community in Qumran and the New Testament*, Cambridge: Cambridge University Press, 1965.

Gaster, M., *The Samaritans: Their History, Doctrine, and Literature*, London: The British Academy, 1925.

Goshen-Gottstein, M. H., "The Psalms Scroll (11QPs[a]): A Problem of Canon and Text," *Textus* 5 (1966) ed. by S. Talmon, 22–23.

Grant, R. M., *Gnosticism and Early Christianity*, Columbia University Press, 1966 (2nd ed.).

Greenfield, J. C. & Shaked, S., "Three Iranian Words in the Targum of Job from Qumran," *ZDMG* 122 (1972) 37–45.

Gruenwald, I., "Knowledge and Vision—Towards a Clarification of Two Gnostic Concepts in the Light of Their Alleged Origin," *Israel Oriental Studies* III (1973) 63–107.

————, *Apocalyptic and Merkavah Mysticism*, Leiden: Brill, 1980.

————, "Aspects of the Jewish-Gnostic Controversy," in *The Rediscovery of Gnosticism*, vol. 2, ed. B. Layton, Leiden: Brill, 1981, 713–23.

Gundry, R. H., *The Use of the Old Testament in St. Matthew's Gospel with Special Reference to the Messianic Hope*, Leiden: Brill, 1967.

Haas, N., "Anthropological Observations on the Skeletal Remains from Giv'at ha-Mivtar," *IEJ* 20 (1970) 38–59.

Halperin, D. J., *The Merkabah in Rabbinic Literature*, American Oriental Society, 1980.

————, "Crucifixion, the Nahum Pesher, and the Penalty of Strangulation," *JJS* 32 (1981) 32–46.

Harris, J. B., *The Qumran Commentary on Habakkuk*, London: A. R. Mowbry, 1966.

Haenchen, E., *The Acts of the Apostles: A Commentary*, Westminister Press, 1971.

Hengel, M., *Judaism and Hellenism*, 2 vols., tr. by J. Bowden, Fortress Press, 1974.

————, "Zeloten und Sikarier," in *Josephus-Studien, Otto Michel zum 70 Geburstag gewidmet*, ed. by O. Betz, et al., Göttingen: Vandenhoeck & Ruprecht, 1974, 175–96.

————, *Zeloten,* Leiden: Brill, 1976 (2nd ed.).

————, *Acts and the History of Earliest Christianity,* Fortress Press, 1980.

Hoegenhaven, J., "The First Isaiah Scroll from Qumran (1QIs^a) and the Masoretic Text. Some Reflections with Special Regard to Isaiah 1–12," *JSOT* 28 (1984) 17–35.

Horgan, M. P., *Pesharim: Qumran Interpretation on Biblical Books,* Catholic Biblical Association, 1979.

Horsley, R. A., "Josephus and the Bandits," *JSJ* 10 (1979) 37–63.

————, "Popular Messianic Movements around the Time of Jesus," *CBQ* 46 (1984) 471–95.

Horst, P. W. van der, "Moses' Throne Vision and Ezekiel the Dramatist," *JJS* 34 (1983) 21–29.

Howard, G., "Hebrews and Old Testament Quotations," *Novum Testamentum* 10 (1968) 208–216.

————, "Frank Cross and Recensional Criticism," *Vetus Testamentum* 21 (1971) 440–50.

Janzen, J. G., *Studies in the Text of Jeremiah,* Harvard University Press, 1973.

Jaubert, A., "Le Calendrier des Jubilés et de la Secte de Qumrân: Ses origines bibliques," *Vetus Testamentum* 3 (1955) 250–64.

————, *The Date of the Last Supper,* tr. by I. Rafferty, Alba House, 1965.

Jeremias, Jerd, *Der Lehrer der Gerechitigkeit,* Göttingen: Vanderhoeck & Ruprecht, 1963.

Jeremias, Joachim, "Der Ursprung der Johannestaufe," *ZNW* 28 (1929) 312–20.

―――, "Proselytentaufe and Neues Testament," *TZ* 5 (1949) 419–28.

Jongeling, B., "The Job Targum from Cave 11 (11QtgJob)," *Folia Orientalia* 15 (1974) 181–96.

―――, Laberschagne, C. L., & Woude, A. S. van der, *Aramaic Texts from Qumran,* Leiden: Brill, 1976.

Kahle, P., *The Cairo Geniza,* Oxford: Blackwell, 1959 (2nd ed.).

Kanael, B., "Notes on the Dates Used During the Bar Kokhba Revolt," *IEJ* 21 (1971) 39–46.

Käsemann, E., "The Disciples of John the Baptist in Ephesus," in *Essays on New Testament Themes,* Fortress, 1982, 136–48.

Kaufman, S. A., "The Temple Scroll and Higher Criticism," *HUCA* 53 (1982) 29–43.

Kittel, B. P., *The Hymns of Qumran,* Scholars Press, 1981.

Klinzing, G., *Die Umdeutung des Kulte in der Qumrangemeinde und im Neuen Testament,* Göttingen: Vandenhoeck & Ruprecht, 1971.

Kloner, A., "The Subterranean Hideaways of the Judaean Foothills and the Bar-Kokhba Revolt," in *The Jerusalem Cathedra* 3, ed. by L. I. Levine, Jerusalem: Yad Izhak Ben-Zvi Institute/Wayne State University Press, 1983, 114–35.

Knibb, M. A., "The Date of the Parables of Enoch: A Critical Review," *NTS* 25 (1978–79) 345–59.

Kobelski, P. J., *Melchizedek and Melchireša,* The Catholic Biblical Association, 1981.

Koester, H., *History and Literature of Early Christianity,* 2 vols., Fortress Press, 1982.

Kooij, A. van der, "On the Place of Origin of the Old Greek of the Psalms," *Vetus Testamentum* 33 (1983) 67–74.

Kraeling, C. H., *John the Baptist,* Scribners, 1951.

Kuhn, H.-W., *Enderwartung und gegenwärtiges Heil: Untersuchungen zu den Gemeindeliedern von Qumran,* Göttingen: Vandenhoech & Ruprecht, 1966.

Kutscher, E., "The Language of Genesis Apocryphon; A Preliminary Study," *Scripta Hierosolymitana* 4, ed. by C. Rabin & Y. Yadin, (1965) 1–35.

————, The Language and Linguistic Background of the Isaiah Scroll (1QIsᵃ). Leiden: Brill, 1979.

Lagarde, P. de, *Anmerkungen zur griechischen Übersetzung des Proverbien,* Leipzig: Brockhaus, 1863.

Laperrousaz, E.-M., *Quomrân: L'establissment essénien des bords de la Mer Morte. Historie et archéologie des site,* Paris: Picard, 1976.

Lang, F., "Erwähnungen zur eschatologischen Verkündigung Johannes des Täufers," in *Jesus Christus in Historie und Theologie, Festschrift für H. Conzelmann,* ed. by G. Strecker, Tübingen: J. C. B. Mohr, 1975, 466–73.

Lapp, Paul and Nancy, *Discoveries in the Wadi ed-Daliyeh (The Annual of the American School of Oriental Research XLI)* 1974.

Leaney, A. R. C., "Greek Manuscripts from the Judaean Desert," in *Studies in New Testament Language and Text: Essays in Honor of G. D. Kilpatrick,* ed. J. K. Elliot, Leiden: Brill, 1976, 283–300.

Lehman, M. R., "Studies in the Muraba'at and Naḥal Ḥever Document," *RQ* 13 (1963) 51–81.

Levy, R., "First 'Dead Sea Scrolls' Found in Egypt Fifty Years Before Qumran Discoveries," *BAR* 8 (1982) 38–53.

Licht, J., "An Ideal Town Plan from Qumran—The Description of the New Jerusalem," *IEJ* 29 (1979) 44–59.

Lierbermann, S., *Greek in Jewish Palestine in the II-IV Centuries CE,* Jewish Theological Seminary of America, 1942.

————, "Light on the Cave Scrolls from Rabbinic Sources," in *Proceedings of the American Academy for Jewish Research,* 1951, 394–404.

MacCarter, P. K., *I Samuel, The Anchor Bible,* Doubleday, 1980.

MacDonald, J., *The Theology of Samaritans,* London: SCM Press, 1964.

MacRae, G. M., "The Jewish Background of the Gnostic Sophia Myth," *Novum Testamentum* 12 (1970) 86–101.

Mansoor, M., "The Nature of Gnosticism in Qumran," in *The Origin of Gnosticism,* ed. by U. Bianchi, Leiden: Brill, 1970, 389–400.

Mazar, B., *The Mountain of the Lord: Excavation in Jerusalem,* Doubleday, 1975.

McKelvey, R. J., *The New Temple: The Church in the New Testament,* Oxford: Oxford University Press, 1969.

McNamara, M., *Targum and the New Testament,* Eerdmans, 1972.

Mearus, C. L., "Dating the Similitudes of Enoch," *NTS* 25 (1978–79) 360–69.

Meeks, W., *The First Urban Christians: The Social World of the Apostle Paul,* Yale University Press, 1983.

Meier, J. P., "John the Baptist in Matthew's Gospel," *JBL* 99 (1980) 383–405.

Merrill, E. H., *Qumran and Predestination: A Theological Study of the Thanksgiving Hymns,* Leiden: Brill, 1975.

Meshorer, Y., *Jewish Coins of the Second Temple Period,* tr. by I. H. Levine, Tel Aviv: Am Hassefer, 1967.

Meyers, E. M. & Strange, J. F., *Archaeology, the Rabbis and Early Christianity,* Abingdon, 1981.

Milgrom, J., "'Sabbath' and 'Temple City' in the Temple Scroll," *BASOR* 232 (1978) 25–27.

————, "The Temple Scroll: Aspects of Its Historical Provenance and Literary Character," *ibid.,* 5–22.

Milik, J. T., *Ten Years of Discovery in the Wilderness of Judaea,* tr. by J. Strugnell, London: SCM Press, 1959.

————, "The Monastery of Kostellion," *Biblica* 42 (1961) 21–27.

————, "Turfen et Qumran, Livre de Géants juif et manichéen," in *Tradition und Glaube: Das frühe Christentun in seiner Umwelt, Festgabe für K. G. Kuhn,* ed. by G. Jeremias, *et al.,* Göttingen: Vanderhoeck & Ruprecht, 1971, 117–27.

———— and Black, M., *The Books of Enoch,* Oxford: Clarendon Press, 1976.

Montgomery, J., *The Samaritans: The Earliest Jewish Sect,* J. C. Winston, 1907.

Moule, C. F. D., "Once More, Who Were the Hellenists?" *Expository Times* 70 (1958–59) 100–102.

————, "Fulfillment-Words in the New Testament: Use and Abuse," *NTS* 14 (1968) 293–320.

Muraoka, T., "The Aramaic of the Old Targum of Job from Qumran Cave XI," *JJS* 25 (1974) 425–443.

————, "The Greek Texts of Samuel-Kings: Incomplete Translations or Recensional Activity?" *Abr-Naharain* 21 (1982–83) 20–49.

Murphy-O'Connor, J. (ed.), *Paul and Qumran: Studies in New Testament Exegesis,* Priority Press, 1968.

————, "La genèse litérire de la Règle de la Communauté," *RB* 76 (1969) 528–49.

————, "The Essenes and Their History," *RB* 81 (1974) 215–44.

————, "The Essenes in Palestine," *BA* 40 (1977) 94–124.

Neusner, J., *A Life of Rabban Yohanan ben Zakkai,* Leiden: Brill, 1962.

————, "Jews and Judaism under Iranian Rule: Bibliographical Reflection," *History of Religions* 8 (1968) 159–77.

————, *Rabbinic Traditions About the Pharisees Before 70,* 3 vols., Leiden: Brill, 1971.

————, "Pharisaic-Rabbinic Judaism: A Clarification," *History of Religions* 12 (1972–73) 250–70.

————, *First Century Judaism in Crisis,* KTAV, 1982 (Augmented ed.).

Newsom, C., & Yadin, Y., "The Masada Fragment of the Qumran Songs of the Sabbath Sacrifice," *IEJ* 34 (1984) 77–88.

Nickelsburg, G. W. E., *Jewish Literature Between the Bible and the Mishnah,* Fortress Press, 1981.

Nolland, J. M., "A Misleading Statement of the Essene Attitude to the Temple," *RQ* 9 (1978) 555–62.

Patte, D., *Early Jewish Hermeneutic in Palestine,* Scholars Press, 1975.

Pearson, B. A., "Jewish Elements in Gnosticism and the Development of Gnostic Self-Definition," in *Jewish and Christian Self-Definition,* vol. 1, ed. by E. P. Sanders, Fortress Press, 1980, 151–160.

Pixner, B., *An Essene Quarter in Mount Zion?* Franciscan Printing House, 1976.

Ploeg, J. van der, *Le rouleau de la Guerre: Traduit et annoté avec une introduction,* Leiden: Brill, 1959.

———, "Fragments d'un manuscrit de Psalmes de Qumran (11QPs^b)," *RB* 74 (1967) 408–12.

——— and Woude, A. S. van der, *Le Targum de Job de la Grott XI de Qumran,* Leiden: Brill, 1971.

Pummer, R., "The Present State of Samaritan Studies: I," *JSS* 21 (1976) 39–61.

———, "The Present State of Samaritan Studies, II," *JSS* 22 (1977) 27–47.

Quispel, G., *Gnosis als Weltreligion,* Zürich: Origo Verlag, 1951.

———, "Ezekiel 1:26 in Jewish Mysticism and Gnosis," *Vigilae Christianae* 34 (1980) 1–13.

Rabin, C., *The Zadokite Fragments,* Oxford: Clarendon Press, 1958.

————, *Qumran Studies,* Schocken Books, 1975.

————, "Hebrew and Aramaic in the First Century C.E.," in *The Jewish People in the First Century,* vol II, ed. by S. Safrai & M. Stein, Assen/Amsterdam: Van Gorcim, 1976.

Rabinowitz, I., "'Pèsher/pittārōn' Its Biblical Meaning and Its Significance in the Qumran Literature," *RQ* 8 (1975) 219–32.

Rajak, T., "Josephus and 'Archaeology' of the Jews," *JJS* 33 (1982) 465–77.

————, *Josephus: The Historian and His Society,* Fortress, 1983.

Reike, Bo, "Traces of Gnosticism in the Dead Sea Scrolls?" *NTS* 1 (1954–55) 137–41.

Rhoads, D. M., *Israel in Revolution 6-74 C.E. A Political History Based on the Writings of Josephus,* Fortress Press, 1976.

Ringgren, H., *The Faith of Qumran: Theology of the Dead Sea Scrolls,* Fortress Press, 1963.

————, "Qumran and Gnosticism," in *The Origin of Gnosticism,* ed. by U. Bianchi, Leiden: Brill, 1970, 379–88.

Robinson, J. M., "The Coptic Gnostic Library Today," *NTS* 14 (1968) 356–401.

Rosenbloom, J. R., *The Dead Sea Isaiah Scroll: A Literary Analysis,* Eerdmans, 1970.

Rowland, C., *The Open Heaven: A Study of Apocalyptic in Judaism and Early Christianity,* Crossroad, 1982.

Rowley, H. H., "The Samaritan Schism in Legend and History," in *Israel's Prophetic Heritage,* ed. B. W. Anderson & W. Harrelson, Harper & Row, 1962, 208–222.

————, "Sanballat and the Samaritan Temple," in *Men of God: Studies in Old Testament History and Prophecy,* London: Thomas Nelson, 1963, 246–76.

Rudolph, K., *Gnosis: The Nature and History of Gnosticism,* tr. by R. Mcl. Wilson, Harper & Row, 1983.

————, "'Gnosis' and 'Gnosticism'—The Problems of Their Definition and Their Relation to the Writings of the New Testament," in *The New Testament and Gnosis: Essays in Honor of Robert Mcl. Wilson,* ed. by A. H. B. Logan & A. J. M. Wedderburn, Edinburgh: T. & T. Clark, 1983, 21–37.

Sanders, E. W., "The Colossian Heresy and Qumran Theology," in *Studies in the History and Text of the New Testament in Honor of K. W. Clark,* ed. by B. L. Daniels & N. J. Suggs, University of Utah Press, 1967, 133–45.

Sanders, J. A., *The Dead Sea Psalm Scroll,* Cornell University Press, 1967.

————, "The Qumran Psalm Scroll (11QPs^a) Reviewed," in *On Language, Culture, and Religion: In Honor of Eugene A. Nida,* ed. by M. Black & W. A. Smalley, The Hague: Mouten, 1974, 79–99.

Schäfer, P., "Rabbi Aqiva and Bar Kokhba," in *Approaches to Ancient Judaism* 2, ed. W. S. Green, Scholars Press, 1980, 113–30.

————, *Der Bar Kokhba-Aufstand: Studien zum zweiten judischen Krieg gegen Rom,* Tübingen: J. C. B. Mohr, 1981.

————, "New Testament and Hekhalot Literature: The Journey into Heaven in Paul and in Merkavah Mysticism," *JJS* 33 (1982) 19–35.

Schechter, S., *Documents of Jewish Sectaries,* Cambridge: Cambridge University Press, 1910.

Schiffman, L. H., *The Halakha at Qumran,* Leiden: Brill, 1975.

—————, "The Temple Scroll in Literary and Philological Perspective," in *Approaches to Ancient Judaism* 2, ed. W. S. Green, Scholars Press, 1980, 143–58.

—————, "Jewish Sectarianism in Second Temple Period," in *Great Schisms in Jewish History,* ed. by R. Jospe & S. M. Wagner, Center for Judaic Studies, University of Denver & KTAV Publishing House, 1981, 1–46.

—————, "Merkavah *Speculation at Qumran:* The 4Q Serek Shirot 'Olat ha-Shabbat," in *Mystics, Philosophers, and Politicians, Essays in Jewish Intellectual History in Honor of A. Altman,* ed. by J. Reinharz, & D. Swentschinski, Duke University Press, 1982, 15–47.

—————, *Sectarian Law in the Dead Sea Scrolls: Courts, Testimony, and the Penal Codes,* Scholars Press, 1983.

Schmithals, W., *The Office of the Apostles in the Early Church,* tr. by J. E. Steely, Abingdon, 1969.

—————, *Gnosticism in Corinth: An Investigation of the Letters to the Corinthians,* tr. by J. E. Steely, Abingdon, 1971.

—————, "The *Corpus Pantinum* and Gnosis," in *The New Testament and Gnosis: Essays in Honor of Robert Mcl. Wilson,* ed. by A. H. B. Wedderburn, Edinburgh: T. & T. Clark, 1983, 117–21.

Schoeps, H.-J., *Theologie und Geschichte des Judentums,* Tübingen: J. C. B. Mohr, 1949.

—————, *Jewish Christianity: Factional Dispute in the Early Church,* tr. by D. R. A. Hare, Fortress Press, 1969.

Scholem, G., *Major Trends in Jewish Mysticism,* Schocken Books, 1961.

————, *Jewish Gnosticism, Merkavah Mysticism, and Talmudic Tradition,* The Jewish Theological Seminary of America, 1965 (2nd ed.).

————, "Jaldabaoth Reconsidered," in *Mélanges d'Histoire des Religions offerts H.-C. Puech,* Paris: Press Universitaires de France, 1974, 405–21.

Schürer, E., *The History of the Jewish People in the Age of Jesus Christ,* 2 vols., rev. & ed. by G. Vermes, *et al.,* Edinburgh: T. & T. Clark, 1979.

Schütz, R., *Johannes der Täufer,* Zürich/Stuttgart: Zwingli Verlag, 1967.

Schwartz, D. R., "The Three Temples of 4QFlorilegium," *RQ* 10 (1979) 83–91.

Segal, A. F., *Two Powers in Heaven,* Leiden: Brill, 1977.

Segal, M. H., *A Grammar of Mishnaic Hebrews,* Oxford: Clarendon Press, 1927.

Seitz, O. J. F., "The Future Coming of the Son of Man: Three Midrashic Formulations in the Gospel of Mark," *SE* VI (1973) 478–94.

Shaked, S., "Qumran and Iran: Further Consideration," *Israel Oriental Studies* 2 (1972) 433–46.

Silbermann, L., "Unriddling the Riddle: A Study in the Structure and Language of the Habakkuk Pesher (1QpHab)," *RQ* 3 (1961) 323–64.

Simon, M., *Jewish Sects at the Time of Jesus,* tr. by J. H. Farley, Fortress Press, 1967.

Sinclair, L. A., "A Qumran Biblical Fragment: Hosea 4QXXII^d,"*BASOR* 239 (1980) 61–65.

————, "Hebrew Text of the Qumran Micah Pesher and Textual Traditions of the Minor Prophets," *RQ* 11 (1983) 253–63.

Skehan, P. W., "A Fragment of the 'Song of Moses' (Deut. 32) from Qumran," *BASOR* 136 (1954) 12–15.

————, "A Liturgical Complex in 11QPs^a," *CBQ* 35 (1973) 195–205.

————, "Exodus in the Samaritan Recension from Qumran," *JBL* 74 (1955) 182–87.

Smallwood, E. M., *The Jews under Roman Rule from Pompey to Diocletian,* Leiden: Brill, 1976.

Smith, M., "Zealots and Sicarii, Their Origins and Relation," *HTR* 64 (1971) 1–19.

————, "The Samaritan Problem: A Case Study in Jewish Sectarianism in the Roman Era," in *Traditions in Transformation. Turning Points in Biblical Faith,* ed. by B. Halperin & J. D. Levenson, Eisenbrauns, 1981, 323–50.

Sokolof, M., *The Targum to Job from Qumran Cave XI,* Ramat-Gan: Bar-Illan University, 1974.

Sowers, S. G., *The Hermeneutics of Philo and Hebrews,* Zürich: EVZ-Verlag, 1965.

Spicq, C., "L'Épître aux Hébreux, Apollos, Jean-Batiste, les Hellénistes et Qumrân," *RQ* 1 (1959) 365–90.

Stegemann, H., *Die Entstehung der Qumrangemeinde,* Bonn: privately published, 1971.

Stendahl, K. (ed.), *The Scrolls and the New Testament,* Harper & Row, 1957.

————, *The School of Matthew and Its Use of the Old Testament,* Fortress Press, 1968 (2nd ed.).

Stern, M., "Society and Religion in the Second Temple Period," in *Society and Religion in the Second Temple Period, The World History of the Jewish People,* ed. M. Avi-Yona & Z. Baras, Jerusalem: Masad Publication Ltd., 1977, 263–302.

Strugnell, J., "The Angelic Liturgy at Qumran—4Q Serek Šîrôt 'Olat Haššabbāt," *Vetus Testamentum,* supple. VII (1960) 318–45.

————, "Notes on the Text and Transmission of the Apocryphal Psalms 151, 154 (= Syr. II) and 155 (= Syr. III)," *HTR* 59 (1966) 257–81.

Svenster, J. N., *Do You Know Greek? How Much Greek Could the First Jewish Christians Have Known?* Leiden: Brill, 1968.

Talmon, S., "The Calendar Reckoning of the Sect from the Judaean Desert," *Scripta Hierosolymitana* IV (1965) 162–99.

————, "Psqah Be'emṣa' Pasuq and 11QPsᵃ," *Textus* 5 (1966) ed. by S. Talmon, 11–21.

Tcherikover, V., *Hellenistic Civilization and the Jews,* tr. by S. Applebaum, The Jewish Publication Society, 1959.

Teicher, J., *Urgemeinde Judenchristentum, Gnosis,* Tübingen: J. C. B. Mohr, 1956.

Theissen, G., *The First Followers of Jesus: A Sociological Analysis of the Earliest Christianity,* SCM Press, 1978.

Thiering, B. E., "Inner and Outer Cleansing at Qumran as a Background to New Testament Baptism," *NTS* 26 (1980) 266–77.

Thomas, J., *Le Mouvement Batiste en Palestine et Syrie (150 av. J.-C.—300 ap. J.-C.)*, Gembloux: J. Duculot, 1935.

Tov, E., "The Textual Affiliations of 4QSamᵃ," *JSOT* 14 (1979) 37–53.

————, *The Text-Critical Use of the Septuagint in Biblical Research*, Jerusalem: Simor Ltd., 1981.

————, "A Modern Textual Outlook Based on the Qumran Scrolls," *HUCA* 53 (1982) 11–27.

Trever, J. C., "1QDanᵃ, the Latest of the Qumran Manuscripts," *RQ* 7 (1970) 277–86.

Tröger, K. W., "The Attitude of the Gnostic Religion toward Judaism as Viewed in a Variety of Perspectives," in *Bibliothéque Copte de Nag Hammadi Section ≪ Etudes ≫—1—Colloque International sur les Textes de Nag Hammadi*, ed. by B. Barc, Quebec: Les Press de L'université Lavel; Louvain: Editions Peaters, 1981, 86–98.

Tzaferis, V., "Jewish Tombs at and near Giv'at ha-Mivtar, Jerusalem," *IEJ* 20 (1970) 18–32.

Ulrich, E. C., *The Qumran Text of Samuel and Josephus*, Scholars Press, 1978.

————, "4QSamᶜ: A Fragmentary Manuscript of 2 Samuel 14–15 from the Scribe of the Serek Hayyahad (1QS)," *BASOR* 235 (1979) 1–25.

VanderKam, J. C., "The Origin, Character, and Early History of the 364-day Calendar: A Reassessment of Jaubert's Hypothesis," *CBQ* 41 (1979) 390–411.

————, "2 Maccabees 6, 7a and Calendrical Change in Jerusalem," *Journal for Study of Judaism* 12 (1981) 52–74.

Vaux, R. de, *Archaeology and the Dead Sea Scrolls,* Oxford: Oxford University Press, 1973.

Venetz, H. J., *Die Quinta des Psalteriums, Ein Beitrag zur Septuaginta und Hexaplaforschung,* Heidelscheim, 1974.

Vermes, G., *Scripture and Tradition in Judaism: Haggadic Studies,* Leiden: Brill, 1961.

————, "The Impact of the Dead Sea Scrolls on the Study of the New Testament, *JJS* 27 (1966) 106–116.

————, *The Dead Sea Scrolls: Qumran in Perspective,* Collins & World Publishing Co., 1978.

Waard, J. de, *A Comparative Study of the Old Testament Text in the Dead Sea Scrolls and in the New Testament,* Leiden: Brill, 1965.

Walker, W. O., "The Son of Man: Some Recent Developments," *CBQ* 45 (1983) 584–607.

Weiss, R., "Recensional Variations between the Aramaic Translations to Job from Qumran Cave ll and the Masoretic Text," *Shnaton* 1 (1975) 123–27.

Wenschkewitz, H., *Die Spiritualisierung der Kultbegriffe Tempel, Priester, und Opfer im Neuen Testament (Angelos Beiheft* 4) Leipzig: Pfeiffer, 1932.

Wernberg-Møller, P., *The Manual of Discipline,* Leiden: Brill, 1957.

————, "A Reconsideration of the Two Spirits in the Rule of the Community (1QSerek III, 13–IV, 26)," *RQ* 3 (1961–62) 413–441.

Wilkinson, J., *Jerusalem as Jesus Knew It,* London: Thomas & Hudson, 1978.

Wilcox, M., "Upon the Tree—Deut. 21:22–23 in the New Testament," *JBL* 96 (1977) 85–99.

Williamson, R., *Philo and the Epistle to the Hebrews,* Leiden: Brill, 1970.

Wilson, R. Mcl., "Simon Dositheus and the Dead Sea Scrolls," *Zeitschrift für Religions-und Geistes-Geschichte* 9 (1957) 21–30.

———, "Gnosis, Gnosticism and the New Testament," in *The Origin of Gnosticism,* ed. by U. Bianchi, Leiden: Brill, 1967, 511–27.

———, "Jewish Gnosis and Gnostic Origins: A Survey," *HUCA* 45 (1974) 177–89.

———, "Nag Hammadi and the New Testament," *NTS* 28 (1982) 289–302.

Wink, W., *John the Baptist in the Gospel Tradition,* Cambridge: Cambridge University Press, 1968.

Winston, D., "The Iranian Component in the Bible, Apocrypha, and Qumran: A Review of the Evidence," *History of Religions* 5 (1966) 183–216.

Woude, A. S. van der, "Melchisedek als himmlische Erlösergestalt in den neugefundenen eschatologischen Midrashim aus Qumran Höhle XI," *Oudtestamentische Studien* XIV (1965) 354–73.

———, "Fragmente einer Rolle der Leider für das Sabbatopfer aus Höhle XI von Qumran (11QSirSabb)," in *Von Kanaan bis Kerala: Festschrift für J. P. M. van der Ploeg,* ed. by W. C. Delsmann, *et al.,* Kevelaer: Butzon & Bercker; Neukirchen-Vlyn: Neukirchener Verlag, 1982, 311–37.

————, "Wicked Priests or Wicked Priest? Reflections on the Identification of the Wicked Priest in the Habakkuk Commentary," *JJS* 33 (1982) 349–59.

Wright, A., *The Literary Genre Midrash,* Alba house, 1967.

Wright, G. R. H., "The Archaeological Remains at El Mird in the Wilderness of Judaea," *Biblica* 42 (1961) 1–12.

Yadin, Y., "A Midrash on 2 Sam 7 and Ps 1–11 (4QFlorilegium)," *IEJ* 9 (1959) 95–98.

————, *The Scroll of the War of the Sons of Light against the Sons of Darkness,* tr. by Batya and Chaim Rabin, London: Oxford University Press, 1962.

————, *The Finds from the Bar Kokhba Period in the Cave of Letters,* Jerusalem: Israel Exploration Society, 1963.

————, "The Excavation of Masada—1963/4, Preliminary Report," *IEJ* 15 (1965) 1–120.

————, *The Ben Sira Scroll from Masada,* Jerusalem: Israel Exploration Society & The Shrine of the Books, 1965.

————, *Masada: Herod's Fortress and the Zealots' Last Stand,* tr. by H. Pearlman, Random House, 1966.

————, *Bar-Kokhba,* Random House, 1971.

————, "Pesher Nahum (4QpNahum) Reconsidered," *IEJ* 21 (1971) 1–12.

————, "Epigraphy and Crucifixion," *IEJ* 23 (1973) 18–22.

————, *The Temple Scroll: The Hidden Laws of the Dead Sea Sect,* Random House, 1985.

Yamauchi, E. M., *Pre-Christian Gnosticism: A Survey of the Proposed Evidence,* Baker Book House, 1983 (2nd ed.).

Zeitlin, S., *The Dead Sea Scrolls and Modern Scholarship,* Dropsie College, 1956.

Index of Biblical References

OLD TESTAMENT

292   *Index*

Apocrypha and Pseudepigrapha References

Qumran Documents References

CD (Damascus Document)		11:18–21	141
1:13	127	11:20	126
2:5	114	12:10	36
2:6	114	15	158
2:18–3:12	42	19:7	127
3:12–14	42	19:26	127
3:14	45	19:33	42
3:14–16	46	20:16	127
3:18	159	20:22	141
3:19	144		
4:1	35	*1QIs^a* (Isaiah Scroll)	
4:4	35	7:14	88
4:17	130	9:5	88
4:20	129, 130	11:6	88–89
5:5	35	14:30	90
5:8	127	21:8a	90
5:11–12	105	33:8b	89
6:3	123	40:6	91
6:8	127	49:17	91
6:13	127	49:24	91
7:9	127	51:5	92
7:10	127	51:19	91
7:14	127	53:11a	93
7:16	127	60:19a	92
7:18ff.	67	62:11	93
8:9	127		
8:14	127	*1QS* (Manual of Discipline)	
9:5	127	1:9–11	143
9:7	127	2:7–8	114
9:21	111	2:16ff.	143
9:23	111, 159	3:4–8	111, 115
11:14	131	3:13	197
11:18	126, 141	3:15	168

294

Ancient Historical Writings

Author Index

Wink, W., 117
Woude, A.S. van der, 47, 48
Wright, A., 123, 124
Wright, G., 30

Yadin, Y., 3, 9, 16–18, 20, 22, 24, 25, 52, 56, 63, 67, 95, 133, 135, 148

Zeitlin, S., 52

Subject Index